FIRST

EXPERT

COURSEBOOK

Jan Bell and Roger Gower

Contents

Contents

Exam overview

➤ See pages 175–181 for more detailed information and task strategies.

Cambridge English: First has four papers. Paper 1 receives 40 percent of the total marks and the other three papers have 20 percent each. The pass mark is based on an overall mark (you do not need to pass every paper to pass the exam). There are three pass grades (A, B and C) and two fail grades (D and E).

Paper	Task type	Task description
Paper 1: Reading and Use of English 1 hour 15 minutes 7 parts 52 questions in total	**Part 1:** multiple-choice cloze (8 questions)	**Part 1:** Choosing a word or phrase from four options to fill in gaps in a text
	Part 2: open cloze (8 questions)	**Part 2:** Filling in gaps in a text with an appropriate word
	Part 3: word formation (8 questions)	**Part 3:** Changing the form of a given word to make it fit the gaps in a text
	Part 4: key word transformations (6 questions)	**Part 4:** Using a given word to complete a sentence so that it means the same as a previous sentence
	Part 5: multiple choice (6 questions)	**Part 5:** Answering four-option multiple-choice questions on a text
	Part 6: gapped text (6 questions)	**Part 6:** Completing a gapped text with sentences which have been removed and placed in jumbled order
	Part 7: multiple matching (10 questions)	**Part 7:** Matching information to 4–6 different texts (or different parts of a text)
Paper 2: Writing 1 hour 20 minutes 2 tasks (one compulsory, the other a choice out of three options) 140–190 words each	**Part 1:** essay (compulsory)	**Part 1:** An essay based on a title and notes
	Part 2: one writing task: the choice may include an email/letter, an article, a review, a report	**Part 2:** Carrying out a writing task, using an appropriate format and style. There are three task types to choose from.
Paper 3: Listening Approximately 40 minutes 4 parts 30 questions in total	**Part 1:** multiple choice (8 questions)	**Part 1:** Eight short unrelated extracts of around 30 seconds each, each with a three-option multiple-choice question
	Part 2: sentence completion (10 questions)	**Part 2:** A 3–4-minute monologue with ten sentence completion questions
	Part 3: multiple matching (5 questions)	**Part 3:** Five short related monologues of around 30 seconds each, to match to a list of eight options
	Part 4: multiple choice (7 questions)	**Part 4:** A 3–4-minute interview or discussion with seven three-option multiple-choice questions
Paper 4: Speaking Approximately 14 minutes 4 parts	**Part 1:** conversation: giving personal information (2 minutes)	**Part 1:** The interlocutor asks each candidate questions about themselves
	Part 2: 'long turn': giving information and expressing opinions (4 minutes)	**Part 2:** Each candidate, individually, compares two photos (1 minute) and comments briefly on the other candidate's photo (30 seconds)
	Part 3: collaborative task: exchanging information and ideas (4 minutes)	**Part 3:** The candidates work together for 2 minutes and discuss a task based on a diagram. They then try to reach a decision in 1 minute.
	Part 4: discussion: developing the topic of Part 3 (4 minutes)	**Part 4:** The interlocutor leads a discussion between the two candidates, developing the topic of Part 3.

1 Lifestyles

1A
- **Reading and Use of English:** Developing skills: Skimming and scanning
- **Language development:** Present and past situations, habits and states
- **Writing:** Informal email (Part 2)

1B
- **Speaking:** Vocabulary: Special occasions; Developing skills: Comparing photos
- **Listening:** Developing skills: Listening for gist; Listening for specific information
- **Language development:** Comparatives and superlatives; Modifying adjectives and adverbs; Adjective + noun collocations; Phrasal verbs with *up* and *down*
- **Reading and Use of English:** Key word transformations (Part 4); Multiple-choice cloze (Part 1)

Lead-in

1   Look at the entry from the *Longman Exams Dictionary*. Mark the key points that define *lifestyle*.

> **life·style** /ˈlaɪfstaɪl/ *n* [C] the way a person or group of people live, including the place they live in, the things they own, the kind of job they do and the activities they enjoy: *Regular exercise is part of a **healthy** lifestyle.* | **lavish/comfortable/simple/etc. lifestyle** *They lead an extremely **lavish** lifestyle.*

2   Discuss the questions.
   1   The photos show typical aspects of a student's lifestyle in the UK. Which would you most/least enjoy? Why?
   2   Think of one adjective that describes your lifestyle best.

Reading: Developing skills

Before you read   1   Read the title of the article on page 9 and the introduction. In what ways can parents be 'pushy'?

Skimming   2   Skim the article and match the summary sentences (1–4) with the sections of the article (A–D).
1 Some children are expected to do activities for the wrong reasons.
2 The more activities children do, the better.
3 Children don't need pressure at their age.
4 Technology has advantages for children.

Scanning   3   Look at the questions in the task below. The key words are highlighted for you. Now look at the example (0). The highlighted words link to the highlighted part of section C of the text. Then read the strategies and do the task.

EXPERT STRATEGY
Skimming
- Use the title, introduction and any pictures to get an idea of the topic and what a text will be about. This will make it easier to understand the text.
- To get a general understanding of a text, read through it quickly, focusing only on the main ideas. These are found in 'topic sentences', often the first or last sentences of each paragraph.

EXPERT STRATEGY
Scanning
When you know what information you want to find, you can save time by scanning the text for it, rather than reading the whole text. Read the questions first, identify the key words and look for phrases or information in the text that express the same ideas.

You are going to read an article in which different families give their views on how children should spend their free time. For questions 1–10, choose from the sections (A–D). The sections may be chosen more than once.

Which section mentions:

the anxiety some parents have about aspects of modern life?	0 C
an attempt to limit the time spent playing computer games?	1
the practical difficulties of getting children to their activities?	2
the pressure that many children are under to succeed?	3
a suspicion that the activities which some children go to may not be their own choice?	4
the benefits to children of having access to a computer?	5
worrying about letting children be independent?	6
the value of playing music for pleasure?	7
the difficulty of being a 'one-parent family'?	8
the link between practising new skills and making progress?	9
a negative view of competitive parents?	10

4   Which of the skills, skimming or scanning, did you find the most useful for the task in Exercise 3? Why?

Vocabulary   5   Look at the underlined words and phrases in the article and guess what they mean.

Discussion   6   Which family's lifestyle is most similar to/different from yours?

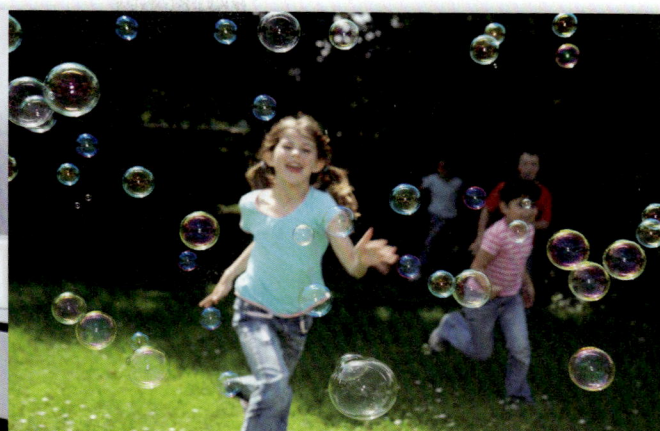

Our lost childhood?

Last week a group of teachers, authors and psychologists said video games and 'pushy parents' were robbing children of their happiest years. But is that true? Here we speak to four very different families.

A The Thomases

Our children like to chill out in front of the TV or play computer games just like every child all over the world. But parents also need to give their children the chance to try out as many different things as they can afford. Both our boys play football for a club and their school, so they train a couple of times a week and play at the weekend. Charlie also plays basketball and the drums. William learns the electric guitar and Laura sings and has kickboxing and trampolining lessons. But we make it clear to them that if they want to improve at something, they need to work hard and keep doing it over and over again. There's only Friday when someone is not out. It's spent eating pizzas and deciding on the logistics of how and when we are going to get the children to their different classes over the weekend.

B The Luckhursts

The best thing you can give your children is time. Proper time. Not a few snatched minutes here and there while you rush them off to ballet or violin lessons but time spent talking and listening to them.

These days children are packed off to all sorts of lessons at an ever younger age. They are expected to achieve more and more younger and younger, and are made to feel a failure if they don't reach the targets set for them. I encourage my kids to play the piano but only for fun – that's just as important. Childhood is the only time in your life when you can play and not have the worries that adults have. So why are we trying to rush it? I think the rivalry between parents at school is particularly depressing – as if anyone cares whose child learns to ride a bike first or learns to read before anyone else!

C The McGraths

Here in Britain, we tend to complain that children don't play in the garden and go out on their bikes the way we did. Computer games and the internet have taken over from playing outside but, although I worry about this, I doubt I'd have been riding bikes if we'd had the internet. Maybe as adults we're scared of the world they're growing up in because we don't really understand it. In any case, since I separated from my husband, it's not easy to keep the children constantly entertained and I'm happy for them to go on the computer because it gives me a break. Both my kids love computer games. Natalie spends a lot of time on Facebook and, actually, it's a good way for her to keep in touch with her friends in Spain and keep up her Spanish at the same time.

D The Clarkes

If my kids had their way, they'd be on the computer the minute they got home from school but I try to keep an eye on this because we do have rules about how long they're allowed to spend playing games on their computer. When they're not doing this, the boys play football together and Julia does cheerleading and goes to a youth club. She wants to go ice-skating but the nearest rink is a bus ride and a walk away, and I'm worried that she's still a bit young to do this on her own.

I can't afford to send my kids to extra lessons. In any case, too many people push their kids into doing something because they themselves used to do it or wanted to. Living your life through your kids has its own dangers, in my view. Julia loves horses but riding lessons cost a fortune, so that's out.

Language development 1

Present situations and habits

➤ EXPERT GRAMMAR page 182

1a Match the people in the picture (A–E) with the sentences (1–6).
  1 She lives in a small house with her husband and children.
  2 His children are growing up fast!
  3 He'll sit and doze in an armchair all evening.
  4 She's always making long calls on the phone.
  5 He's staying with the family at the moment.
  6 She usually goes out in the evening.

b Match the uses (a–f) with the sentences (1–6) in Exercise 1a.
  a a regular action
  b an annoying or surprising habit
  c characteristic behaviour
  d a long-term situation
  e a changing situation
  f a temporary situation

c Now complete the table with the uses and sentences from Exercise 1b.

Form	Use	Examples
Present continuous	(1) _____ (3) _____	(2) _____ (4) _____
Present continuous + *always*	(5) _____	(6) _____
Present simple	(7) _____ (9) _____	(8) _____ (10) _____
will + infinitive	(11) _____	(12) _____

2a Complete the conversations with the correct form of the verbs in brackets. Use the present simple, present continuous or *will*.
  1 A: _____ (you/live) in a house or a flat?
     B: We _____ (live) in a flat for now but we _____ (look for) a house.
  2 A: Who _____ (you/get on) best with in your family?
     B: My father. He _____ (tell) us endless funny stories.
  3 A: _____ (anyone/annoy) you in your family?
     B: Yes, my brother. He _____ (always/take) my CDs without asking me!
  4 A: How often _____ (you/go out)?
     B: I usually _____ (go out) every night but I _____ (study) a lot at the moment, so I _____ (only/go out) at weekends until my exams are finished.
  5 A: _____ (you/like) learning English?
     B: Yes, I do. It was difficult at first but it _____ (get) easier now.

b Work in pairs. Take it in turns to ask each other the questions in Exercise 2a and give answers which are true for you.

State verbs

➤ EXPERT GRAMMAR page 182

3a Read the sentences. Does each one describe a state (S) or an action (A)?

1 I don't understand. ____
2 Do you know Peter? ____
3 We don't have a big house. ____
4 Sorry, I'm having lunch. ____

b Read the information and complete it with the verbs from Exercise 3a.

A Some verbs are not used in the continuous because they describe states, not actions (e.g. *believe*, *like*, *seem*, *want*, *own*, _____ , _____).
B Some verbs are not used in the continuous when they describe states, but can be used in the continuous when they describe actions (e.g. *look*, *appear*, *see*, *think*, *feel*, _____).

4 Correct the mistakes in the sentences.

1 I'm having two brothers.
2 Jan has a shower – can you call back later?
3 I don't understand this word. What is it meaning?
4 Marina thinks about getting a car. Do you think it's a good idea?
5 We are not owning our house; we rent it.
6 The house is looking old but it's quite modern inside.
7 What do you look at? Oh, yes! I can see it now!
8 Phil sees a client at the moment. He won't be long.

Past habits and states

➤ EXPERT GRAMMAR page 182

5a Read the quote from the singer Rihanna. Mark two past habits and one past state.

Early memories

'When I was a child, we used to live in Bridgetown, Barbados, and I used to sell clothes on a stall with my father. In the evenings I would help my mother with the cooking.'

b Read the quote in Exercise 5a again and answer the questions.

1 Did Rihanna sell clothes with her father once or many times?
2 Did she help her mother with the cooking once or many times?
3 What verb forms are used to describe these past habits?
4 Choose the correct answers: *sell* / *live* is a state verb. You can't use *would* / *used to* with a state verb.

c Read the information and complete it with *used to*, *would* or the past simple form of verbs from the quote in Exercise 5a.

A To talk about past habits, use _____ (e.g. *I used to sell clothes on a stall with my father.*) or *would* (e.g. *I _____ my mother with the cooking.*).
B To talk about past states, use _____ (e.g. *We _____ in Bridgetown.*).
C The past simple can also be used for past habits and states (e.g. *I _____ in Bridgetown. I _____ my mother with the cooking.*)

6 Complete the sentences with the correct form of the verbs in brackets. Use *used to*, *would* or the past simple. Only use the past simple if *used to* or *would* are not possible. More than one answer may be possible.

1 Sorry I _____ (forget) to write to you last week.

2 I _____ (live) in France when I was a child.
   We _____ (have) two beautiful cats.

3 When I was younger, my family _____ (always/go) to the beach in summer. We _____ (have) some great beach parties!

4 My father _____ (be) a businessman.
   He _____ (often/work) six or seven days a week, until he _____ (retire) in 1995.

7a Write true sentences about you.

1 My … is always …
2 I used to … but now …
3 As a child, I would often …

b Now compare your experiences with other students.

8 Match the sentence halves.

1 I'm writing to tell you
2 I live in Poznań,
3 I live in a flat with
4 We don't look like each other
5 When I'm not surfing the internet,
6 When I was a child,

a but we have very similar personalities.
b we used to visit your country every summer.
c something about myself.
d I like going out with my friends.
e a city in the west of Poland.
f my parents and my brother.

Writing (Paper 2 Part 2: Informal email)

Lead-in

1 Discuss the questions.

1 Who do you write informal emails to?
2 What kind of things would you write in an email to a new friend?

Understand the task

2 Read the exam task. What is the purpose of the email?

a to ask for information
b to give information
c to entertain the reader

You have received this email from an English-speaking boy called Simon.

> Hello,
> I would like to get to know someone from your country and a friend has told me that you would like to practise your English. Perhaps we could email each other. Could you tell me a bit about yourself and your family? Could you suggest how we might meet sometime in the future?
> Thanks,
> Simon

*Write your **email** in **140–190** words in an appropriate style.*

Plan your email

3a What information are you going to include in your email? Make a list.

job, hobbies, ...

b Copy and complete the paragraph plan with the information from Exercises 2 and 3a.
Paragraph 1: why you are writing
Paragraph 2: about you
Paragraph 3: about your family
Paragraph 4: suggesting meeting

Language and content

4a These extracts from a student's email are inappropriate. Rewrite them using informal language from the table on page 13.

1 It would be a pleasure to become acquainted with you.

2 I am an inhabitant of a small town in Spain.

3 My sister and I have a very good relationship.

4 At the next opportunity to write, I will forward a photograph of us all.

5 When I was a child, it was customary for us to spend our vacations by the sea.

6 She has a similar appearance to me. However, she can seem rather talkative.

7 I understand you wish to make contact with someone from my country.

8 Does the possibility ever arise for you to visit my country?

9 I take pleasure in your interest.

10 I should like to take this opportunity to inform you of my family situation.

Responding to a suggestion	I'm glad you're … So you'd like to get in touch … As your friend said, I'd like … because …
Introducing yourself	My name's … I live in …
Talking about people	Let me tell you about my family. She looks like me but she can be a bit … We get on (well) …
Lifestyles	We like to … We would always go on holiday … I often used to … We both enjoy …
Talking about the future	Do you ever get the chance to … ? It would be great to meet up sometime. Perhaps we could … Next time I write, I'll …

b Read the statements giving advice about informal emails. Do you think they are *Right* (R) or *Wrong* (W)?

1 Use a personal, conversational style.
2 Avoid simple words.
3 Avoid phrasal verbs.
4 Avoid direct questions to the reader.
5 Use short, simple sentences.
6 Use contractions.

c Find examples in the table above to justify your answers in Exercise 4b.

d Which of the options (1–9) would be appropriate to open and close your email? Which ones would not be appropriate? Why?

1 Dear Mr Jones,

2 I hope to hear from you at your earliest convenience.

3 Lots of love,

4 Hello Simon,

5 Looking forward to hearing from you.

6 Best wishes,

7 Dear friend,

8 Well, that's all for now. Do write back soon.

9 Yours sincerely,

EXPERT LANGUAGE: Sentence word order

Put the words in the correct order to make sentences.

1 very / always / English / I / speak / don't / well
_____

2 always / my mother and father / Fridays / fish / on / eat
_____

3 having / great / right now / Paris / my sister's / in / time / a
_____

4 usually / her / gave / help / friends / a lot of / her
_____

5 bed / music / in / would / my grandmother / listen to / always
_____

6 the party / very much / everyone / themselves / enjoyed / at
_____

7 you / I'll / next week / email / send / on Tuesday / an
_____

8 as / write / please / back / as / can / you / soon
_____

Write your email

➤ EXPERT STRATEGIES pages 177–178

5 Now write your email using the ideas and some of the language above. Do not include any addresses.

Check your email

➤ EXPERT WRITING page 202

6 Edit your work using this checklist. (There is a full checklist on page 198.)
Check your:
• paragraph plan. Have you included all the points?
• use of present and past tenses.
• use of time expressions.
• style.
• spelling.
• number of words.

Speaking: Developing skills

A

B

C

D

Vocabulary: Special occasions

1 Match the photos (A–D) with the special occasions (1–3).

1 birthday party
2 graduation ceremony
3 wedding

2a Match the verbs in A with the nouns in B. More than one answer may be possible.

A

be awarded   blow out   blow up   cut   exchange   make
propose   rent   send out   take   unwrap   walk down

B

the aisle   balloons   the cake   the candles   a certificate   invitations
a marquee   photos   presents   rings   a speech   a toast

b Match each of the phrases in Exercise 2a with one of the photos above and say:

1 how it links to the special occasion.
2 if there are other special occasions where you do this.

3a Match the words and phrases in the box with the definitions.

anniversary   best man   bridesmaid   honeymoon   reception
registry office   witnesses

1 a place where people get married _____
2 a person who supports the bride _____
3 the person who helps the groom _____
4 the people who watch, and sign the marriage certificate at a wedding _____
5 the formal party after a wedding _____
6 a holiday after the wedding _____
7 exactly a year or number of years after the wedding _____

b Underline the stressed syllable(s) on each of the words and phrases in the box in Exercise 3a.

4   Read the conversations and choose the correct answers (1–5). Then complete the gaps (a–e) with the correct form of words and phrases from Exercises 2 and 3.

> Alex: Did you **(1)** *go / get* married in a church or did you have a civil wedding in a(n) **(a)** ____ ?
>
> Peter: When we first **(2)** *got / were* engaged, Tania wanted a white wedding with lots of **(b)** ____ to look after her but later she wanted something less formal.
>
> Alex: Where did you hold the **(c)** ____ ?
>
> Peter: At my parents' house. Everyone had a good time eating and drinking until we disappeared off on our **(d)** ____ .

> Linda: Why did you decide to **(3)** *hold / break up* such a small wedding reception?
>
> Ivana: Because we haven't got much money.
>
> Linda: Did you **(e)** ____ formal invitations to all your **(4)** *guests / visitors*?
>
> Ivana: No, no, it was all very casual. Nobody was expected to dress **(5)** *up / down*.

5   Think of a special occasion that you celebrate in your country (e.g. a wedding, a baby being born, coming of age, passing exams) and a special day (e.g. New Year's Day, Mother's Day). Discuss how you celebrate both occasions. What similarities/differences are there?

Comparing photos

6a You are going to talk for one minute about two of the photos on page 14. (Note: in the exam, you only get two photos.) Choose two that you would like to compare and make notes about them under these headings.

*   similarities between the two photos
*   differences between the two photos
*   why the celebrations are important to the people

b   🎧 02 Listen to a student talking about two of the photos and answer the questions.

1   Which two photos is she talking about?
2   Why does she say the celebrations are important to the people?

c   🎧 02 Look at the table. Then listen again and tick the expressions the speaker uses.

EXPERT STRATEGY

If you have to speak for an extended period such as a minute, divide the time into smaller sections and think about what to say in each section. Don't try to say everything at once!

Similarities	Both of … are … They both seem to be … Neither of them … In this one … and this one …
Differences	One thing which is different in this one … The main difference between … and … is … This one is … whereas … is …
Expressing opinion	Although … , I think … (because …) On the other hand, … is probably … I believe it would be …

d   Take turns to speak for a minute about the two photos you have chosen. Use your notes and expressions from the table above.

Discussion

7   Think of a memorable celebration you've taken part in. Who took part and what happened? How would you describe the occasion (e.g. moving, funny, exhilarating)? Give reasons.

Listening: Developing skills

Before you listen

1 Discuss the questions.

1 What are the most common reasons for people going to live in another country?
2 Think of a few different countries. What do you think the advantages and disadvantages of living there would be?

Listening for gist

2 🎧 03 **Listen to three people talking about living abroad. Why did each of the speakers first go abroad?**

Speaker 1: _____

Speaker 2: _____

Speaker 3: _____

a to study
b for work
c for a holiday

Listening for specific information

3 🎧 03 **Look at the task and mark the key words in the statements. The first item has been done for you. Then listen again and do the task. (Note: in the exam, there will be five speakers and you will choose one option for each speaker from eight available options.)**

For questions 1–3, choose from the list (A–E) what each speaker says. Use the letters only once. There are two extra letters which you do not need to use.

A People have been very kind to me.

B The climate is the reason I came here.   1 ☐

C It feels very remote living here.   2 ☐

D The people are exactly as I'd imagined.   3 ☐

E Mealtimes have a high priority.

Discussion

4 Discuss how you would feel about living in another country. Talk about:

• which countries you have visited or lived in and how you felt about them.
• which countries you would like to live in and why.
• what you missed/would miss most about your own country.

Language development 2

Comparatives and superlatives

➤ **EXPERT GRAMMAR** pages 182–183

1a Correct the mistakes in the sentences.

1 Burns Night celebrates the birth of the poet Robert Burns. It is one of most important nights in Scotland.
2 For many Scots, Burns supper is the most good event of the year.
3 Usually, more late it gets, more noisy it gets.
4 The speech before the toast was funnyiest I have heard.
5 The music was more loud that last year.
6 The celebration was more lively one I've ever been to.
7 Outside, it was just as chilly than last year.
8 Next year I'll leave more early. I couldn't get hold of a taxi.

b Read about comparatives and superlatives on pages 182–183 and check your answers in Exercise 1a.

c Complete the article with the comparative or superlative form of the adjectives and adverbs in brackets.

The Mexican holiday Cinco de Mayo (5 May), which remembers the Mexican defeat of the French army in 1862, is celebrated **(1)** _____ (enthusiastically) in the state of Puebla than in other parts of Mexico. It is not the **(2)** _____ (popular) holiday in Mexico. In fact, it is celebrated **(3)** _____ (widely) by Mexicans in the USA than in Mexico, and the holiday is **(4)** _____ (well known) in the USA than Mexican Independence Day. In recent years, Cinco de Mayo has become **(5)** _____ (big) than ever and is promoted as a celebration of Mexican culture, food and music. Participation is now **(6)** _____ (wide) than before and non-Mexican Americans are **(7)** _____ (enthusiastic) about it as Mexicans. In California, the **(8)** _____ (lively) and **(9)** _____ (sensational) parties take place in Los Angeles. Celebrations have become **(10)** _____ (commercialised) in recent years but Cinco de Mayo is still a great festival.

Modifying adjectives and adverbs

A To express a big difference:
 • *far/a lot/much + comparative*
 He is **far better** than the other singers in the band. (~~very better~~)
 The food is **a lot nicer** in this café. (~~very nicer~~)
 The festival is **much more popular** this year. (~~very more popular~~)
 • *by far/easily + superlative*
 He is **by far the best** singer in the band.
 The festival is **easily the most popular** in the country.
 • *not nearly as ... as ...*
 This party is **not nearly as** good **as** last year's.
 This is **not nearly as** good a party **as** last year's.

B To express a small difference:
 • *slightly/a bit/a little + comparative*
 The music is (only) **slightly better** than before.
 The concert was **a bit/a little better** than I expected.
 • *just about + superlative*
 It was **just about the longest** carnival procession ever.
 • *nearly/not quite as ... as*
 The first show was **nearly as good as** the second one.
 The weather **isn't quite as hot as** it was last time.

2 Read the information above and complete the sentences with the comparative or superlative form of the adjectives in brackets.

1 Fiesta Broadway in Los Angeles is _____ (by far/large) Cinco de Mayo celebration in the USA.
2 This year it was _____ (much/crowded) than it was last year.
3 This year's parade wasn't _____ (quite/long) last time.
4 The costumes were _____ (a lot/colourful) than before.
5 The food is _____ (far/spicy) than I remembered.
6 I tried _____ (easily/mild) dish and it still made my mouth burn!
7 And I'm sure I was _____ (just about/bad) dancer there!

3a Choose one item from the list and write four sentences.
Compare:
 • three types of dance you know (e.g. salsa, tango, ballet; fast/slow, easy/hard, cheap/expensive).
 • three types of music (e.g. rap, jazz, opera; interesting/boring, noisy/quiet).
 • three types of food (e.g. Italian, French, Chinese; spicy/mild, light/heavy, tasty/bland).

b Discuss your answers to Exercise 3a. Give reasons for your opinions.

Use of English 1 (Paper 1 Part 4)

Key word transformations

EXPERT STRATEGY

- Read both sentences carefully.
- Identify what is missing from the second sentence.
- Identify what kind of word the key word is (noun, verb, etc.) and what structure it could be used with.
- Look at the words before and after the gap to see what kind of structure could fit.
- Write 2–5 words without changing the key word. Contractions count as two words.
- Read your sentence to check that it makes sense and is correct.
- Make a guess if necessary.

➤ **HELP**

1 Do you need an active or passive form?

2 Do you need an adjective or an adverb?

1a Look at sentences 1 and 2 and read the strategy. Then answer questions a and b below.

1 Peter is a lot older than Martin.
AS
Martin is _____ Peter.

2 The only person Jane didn't like was her boss.
APART
Jane liked everyone _____ her boss.

a What area of grammar is focused on in sentence 1?
A modifying adverbs   B comparison of adjectives

b What area of vocabulary is focused on in sentence 2?
A prepositional phrases   B phrasal verbs

b Now complete sentences 1 and 2 with 2–5 words. Follow the steps in the strategy.

2a Do the first half of the task. Use the Help notes for support with certain items.

Complete the second sentence so that it has a similar meaning to the first sentence, using the word given. **Do not change the word given.** *You must use between* **two** *and* **five** *words, including the word given.*

1 Fewer people read Carlton's books these days.
WIDELY
Carlton's books _____ these days.

2 Lucy doesn't swim nearly as well as Kate.
SWIMMER
Kate is _____ Lucy.

3 Rap music isn't nearly as popular as it was ten years ago.
LESS
Rap music is _____ it was ten years ago.

b Now do the second half of the task. This time there are no Help notes.

4 I find studying more difficult as I become older.
IS
I find it _____ as I become older.

5 My brother never asks when he borrows my things.
ALWAYS
My brother is _____ asking.

6 Traffic today doesn't move much faster than 100 years ago.
LITTLE
One hundred years ago traffic moved _____ than today.

Task analysis

3 Discuss the questions about the task.

1 Which questions test:
   a verb forms?
   b comparative or superlative structures?

2 Which of the questions did you find the most difficult? Why? Which of these areas of language do you need more practice in?

Use of English 2 (Paper 1 Part 1)

Lead-in

1 What hospitality customs do you have in your country?

Multiple-choice cloze

2a Read the title and text quickly and answer the questions. Ignore the gaps at this stage.

1 What were travellers often given in ancient times?
2 What might be given to a guest in Japan?
3 Why might guests eat too much in a foreign country?

b Read the strategy and do the task. Use the Help notes for support with certain items.

EXPERT STRATEGY

- Read the title and whole text quickly, ignoring the gaps.
- Read the text again. Try to guess what kind of word fits each gap.
- Choose which answer (A–D) fits the grammar and meaning.
- If you aren't sure, cross out answers which you know are incorrect.
- Read the text again to check.

➤ HELP

1 Which word can mean 'civilisation'?
2 Which word means 'continued to live in spite of many problems'?
3 Which verb is always followed by an infinitive?
8 Which verb is used with *down* to form a phrasal verb that means 'refuse'?

For questions 1–8, read the text below and decide which answer (A, B, C or D) best fits each gap. There is an example at the beginning (0).

Hospitality

Hospitality – looking after visitors – is universal but in different cultures hosts are (0) _C_ to receive guests in different ways. In much of the ancient (1) __ it was the custom to provide passing travellers with food and water. Today some old customs have (2) ___ . In a traditional Japanese household, if a guest admires a particular object in the house, the host will (3) ___ to give it to the guest straightaway. And in parts of Russia guests are greeted with bread and salt on a special cloth. The guest is (4) ___ to kiss them and hand them back to the host. Sometimes the guest breaks (5) ___ a small piece of bread, dips it in the salt and eats it.
In some countries, when (6) ___ guests arrive from abroad, they may feel they have been given a particularly (7) ___ meal. But this is probably because the host politely offers more and more food and drink and the guest is too embarrassed to (8) ___ anything down.

0	A hoped	B considered	C expected	D intended
1	A globe	B earth	C world	D planet
2	A supported	B survived	C preserved	D existed
3	A provide	B fancy	C consider	D want
4	A needed	B demanded	C required	D desired
5	A off	B down	C out	D in
6	A strange	B foreign	C alien	D unfamiliar
7	A strong	B dense	C wide	D heavy
8	A slow	B turn	C keep	D take

Task analysis

3a Discuss the questions about the task.

1 Did you guess any words before looking at the options?
2 Which questions test:
   a the correct word from a set with similar meanings?
   b phrasal verbs?
   c adjective + noun collocations?

b Make a note of any expressions, phrasal verbs or adjective + noun collocations you want to remember in your vocabulary notebook.

Language development 3

Adjective + noun collocations

1 Read the information. Then find six more adjective + noun collocations in the text on page 19.

> Look at this adjective + noun collocation from the text on page 19:
>
> *a **heavy** meal* (*a **strong** meal*)
>
> but:
>
> *a **strong** drink* (*a **heavy** drink*)
>
> When you learn an adjective, note which nouns it collocates with.

2 Look at the dictionary entry and complete the spidergram. Use nouns from the dictionary entry.

> **sour** *adj* **1** having a sharp acid taste that stings your tongue like the taste of a lemon: *sour apples* **2** milk or other food that is sour is not fresh: *In warm weather, milk can go sour.* **3** unfriendly or looking bad-tempered: *Rob gave me a sour look.* **4 sour grapes** the attitude of someone who pretends to dislike something they really want

_____   _____

(sour)

_____   _____

3 a Complete the spidergrams with the nouns in the box.

~~argument~~ choice clothes English feelings gap
grin heels influence number possibility
speed variety

(strong) (plain) (wide) (high)

|
argument

b Complete the sentences with adjective + noun collocations from Exercise 3a. More than one answer may be possible.

1 My grandparents have _____ on the subject of hospitality.
2 Can you give me directions to your house in _____ so that I can understand them?
3 Dan's face broke into a _____ when I invited him in.
4 Everyone drives at such _____ today – it's so dangerous.
5 Four different types of tea – what a _____ !
6 In more traditional cultures, grandparents have a _____ on children.

7 Please take your shoes off in the gym. _____ can damage the floor.
8 If you call Toni, there's a _____ that he'll invite you to visit him.

Phrasal verbs with *up* and *down*

4 Look at the sentences with the phrasal verb *pick up*. Which one has an obvious meaning? Which one has an idiomatic meaning?

1 I *picked up* a cup that was lying on the floor.
2 She *picked* me *up* at the hotel and took me to the party.

5 a In these sentences the meanings of the phrasal verbs are fairly obvious. Complete them with *up* or *down*.

1 The dinner won't cook if you don't turn the heat ___ .
2 We can't afford a big party – we need to keep costs ___ .
3 The old bus station has gone – they've pulled it ___ .
4 When you see someone's glass is empty, go and fill it ___ .
5 He settled ___ on the sofa to read his book.
6 The town's getting bigger – they've put ___ a lot of new houses.

b Some of these phrasal verbs have an idiomatic meaning. Match the sentence halves. Use a dictionary if necessary.

1 Please tidy up   a the apartment and sell it for a
2 I never turn down   big profit.
3 Remember to   b your best friend by breaking a
   wrap up   promise.
4 She took down   c the time of the next train
5 Look up   on the website.
6 They put up   d the mess as soon as possible.
7 Never let down   e the presents before going to
8 He decided to   the party.
   do up   f the offer of a lift home.
                  g the decorations from the wall.
                  h a tent in the garden.

c Match the phrasal verbs (1–8) in Exercise 5b with the definitions (a–h).

a decorate   e refuse
b look for information   f put something in
c disappoint   special paper
d erect   g remove
                  h make neat and
                    organised

6 Make a note of the phrasal verbs you want to remember in your vocabulary notebook. Write the whole sentence and mark the phrasal verb.

7 Discuss the questions.

1 Who tidies up in your house?
2 Has a friend ever let you down? What happened?
3 How often do you look up a word in English?

2 Earning a living

Overview

2A
- ➤ **Reading and Use of English:** Multiple choice (Part 5)
- ➤ **Language development:** Past simple and present perfect simple; Present perfect simple and continuous; *for* and *since*
- ➤ **Writing:** Formal email (Part 2)

2B
- ➤ **Speaking:** Vocabulary: Education; Collaborative task (Part 3)
- ➤ **Listening:** Multiple choice (Part 4)
- ➤ **Language development:** Articles; *some/any, something/anything*; Forming adjectives; Phrasal verbs: Education
- ➤ **Reading and Use of English:** Open cloze (Part 2); Word formation (Part 3)

Lead-in

1 Discuss the questions.
  1 Which of the jobs in the photos do you think are the most/least difficult, demanding or interesting?
  2 Some people 'work to live' and others 'live to work'. Which do you think is best? What do people you know do?

21

Reading (Paper 1 Part 5)

Before you read

1 Look at the title of the article and the photo and discuss the questions.
1 What do you think the men's business is?
2 What might the problems be with setting up this kind of business?

Skimming

2 Read the strategies on page 8 again. Then skim the article and check your answers to Exercise 1.

Multiple choice

3 Read the strategies and do the task. The first item has been done for you. (The highlighted words in the text show how the answer was found.)

> **EXPERT STRATEGY**
> * Read the question stems and mark the key words. Don't look at the options yet.
> * Find and mark the parts of the text that contain the information you need.
> * Read the options. The correct option will match the meaning of the text but use different words.
> * Read the part of the text you have marked again carefully and choose the correct option.

> **EXPERT STRATEGY**
> Reading for detail: to understand the details in a text, read it slowly and carefully. You may need to read parts of the text more than once.

> **EXPERT STRATEGY**
> Deducing meaning: You can't use a dictionary in the exam. Use clues like these to help you guess words you don't understand.
> * Is it like a word in your own language?
> * Can you work out the meaning from the context?
> * Can you work out the meaning from parts of the word itself (e.g. a prefix or a suffix)?

You are going to read an article about three men who went into business together. For questions 2–6, choose the answer (A, B, C or D) which you think fits best according to the text.

1 The three friends gave up their 'real jobs' because they had
A always dreamt of creating fruit drinks together.
B realised that one of their business ideas might be a success.
C decided their 'real jobs' did not allow them to live healthy lives.
D lost interest in what they were doing before.

2 Innocent's major obstacle to marketing their smoothies was
A deciding how to package the drink attractively.
B getting investors to put money into the business.
C working out how to keep healthy drinks fresh.
D keeping the cost low enough to sell to supermarkets.

3 The expression *not messing about with them* in line 15 suggests that they didn't
A change the basic contents of the drinks.
B worry about which bottles the drinks were in.
C check how long the drinks were kept in the shops.
D allow anyone else to distribute the drinks.

4 The business has become very successful because
A the staff are young and dynamic.
B the ingredients change according to what is popular at the time.
C the company has benefited from the partners' experience in advertising.
D the partners have kept a very clear focus on what they do.

5 Employees are motivated to work for Innocent because they
A are paid more than other people in similar jobs.
B appreciate working for a prize-winning company.
C feel they are valued by the organisation.
D get a lot of time off to pursue their own interests.

6 Innocent became a popular company when it was set up because it
A did not allow itself to become too big.
B was much admired for its underlying philosophy.
C believed in encouraging healthy eating.
D did not concern itself with making a lot of money.

Task analysis

4 Discuss your answers, explaining why you chose each option.

Vocabulary

5 Read the strategy and try to work out the meaning of the underlined words in the article.

These men are Innocent!

Back in 1998, three 26-year-olds, Adam Balon, Richard Reed and Jon Wright, made up their minds that it was time they either left their well-paid jobs in management consultancy and advertising and went into business together or stopped talking about it. What kind of business they wanted to set up they weren't quite sure but it was something they had been discussing ever since they were at university together. Deciding that the way forward was to make it easier for busy people to be healthy, the trio bought some fruit and made smoothies, which they then ==tested on people== at a small jazz festival in London. 'We put up a large sign asking, "Should we quit our jobs to make these smoothies?" and put out one bin saying "Yes" and another saying "No".' ==The 'Yes' bin filled up immediately with empty bottles and the next day they resigned from their jobs.==

However, launching Innocent smoothies did not happen overnight. Experts in the food industry told them that their product was too expensive and without the use of <u>additives</u>, the drinks wouldn't last long. Even more worryingly, the numerous banks they approached were not too keen on financing them and it wasn't until their savings were about to run out that a wealthy businessman took a leap of faith and invested in the business. Ignoring most of the advice they'd been given, Innocent then went on to create a range of drinks made from 100 percent fresh fruit and nothing else. Careful production and high-tech packaging gave the drinks the longest possible shelf life but they stuck to their beliefs by 'not messing about with them' at all. The next step was to persuade local shops to <u>stock</u> their product, which they delivered personally in their grass-covered minibus.

line 15

Their airy office in London, affectionately known as 'Fruit Towers', is open plan, the 'grass' floors, table football games, beanbags and casually dressed trendy young staff representing the fresh feeling Innocent is trying to create. But alongside all this <u>quirkiness</u> is an impressive business. New recipes created in the high-tech kitchen are tried out on the people in the surrounding office buildings, although new product ideas, however fashionable, are rejected if they go too far away from their main aim: making a natural, healthy, great-tasting drink. Their confidence that a quality product will sell itself appears to have paid off; despite <u>minimal</u> advertising, Innocent currently sells more than two million smoothies per week.

Aside from the greenery, one of the first things you notice about Fruit Towers is how happy everyone there seems to be. The three partners were convinced that success relies on the well-being and happiness of the people who work there, so as well as financial <u>incentives</u> like company shares, healthcare and extra bonuses, the staff are motivated by snowboarding trips, scholarships to enable them to pursue outside interests and studies, and a wide choice of social and sporting activities. Innocent employees are positive, motivated and proud of where they work, which is why the company has won numerous awards over the years, including *Guardian* Employer of the Year and top place in the *Sunday Times*' 'Best small companies to work for' list.

Wright, Balon and Reed had firm ideas from the very beginning about the kind of company they wanted to run. Their aim was to provide a wide range of healthy drinks, make Innocent a global brand and take its ethical values to the world's consumers. Even when, in February 2013, Coca-Cola took full control of Innocent, Reed denied that his company was 'selling out'. In anticipation of the negative reaction from those who value the Innocent image and reputation, he assured customers that Coca-Cola was 100 percent committed to protecting the brand and its values, including a promise to give 10 percent of profits to charity. In addition, the founders would continue to advise Innocent, which would continue to be run by its own team from 'Fruit Towers'.

Language development 1

Summer camp jobs in California

- Spanish-speaking counsellors required
- good English essential
- must be fun-loving, patient and concerned for the welfare of young people

Past simple and present perfect simple

➤ EXPERT GRAMMAR page 184

1a Read the advert and the extract from Isabel's letter of application. Is she a good candidate? Why/Why not?

My first language is Spanish. However, I have often been to California to visit my American friends and I have learned a lot of English over the years. Last year I spent two months on an internship program in San Francisco. Although I haven't worked at a summer camp before, two years ago I helped at a children's charity here in Peru for a month.

Spelling note:
program =
American English
programme =
British English

b Underline examples of the past simple and circle examples of the present perfect simple in Isabel's letter.

c Do we know exactly when Isabel:
1 visited friends in the USA?
2 learned English?
3 was on an internship program?
4 helped at a children's charity?

d Complete the information with examples from Isabel's letter.

A The **present perfect simple** expresses experience, actions and situations at an unspecified time in the past.
1 _____
2 _____
3 _____

B The **past simple** expresses actions at a specified time in the past.
1 _____
2 _____

2a Complete the extracts from a job interview. Use the past simple or present perfect simple form of the verbs in brackets.

1
A: _____
(you/ever/live/abroad?)
B: _____
(yes)
A: _____
(where/you/live?)
B: In Dublin.
A: _____
(when/you/go/there?)
B: In 2012.

2
A: _____
(you/ever/work/in an office?)
B: _____
(no)

3
A: _____
(you/ever/go/to the USA?)
B: _____
(yes)
A: _____
(when/you/go/there?)
B: Last year.
A: _____
(why/you/go/there?)
B: To study English.

4
A: _____
(you/use/English in your work before?)
B: _____
(no)

b Ask each other the questions in Exercise 2a and give answers which are true for you.

Present perfect simple and continuous

➤ EXPERT GRAMMAR pages 184–185

3a Read the next part of Isabel's letter. Underline examples of the present perfect simple and circle examples of the present perfect continuous.

> I have lived in Lima since 2011. I have been studying for a degree in education for two years and I have just taken my second-year exams, though I haven't had the results yet. Recently, I have been taking part in a series of workshops on children's games, which I find very interesting.

b Answer the questions.
1 Does Isabel live in Lima now?
2 Is she still studying for a degree?
3 Which of the two actions above is more permanent, 1 or 2?
4 Has she finished her exams?
5 Has she finished taking part in the workshops?

c Complete the information with examples from Isabel's letter in Exercise 3a.

A The present perfect simple expresses more permanent actions or states which started in the past and continue to the present.
_____

B The present perfect continuous expresses more temporary actions or situations which started in the past and continue to the present.
_____

C The present perfect simple expresses recent finished actions, including repeated actions.
_____

D The present perfect continuous expresses recent longer activities, which may not be finished.
_____

for and *since*

➤ EXPERT GRAMMAR page 185

> Use *for* with a period of time, and *since* with a point in time:
> *for* two years   *since* 1990

4 Read the information above and complete the phrases with *for* or *since*.
1 ___ ages
2 ___ my birthday
3 ___ a long time
4 ___ six o'clock
5 ___ half an hour
6 ___ I was born

5 Tick the correct sentences. Correct the mistakes in the wrong ones.
1 Sorry we're late. We've been sitting in traffic.
2 I've been having some good news: I've got the job!
3 Marta's been taking exams all week – she's exhausted.
4 I've read the book. Do you want it back?
5 Emma's been falling over and hurt her knee.
6 The lift isn't working, so we've used the stairs all day.

6 Complete the extract from a letter with the correct form of the verbs in brackets. Use the past simple, present perfect simple or present perfect continuous. More than one answer may be possible.

> I **(1)** _____ (be) here for two months now and I **(2)** _____ (not write) to you yet. Sorry! I hope you **(3)** _____ (not wait) for a letter. I **(4)** _____ (work) a lot and I **(5)** _____ (not have) much free time. At first I **(6)** _____ (feel) a bit lonely but recently I **(7)** _____ (make) some friends. I **(8)** _____ (try) to find somewhere to live for weeks and I think I **(9)** _____ (find) a flat at last. Up to now I **(10)** _____ (stay) with a colleague.

7 Complete the sentences so they are true for you.
1 I've written _____ .
2 I've never _____ .
3 I've _____ since _____ .
4 I've been _____ing _____ this year.
5 I haven't _____ this month.

8 Correct eight mistakes in the text.

> I have been born in Peru 26 years ago and I've lived here all my life. I am married for two years but we don't have any children yet. I've been working in a bank since four years and I enjoy it a lot. In my spare time I'm trying to improve my English – I've had private lessons for six months now. I also love reading. Last year I have tried to read a novel in English. I go to the mountains for my holidays during six years because I love walking. I've also gone to Brazil two years ago to stay with some friends.

Writing (Paper 2 Part 2: Formal email)

Lead-in

1 Look at the different types of email or letter. Which ones are likely to be very formal? Semi-formal? Informal? For some contexts, your answer might be different. Why?

a inviting a neighbour to dinner
b asking for information from a work colleague
c requesting a brochure from a university
d complaining to a travel agent
e applying for a job
f giving news to a friend

Understand the task

2 Read the task and answer the questions.

1 Who are you writing to?
2 What is the purpose of your email?
3 What information will you include in your email? (Read the question carefully.)
4 What effect do you want to have on the reader? How do you want them to feel about you?

You see this advertisement in a student newspaper.

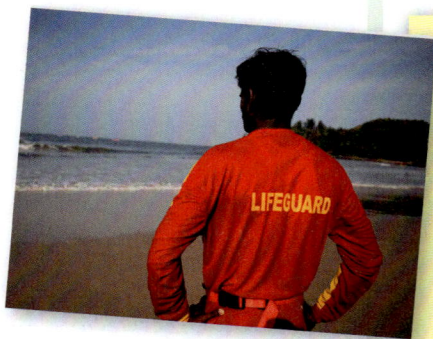

Lifeguard assistants wanted

We are looking for someone in August to assist our lifeguards, provide supervision during beach activities and observe swimmers.

Write to the Lifeguard Manager, saying what your experience and qualifications are and stating the reasons why you are suitable for the job.

*Write your **email** in **140–190** words in an appropriate style.*

Plan your email

3a Tick the points you should include in your email.
1 **Paragraph 1**: reason for writing:
   a your name
   b where you heard about the job
2 **Paragraph 2**: about you:
   a your age
   b where you are from
   c where you live
   d number of brothers and sisters
   e your education
   f your training/qualifications
   g your work experience
   h your hobbies
   i your appearance
   j what kind of person you are
3 **Paragraph 3**: your reason for applying:
   a your present job
   b what you hate about your present job
   c why you are suitable for the job
4 **Paragraph 4**: conclusion:
   a when you are available for interview
   b names and addresses of two people who can give references

b Make notes for each paragraph.

Language and content

4a Look at the sentences from a student's email. Which are appropriately formal and which are too informal?

1 I noticed the lifeguard job in the student magazine and I want to have a go.
2 I am 20 years old and I live in the Netherlands.
3 I'm studying at uni right now and I'm pretty good at PE.
4 I've never done this kind of stuff before but I'm a great swimmer.
5 I suppose you could say I really like working with different people.
6 The job would give me valuable work experience during the summer holidays.
7 I'd do the job really well – you don't have to worry about that.
8 I'll drop in for a chat.
9 I hope you'll have a good think about it and give me the job.
10 I look forward to hearing from you in the near future.

b Rewrite the inappropriate sentences from Exercise 4a in a more formal style. Use phrases from the table below.

Saying why you're writing	*I would like to apply for the position of ... , which I saw advertised ...* *One of my reasons for applying is ...*
Talking about yourself	*I am ... years old and I ...* *At present I am (working for/a student at) ...* *I am a good (swimmer).* *I regret I have had no experience of (this kind of work).* *For the last (two) years, I have been (studying/working) ...* *When I was at ... , I ...* *I very much enjoy (working with people/travelling).*
Talking about the job	*I feel I would be suitable for the job because ...* *I think I would be a suitable candidate for ... because ...* *The job would give me the opportunity to (get further work experience during the summer).*
Stating availability	*I would be happy/free/able to (attend an interview/provide references).* *I am available to attend an interview ...*
Concluding	*I hope you will consider my application.* *I look forward to hearing from you in the near future.*

c Tick the words or phrases you could use to open and close your email.

1 Dear Sue,
2 Dear Sir or Madam,
3 Hi!
4 Dear Ms Smith,
5 Hello,

6 Regards,
7 Yours faithfully,
8 Yours,
9 Yours sincerely,
10 Yours truly,

Write your email

➤ EXPERT STRATEGIES pages 177–178

5 Now write your email using the ideas and some of the language above.

Check your email

➤ EXPERT WRITING page 203

6 Edit your work using this checklist. (There is a full checklist on page 198.)

Check your:
• paragraph plan. Have you included all the points?
• use of the past simple and present perfect.
• style.
• number of words.

Speaking (Paper 4 Part 3)

Vocabulary: Education

1 Match the photos (A–D) with the stages of education (1–4). At what age do you go to schools/colleges in your country?

1 nursery school
2 primary school
3 secondary school
4 college/university

2a Which of the photos do you associate with the words and phrases in the box?

continuous assessment   curriculum   degree   exams   head teacher
higher education   homework   lecturer   playground   playgroup
strict discipline   tutorial   undergraduate   uniform

b 🎧 04 Underline the stressed syllable(s) in each of the words and phrases in the box in Exercise 2a. Then listen and check your answers.

3 Look at the subjects in the box and discuss the questions.

drama   economics   engineering   history   languages   mathematics
philosophy   science   sociology

1 Which of the subjects have you studied? At what age did you study them? Which would you like to study?
2 What is a person called who specialises in each of the subjects? Underline the stressed syllable in each word.
3 Which subjects are/were you good at at school? Which do/did you enjoy most?
4 Which ones would be the most/least useful in future life?

4 Complete the texts with the correct form of the verbs in the box.

apply   attend   do   fail   get   pass   pay   resit   revise   skip   study

A

I hated maths at school. I didn't do any of the homework, never
(1) _____ attention to the teacher and (2) _____ classes whenever I could.
Of course, the first time round I (3) _____ my exams and had
to (4) _____ them the following year. Luckily, I (5) _____ them the second
time and decided to (6) _____ to one of the better universities. I'm there
now and I am (7) _____ very well – studying maths!

B

Marc's very bright. I'm sure he'll (8) _____ a good degree, even though
he doesn't (9) _____ very hard. Of course, he hardly ever
(10) _____ lectures or (11) _____ the things we've done. I sometimes
resent the fact he's so clever!

5 What sort of student are/were you? What are/were the good and bad things about the schools you go/went to?

Collaborative task

EXPERT STRATEGY

In a collaborative task, it's important to give your opinion and also to ask for the other person's opinion and respond to it.

6a 🎧 05 Look at the spidergram and listen to the interlocutor's instructions for the first part of the task. What are the candidates required to do?

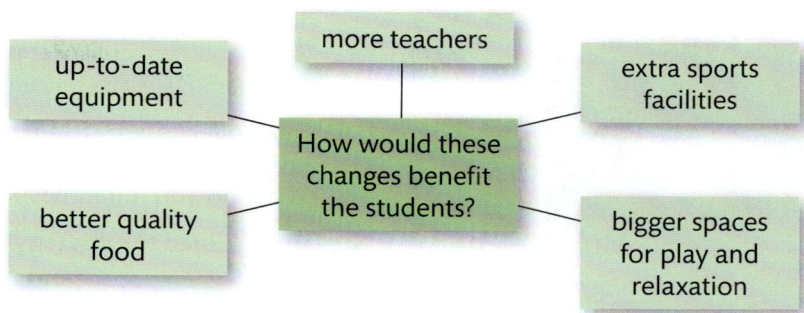

more teachers

up-to-date equipment

extra sports facilities

How would these changes benefit the students?

better quality food

bigger spaces for play and relaxation

b 🎧 06 Read the strategy and listen to two candidates doing the first part of the task. Which points of view do you agree/disagree with? Why?

c 🎧 06 Listen again and complete the phrases the candidates use to give opinions, agree or disagree.

Giving opinions	*Well, (1) _____ they would benefit a great deal from …*
	For (2) _____ , it would be the (3) _____ change in a day school.
Expressing strong agreement	*I couldn't (4) _____ .*
	That's (5) _____ .
Expressing tentative agreement	*Yes, I (6) _____ so.*
Expressing partial agreement	*Yes, I agree (7) _____ , but …*
Disagreeing	*Actually, I (8) _____ smaller classes would …*
	Do you think so? I'm (9) _____ .
	I know (10) _____ many students are not …
	No, I (11) _____ so much.

7 In the next part of the task, you have one minute to try to come to an agreement. Look at the spidergram in Exercise 6a again. Work in pairs and decide which change would have the most benefit.

Task analysis   **8** Did you follow the advice in the strategy?

Discussion   **9a** Look at the statements and decide whether you agree with them.
1 Schooldays are the happiest days of your life.
2 We can learn more from computers than from teachers.
3 Schools don't prepare children for 'the real world'.
4 Life experience is more useful than college or university.

b Discuss the statements in Exercise 9a. Give reasons for your opinions.

Listening (Paper 3 Part 4)

Before you listen

Multiple choice

1a Discuss the questions.

1 How does being at college/university differ from being at school?
2 What do you think the positive and negative aspects might be of continuing your education rather than getting a job?

b Read questions 1–7 in Exercise 2 below (but not the options yet) and mark the key words. The first two have been done for you. What do you think the answers might be?

2 🎧 07 Read the strategy and do the task.

EXPERT STRATEGY

- Read the instructions for information about the speaker and what they will talk about.
- Read the questions and options and mark the key words.
- Listen for the answer to each question. The questions follow the order of the text.
- Choose the option which is closest to what the speaker says. Listen for paraphrases of the words and phrases in the options.
- During the second listening, check that the other options aren't possible.
- To help identify opinions, listen for expressions of agreement and disagreement (e.g. *I (don't) think ...* , *In my opinion ...* , *Yes, absolutely ...* , *I'm sorry, but ...* , *Yes, that's true ...*).

*You will hear a radio interview with a student called Leanne Wilson, who is talking about her first weeks at university. For questions **1–7**, choose the best answer (**A**, **B** or **C**).*

1 What ==advice== does Leanne give about ==getting to know people== in the ==first weeks at university==?
   A Join lots of different sports clubs.
   B Avoid judging people on first impressions.
   C Make friends with people studying the same subject as you.
2 What does she ==regret== about her ==first week at university==?
   A not having more fun
   B not doing more work
   C not saving her money
3 Leanne chose not to live at home because
   A her parents discouraged her.
   B it was too far to travel every day.
   C she wanted to be independent.
4 Leanne was able to manage financially at university by
   A cutting down on her social life.
   B getting an evening job.
   C finding ways of economising.
5 What is Leanne's opinion on attending lectures?
   A It's not worth going.
   B They are useful as an introduction to the subject.
   C You should make detailed notes.
6 What did Leanne find difficult about working without supervision?
   A managing her time
   B motivating herself
   C understanding the task
7 What did she find difficult about university life?
   A being away from her family
   B having to cook for herself
   C getting stressed by work

Task analysis

3 Compare and give reasons for your answers.

Discussion

4 Discuss the question.

What advice would you give to school-leavers starting higher education?

Vocabulary: Collocations

5 Match the verbs (1–8) with the words or expressions they went with (a–h) in the interview.

1 go	a costs
2 make	b advantage of something
3 join	c time (on something)
4 take	d on your own two feet
5 cut	e around (a subject)
6 read	f a club
7 waste	g wrong
8 stand	h friends

Use of English 1 (Paper 1 Part 2)

Lead-in

1 Look at the photo below. What do you know about Albert Einstein?

Open cloze

2a Read the text in Exercise 2b quickly and answer the questions. Ignore the gaps at this stage.

1 In what field is Einstein famous?
2 What problems did he have as a student?

b Read the strategy and do the task. Use the Help notes for support with certain items.

EXPERT STRATEGY

- Read the title and text quickly for a general understanding. Ignore the gaps.
- Decide what type of word is missing in each gap (a noun? an article? a verb?).
- Put only one word in each space and do not use contractions (*isn't, doesn't*, etc.).
- Always write something.
- Read the text again and check that your answers make sense and are correctly spelt.

➤ **HELP**

In this text some gaps require *a/the* or a determiner (*all, both, most*, etc.) of some kind.

1 Choose between *a* and *the*. Think about the difference.
2 Choose a determiner that combines with *nearly* and a plural noun.
4 Which words can be used to add one negative statement to another?

---

*For questions **1–8**, read the text below and think of the word which best fits each gap. Use only **one** word in each gap. There is an example at the beginning (**0**).*

Albert Einstein
(1879–1955)

Albert Einstein is (**0**) *one* of the best-known scientists of the 20th century. Yet he was not (**1**) ___ particularly good student. At school in Munich, he got reasonable grades in nearly (**2**) ___ subjects and was outstanding in mathematics and physics but he disliked doing (**3**) ___ he was told. He didn't like exams and (**4**) ___ did he like attending classes, so he left school early.

(**5**) ___ failing the entrance exam, Einstein was eventually admitted to (**6**) ___ Swiss Federal Institute of Technology in Zurich in 1896. Although he did fairly well, he was unable to get a job in a university after graduation, mainly because he was thought to be extremely lazy. Instead, he worked in a secondary school, (**7**) ___ he taught mathematics and physics, both of which he was good at.

Some two years later, in 1902, Einstein got a job as a low-grade clerk in Bern. In 1905 his special theory of relativity (**8**) ___ published – one of the greatest intellectual achievements in the history of human thought.

Task analysis

c Discuss the questions about the task.

1 Which questions test articles and determiners?
2 Which one of these is also tested?
   a the present perfect
   b the passive
3 Which questions did you find difficult? Why?

Discussion

3 Is/Was your school career similar to Einstein's? In what way is/was it different?

Language development 2

Articles

➤ **EXPERT GRAMMAR** page 185

1a Read the information. Then find examples of the different uses of articles in the text on page 31.

A *a/an*: before singular, countable nouns
- the first time we refer to something
  A man went into a café to ask for directions.
- with jobs
  She's an airline pilot.

B *the*
- to refer to something already known
  The man had seen the café from his car.
- in certain expressions
  I play the piano.
  Are you going to the cinema tonight?
- before most seas, oceans, rivers, groups of islands/mountains, deserts and nationalities
  the Pacific Ocean
  The British can be very reserved.
- when there is only one of something
  The United Nations are meeting in New York.
  The sun rises very early in summer.

C No article
- when talking about something in general
  Schools are too big nowadays.
- before subjects of study
  I study physics.
- before most countries, continents, towns and streets
  I live in France.
- in certain expressions
  at home   in summer/winter

---

b Correct the mistakes in the sentences.

1 The best course was the one I did on the economics. The teacher was very good and I made a good progress.
2 Nina's studying the German at evening classes in the London.
3 My brother is 19. He's at the university in the Africa and wants to become English teacher because it would give him good opportunity to travel.
4 When we were in Japan, we noticed that most Japanese students work harder than the American students I met in USA.
5 I go to college by the train. Unfortunately, the train is often late.

c Complete the text with *a*, *the* or – (no article).

When (1) ___ students in the UK were asked by (2) ___ national newspaper what kind of (3) ___ college they would like to go to, they agreed that one of (4) ___ most important things was (5) ___ location of (6) ___ college and (7) ___ other was (8) ___ state of (9) ___ buildings. (10) ___ majority said they wanted (11) ___ light, well-decorated college with (12) ___ comfortable seats in the lecture rooms. They also wanted (13) ___ college with (14) ___ flexible timetable, where they could spend (15) ___ time on what they enjoy and where learning (16) ___ new skills was fun and exciting. Interestingly, no one said they didn't want to go to (17) ___ college at all.

---

some/any, something/anything

A *some/any (of)*
  *I got **some** good **grades** in my exams.* (countable)
  *The teacher gave me **some** good **advice**.* (uncountable)
  ***Some (of the)** grades were outstanding.* (a limited number)
  ***Some of them** were excellent.* (of before pronouns)
  *Were **any of them** bad?* (it doesn't matter which ones)
  *It was **some weeks/time** before the exam results came out.* (a large number/amount of)
  *Take **any books** you want.* (it doesn't matter which ones)
  *Tell me if you have **any problems**.* (they may not exist)

B *something/anything*
  *I want to give you **something** to read.* (positive)
  *I don't want to give you **anything**.* (negative)
  *Have you got **anything** for me?* (question; I don't know if you have.)
  *Have you got **something** for me?* (question; I hope/think you have.)
  *There's **hardly anything** left to eat.* (= almost nothing)
  *Have you seen **anything** interesting lately?* (something/anything + adjective)

---

2 Read the extract from a student's email to her parents and choose the correct answers.

It's been quite (1) *some / any* time since I've been in touch. Sorry about that. There never seems to be (2) *some / any* time to do (3) *something / anything* these days – except work, of course. Anyway, I've decided to have (4) *some / any* time off in the next few weeks. I'm not promising (5) *something / anything* definite but I'm hoping to get home for at least a couple of days. But I'll need (6) *some / any* money for the train fare – I've got (7) *any / hardly any* left in the bank until my next cheque comes through. Could you lend me (8) *some / any*? I'll be able to get (9) *some / any* work in a restaurant in the holidays, so I'll pay you back then. Apart from that, what I'd like to do more than (10) *something / anything* else when I get home is just relax!

Use of English 2 (Paper 1 Part 3)

Lead-in

1 Discuss the questions.

1 Have you got a good memory? What kind of things do you forget?

2 What techniques do you use to help you remember things?

Word formation

2a Read the article in Exercise 2b quickly and answer the questions. Ignore the gaps at this stage.

1 What can be stressful for students at exam time?

2 What suggestions are there for improving your memory?

b Read the strategy and do the task. Use the Help notes for support with certain items.

*For questions **1–8**, read the text below. Use the word given in capitals at the end of some of the lines to form a word that fits in the gap **in the same line**. There is an example at the beginning (**0**).*

Remembering for exams

It's frustrating for everybody not to be able to remember things but having a bad memory can be a particular (**0**) *disadvantage* for students at exam time.   ADVANTAGE
Anyway, I did a search on the internet and found
(1) ___ ideas for improving your memory. One idea I   COUNT
thought particularly (2) ___ was that we should try and   VALUE
use all our senses when given information to learn.
So, for example, instead of reading (3) ___ , we should   SILENT
record the material and then listen to it. Apparently,
the (4) ___ of speaking and listening helps reinforce   COMBINE
the (5) ___ text. Another theory, which some people   WRITE
might find (6) ___ , is that there is a greater   LIKELY
(7) ___ of our memorising something successfully if   POSSIBLE
we do it when the house is (8) ___ and, preferably,   PEACE
just before bedtime.

EXPERT STRATEGY

• Read the title and whole text first for general understanding. Ignore the gaps.
• Read each sentence. What kind of word is needed in each gap? (a noun? an adjective? an adverb? a verb?)
• Change the form of each word on the right to fit the space.
• Read the whole text again. Check it makes sense.
• Check your spelling. It must be correct.

➤ HELP

Some words might need a prefix or a suffix and some might be negative.

1 Choose from these suffixes to change this verb into an adjective: *-ish*, *-less*, *-ate*.

2 Choose from these suffixes to change this noun into an adjective: *-able*, *-less*, *-ful*, *-est*.

3 Is the missing word an adjective or an adverb?

5 Past participles can be used as adjectives when they come before a noun.

Task analysis

3 Discuss the questions about the task.

1 Are there any answers you would like to check in a dictionary?

2 Which answers required:

a nouns?

b adjectives?

c adverbs?

3 Which answers required

a a suffix?

b a negative prefix?

4 Which questions did you find difficult? Why?

Discussion

4 Do you agree with the ideas in the text? How do you revise for exams?

Language development 3

Forming adjectives

➤ EXPERT GRAMMAR page 186

> A Suffixes:
>   1 Sometimes we add a suffix to form an adjective:
>   *suit* (verb) → *suit**able*** (adjective)
>   *health* (noun) → *health**y*** (adjective)
>   2 Sometimes the stem has to change:
>   *decide* (verb) → *deci**sive*** (adjective)
>   *beauty* (noun) → *beauti**ful*** (adjective)
>
> B Sometimes we make internal changes:
>   *freeze* (verb/noun) → *frozen* (adjective)
>   *heat* (verb/noun) → *hot* (adjective)
>
> C We can add a prefix to change the meaning of an adjective:
>   *regular* → ***ir**regular*; *honest* → ***dis**honest* (opposite)
>   *national* → ***inter**national* (between)

1a Complete the sentences with adjectives formed from the words in brackets and one of the suffixes in the box.

-al   -ate   -ful   -ible   -ic   -ish   -less   -ly   -ous   -y

1 That boy is naughty but he's ___ (harm).
2 It's ___ (nature) for a child to be like that sometimes.
3 Despite his illness, Paul made the ___ (courage) decision to sit his exams.
4 Beth often behaves in a very silly and ___ (child) way.
5 Our teacher gave us some ___ (help) suggestions about studying.
6 Mr Turner has always been ___ (passion) about science.
7 Please clean any ___ (dirt) equipment after you have done the experiment.
8 The sports teacher at my old school was ___ (horror)!
9 There have been ___ (drama) changes in the education system.
10 I like my music teacher as she's very ___ (live).

b Answer the questions about yourself.
1 Have you ever been irresponsible? What happened?
2 Do you think everybody is dishonest on occasions?
3 Is your handwriting the most illegible in the class?

Phrasal verbs: Education

2a Match the phrasal verbs in *italics* in the sentences (1–10) with their definitions (a–j).
1 The principal *handed in* his resignation.
2 The students *turned up* late for class.
3 The teacher *got* her ideas *across* very well.
4 We *worked out* the answers very easily.
5 He *stayed on* at university another year.
6 I *got down to* work as soon as I arrived.
7 A taxi *picked* them *up* and took them to college.
8 She *kept up with* the other students.
9 We *carried out* a survey on staff attitudes.
10 He *went over* the exercise with his students.
a arrived
b collected
c managed to understand
d managed to do as well as
e did
f checked
g gave to a person in charge
h communicated
i started
j remained

b Complete the sentences with the correct form of the phrasal verbs in Exercise 2a.
1 It was a very quiet party. Half the guests never ____ at all!
2 Are you _____ after class tonight or going home?
3 Who's going to _____ that experiment?
4 We're trying to _____ the best way to meet students' needs.
5 _____ your answers carefully.
6 I haven't _____ my homework yet. It's still in my bag.
7 I can't _____ all the latest technology.
8 Come and _____ your old coursework from my office.
9 He didn't really _____ his meaning _____ to the students.
10 It's time I _____ marking the papers.

3 The world around us

The historic centre of Kraków, Poland

Los Glaciares National Park, Argentina

Lead-in 1 **Discuss the questions.**

1 The places in the photos are both World Heritage Sites. Why do you think they were chosen?
2 Why is it important to preserve our natural and cultural heritage?

Reading (Paper 1 Part 6)

Before you read   **1**   How much do you already know about the history of London?

Skimming and scanning   **2**   Read the strategies on page 8 again. Then skim and scan the text to find out what impact the following had on London. Ignore the gaps at this stage.

- the Romans   • the Vikings   • the Normans
- Henry VIII   • the Plague   • the Great Fire
- the Industrial Revolution   • World War II

Gapped text   **3**   Read the strategy and do the task. The first item has been done for you. The highlighted words in D link to the highlighted parts of the text.

EXPERT STRATEGY

- Read the whole of the base text to get an idea of how it's structured.
- Read the text before and after each gap. Predict the missing information and underline any nouns, pronouns, linkers, etc. which may help you.
- Read the options and try to find one that fits the topic. Look for clues such as grammatical links (e.g. tenses), lexical links (e.g. synonyms) and reference links (e.g. pronouns).
- If you're not sure, go on to the next gap.
- Read the text again, with your answers, to check it makes sense.

*You are going to read an article about the history of London. Six sentences have been removed from the article. Choose from the sentences (**A–G**) the one which fits each gap (**1–6**). There is one extra sentence which you do not need to use.*

A   Unfortunately, this new period of wealth was hard hit by a global economic crisis, shortly followed by another attack on the city, in which much of London was ruined.

B   The author Charles Dickens vividly describes the London of that time in his novels as poor, dirty and crime-ridden.

C   During his reign, the River Thames became the focal point of London as the navy was expanded and ships were sent out to explore the world.

D   ==These dreams suffered a huge blow== when ==there was an uprising== against the invaders and this area, later known as London, ==was burnt to the ground== in the first of many disastrous fires.

E   This was a mistake, as it meant very few dogs and cats were left to catch the diseased rats and as a result, around 100,000 people are estimated to have died.

F   But the city's location on the Thames was far too good for its decline to continue.

G   In fact, many of the streets in the city were named after the particular trade which was practised there.

Task analysis   **4**   Compare and give reasons for your answers. What kinds of links helped you?

Discussion   **5**   Discuss the questions.

1   What were the 'highs' and 'lows' of London's history? What were the high and low points of your country's capital city?
2   Which city in the world do you think has had the most interesting history?

Vocabulary: Near synonyms   **6**   Find words or phrases in the text that have similar meanings to these words and phrases.

1   discouraged (paragraph 2)
2   cleanliness (paragraph 3)
3   destroy (paragraph 4)
4   deadly (paragraph 5)
5   disaster (paragraph 5)
6   suddenly appeared (paragraph 7)

A colourful heritage

Twenty-first century London is an exciting place to be. Around 15 million tourists a year visit the city to experience its culture, history and lively nightlife.

Yet it has had more than its fair share of misfortunes. After the invasion of CE43, the Romans developed an area around the River Thames into a trading centre, in the hope of establishing the city as the future capital of England. **1** **D** **Not to be put off**, the new rulers quickly defeated the rebels and went on to rebuild the city. However, the Roman Empire crumbled in the fifth century and with it, the power and influence of London.

2 Trade soon began to expand again, until the Danish Vikings burnt the city to the ground once more in the ninth century. The next 100 years is a confused tale of further invasions but a more settled era began when the Norman King William the Conqueror was crowned in 1066. Within the original Roman walls, the city continued to grow, although wooden houses crowded tightly together meant that fire was a continual hazard and hygiene was so poor that when the Black Death swept through Europe in the 14th century, it killed nearly half of London's inhabitants.

A new London was born in the 16th century, when Henry VIII gave away much of the land previously owned by the church for private development. **3** It was also the period of the first theatres, made famous by Shakespeare's plays. By the 16th century, there were about 200,000 people living in London, although two disasters in the next century would again wipe out much of the population and devastate most of the city itself.

London was no stranger to the Plague but a fatal variety brought over by rats on trading ships caused panic. While those who could escaped the city, sufferers were locked in their houses and orders were given for all household pets to be killed. **4** The next calamity, the Great Fire, put an end to the Plague but burnt down four-fifths of the city. It was during this period that Sir Christopher Wren designed and built many of the well-known London churches we can still see today.

The Industrial Revolution saw the population explode to six million in 100 years as Victorian London became the centre of trade, thanks to the arrival of the railways. However, despite all this economic expansion, living conditions amongst the poor were dreadful. **5**

The boundaries of the City spread outwards in the 20th century, as the population continued to snowball and luxury hotels and department stores sprang up. **6** This time it was bombs which caused the devastation. The period after World War II saw massive rebuilding and also heavy immigration, which was to change the character of the city yet again.

Language development 1

Adjectives and adverbs

> EXPERT GRAMMAR page 186

1a Look at the photos below. Which of the sites do you recognise?

b Read the article. What do these sites have in common? Ignore the words in *italics* at this stage.

The world's *natural* and *cultural* heritage is disappearing *fast* but UNESCO, a United Nations organisation, is working *hard* to preserve it. UNESCO has created a list of more than 900 places, known as World Heritage Sites. The sites on this list should be *actively* protected by all governments. Cultural sites on this list include the Taj Mahal, the *best-known* building in India, the *lively* Islamic centre of Marrakesh and the Statue of Liberty, an *extremely impressive* gift from the people of France to the people of the United States. The World Heritage List also includes natural reserves such as the Galapagos Islands, a place that at one time had *hardly* any tourists but is now in danger of being destroyed by them. UNESCO works *well* and without it, the future of many *fascinating* Heritage Sites would look *bleak*, so it is *worrying* that for *political* reasons, some countries, like the USA and the UK, have withdrawn from *full* membership.

2a Now look at the words in *italics* in the article. Which are adjectives and which are adverbs? Write them in the correct place in the table.

Adjectives	Adverbs
natural	

b Answer the questions.
1 Most adverbs end in *-ly*. What exceptions are there in the article?
2 Which adjective in the article ends in *-ly*?
3 Some adverbs have two forms, each with a different meaning. What example is there of this in the article?

c Read the information on page 186 and check your answers to Exercise 2b.

3a Choose the correct answers.
1 Usually, it's *easy / easily* to know when you're looking at a World Heritage Site.
2 Chartres Cathedral is *incredible / incredibly* well preserved.
3 Our guide round the Summer Palace in Beijing spoke too *fast / quick*.
4 The Kremlin is a *classic / classically* Heritage Site.
5 When we got to Glasgow, it was very *late / lately* in the afternoon and it was snowing *hard / hardly*.
6 Some World Heritage Sites are quite *surprising / surprisingly*. For example, the city of Brasília was *imaginative / imaginatively* created from nothing in 1956.

b Which places in your country would you nominate as World Heritage Sites?

Adverbs of degree

➤ EXPERT GRAMMAR page 187

A to make adjectives and other adverbs stronger: *extremely, very, really, remarkably*
The castle is **really/remarkably** popular.
It's a **very/an extremely** popular attraction.
B to make adjectives and adverbs weaker:
• *rather, fairly, pretty* (positive and negative adjectives)
The city wall is **rather/fairly/pretty** long.
My town is **rather/fairly/pretty** small.
It's **rather a/a rather/a fairly/a pretty** small town. (*fairly a, pretty a*)
• *a bit, a little* (negative adjectives only)
London's **a bit/a little** expensive.
London's **a bit of an** expensive city. (before a noun phrase)
• *quite*
The palace is **quite** interesting.
It's **quite an** interesting palace. (*a quite interesting palace*)
C to emphasise ungradable adjectives: *absolutely*
The temperatures were **absolutely** freezing. (*very freezing, a bit freezing*)
There's an **absolutely** gorgeous view from the top. (*very gorgeous*)

4 Read the information above and choose the correct answer (A, B, C or D).
  1 It was a ___ simple idea.
     A bit   B little   C quite   D remarkably
  2 Karl's got ___ a fast car.
     A pretty   B very   C quite   D extremely
  3 Everybody thinks he is ___ crazy.
     A a little   B a little of   C a bit of   D quite a
  4 Goya's paintings are ___ well known.
     A a bit   B absolutely   C very   D rather a
  5 This is ___ an important day.
     A fairly   B rather   C extremely   D pretty
  6 Your new dress looks very ___ .
     A gorgeous   B wonderful   C marvellous   D beautiful
  7 The weather was ___ wonderful.
     A very   B absolutely   C extremely   D remarkably

5 Use the adjectives in the box with adverbs of degree to talk about 1–3.

dull   fantastic   interesting   lively

  1 a place you have visited
  2 a person you know well
  3 a good film or book

6 Correct the mistakes in the sentences.
  1 It's easy to find my house. There's a very huge statue on the other side of the road.
  2 The park is really lovely and the new theatre is very fantastic.
  3 You don't need to be smart dressed. People dress casually here in summer.
  4 They are working very hardly to restore the Town Hall before the president's visit next month.
  5 It's a fairly lively town, which I like, but the streets are sometimes bit noisy at night.

Writing (Paper 2 Part 1: Essay)

Lead-in 1 Discuss the questions and make notes.
  1 Should governments spend money protecting historic sites? Why/Why not?
  2 Is it more important to keep the past alive or invest in the future?

Understand the task 2 Read the task and answer the questions.
  1 Who is going to read the essay and what is its purpose?
  2 Will you just give your opinion or will you give both sides of the argument (for and against)?
  3 What information must you include?
  4 What style will you use?
  5 What do you think makes a good essay?

> *In your English class, you have been talking about the subject of cultural heritage. Now your English teacher has asked you to write an essay.*
>
> *Write an essay using all the notes and give reasons for your point of view.*
>
> Is it a good thing that countries spend a lot of money on their heritage?
>
> Notes
>
> Write about:
>
> 1 preserving the past
>
> 2 investing in the future
>
> 3 _____ (your own idea)
>
> *Write your **essay** in **140–190** words in an appropriate style.*

Plan your essay 3 a Look at your notes from Exercise 1. Can you use any of the points for Notes 1 and 2 in the task?

  b Do you have any ideas for Note 3? Which of these might make a good extra topic: tourism, the environment, private investment?

c In all essays, you have to give your opinion. In this one, you could agree or disagree, giving reasons; or give arguments for and against, as well as your opinion. Look at this possible paragraph plan for a 'for and against' essay. You need four or five paragraphs. Make notes of the points you will include in each paragraph. Include a maximum of two points per paragraph.

EXPERT STRATEGY

Begin by making a general statement. Then support it with a reason and/or an example.

*Paragraph 1: Introduction: general statement/rhetorical question →
supporting sentence(s)*
*Paragraphs 2/3: Arguments for:
introductory sentence → supporting sentence(s): reason/example*
*Paragraphs 3/4: Arguments against:
introductory sentence → supporting sentence(s): reason/example*
Paragraphs 4 or 5: Conclusion: summing up/balancing the argument/the overall point of view → supporting sentence(s)

Language and content

4a Choose the best sentence for the essay from each pair below.

A
1 On balance, despite the strong arguments against, I think it is important to protect our heritage.
2 Fine, yes you can argue against it, but overall, no, not really.
B
1 I agree with the question.
2 Most countries spend large sums of money protecting their national heritage.
C
1 It's silly not to spend money on things we need now.
2 The problem is that governments need more money for things like housing and roads.
D
1 On the one hand, it is important to protect the past for future generations.
2 No way should we let go of the past.

b Match the sentences you chose in Exercise 4a (A–D) with the paragraphs in Exercise 3c.

c Now decide which of the sentences can be used as the first sentence of each paragraph.

d Think of a second sentence for each of the first sentences.

e Match the sentence openings with the paragraphs in Exercise 3c. (Some may go with more than one paragraph.) Then complete one for each paragraph in your essay with your own ideas.
1 On the other hand, …
2 Another reason for doing it is …
3 However, in my view, …
4 To conclude, there are arguments …
5 The first point I'd like to make is …
6 On the positive side, …
7 Many people claim …
8 Although there are many arguments on both sides, …
9 Though it is true (that) … , we should also bear in mind (that) …

Write your essay

➤ **EXPERT STRATEGIES** pages 177–178

5 Now write your essay, using the ideas and some of the language above.

Check your essay

➤ **EXPERT WRITING** pages 199–200

6 Which of the statements are true about your essay?
1 I have answered the question.
2 The sentences and organisation are clear and logical.
3 Arguments are followed by reasons and examples.
4 Both sides of the argument are given equal treatment.
5 It is clear what I think by the end.
6 The style is consistent and neutral.
7 I have checked: length, grammar, spelling, punctuation and linking expressions.

EXPERT LANGUAGE: Punctuation

Rewrite the paragraph with appropriate capital letters and punctuation.

when youre in england you must visit chester it dates back to roman times so there are lots of fascinating ruins which im sure will interest you and which english heritage a branch of the british government wants to preserve the roman amphitheatre is well worth a visit with its guides dressed up as roman soldiers there is also a cathedral and a church and there are red sandstone walls all around the town it takes about an hour and a half to walk round them but its a lovely walk henry james the american writer wrote about how much he loved these walls unfortunately many of chesters heritage sites were destroyed in the 20th century to make way for a ring road and more are under threat in this century

Speaking (Paper 4 Part 2)

Vocabulary: Animals

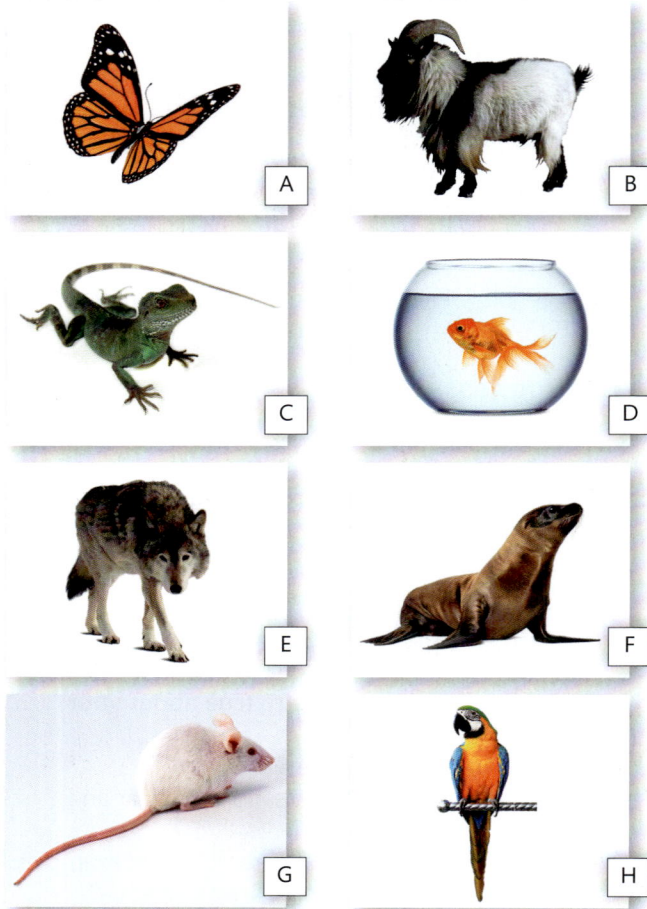

A

B

C

D

E

F

G

H

1a What are the names of the animals in the pictures? Which have an irregular spelling in the plural?

b Which of the animals in Exercise 1a might you find in these places? Name one only for each place. Where might you find each of the others? More than one answer may be possible.
- farm
- jungle
- forest
- house

c Which of the animals in Exercise 1a is an example of the following? More than one answer may be possible.
- insect
- rodent
- reptile
- sea animal
- domestic pet

d Which animal from Exercise 1a has:
1 a tail?	5 a beak?
2 wings?	6 hooves?
3 claws?	7 fur?
4 whiskers?	8 fins?

e Which of the animals in Exercise 1a:
1 squeaks?
2 howls?
3 screeches?

2 Check the meaning and pronunciation of the words in the box in a dictionary. Then write them next to the categories below. Some may go in more than one category.

ant   bear   beaver   bee   beetle   bull   calf
dolphin   giraffe   guinea pig   hamster   leopard
moose   mosquito   penguin   pigeon   rabbit   shark
sheep   squirrel   tortoise   vulture   whale

1 domestic pets
2 farm animals
3 wild animals
4 birds
5 insects

3 Think of an example of an animal which:
1 bites.
2 pecks.
3 stings.
4 scratches.
5 hibernates.
6 builds a nest.
7 is in danger of becoming extinct.

4a Which animals do you associate with adjectives 1–9? You can choose from the animals in the box or any other animals you know.

cat   crocodile   dog   donkey   fox   jaguar   lion
snake   tiger

1 aggressive	6 agile
2 elegant	7 affectionate
3 proud	8 useful
4 fierce	9 intelligent
5 cunning	

b Compare the animals in Exercise 4a using adjectives 1–9 and any other adjectives you know.

5 Which animals:
a do you like most?
b have you kept as a pet?
c have a personality which is similar to yours?

Comparing photos

6 Look at the photos. What jobs do they show?

7 Answer the questions.
1 What do the photos have in common?
2 What is different about them?

They both show …

In the one on the left …, whereas in the other one …

Sample answer

8a 🎧 08 Listen and complete the sentence from the interlocutor's instructions.

I'd like you to compare the photographs and say why _____ .

b 🎧 09 Listen to a candidate doing the task and answer the questions.
1 Did he mention the same similarities and differences as you?
2 Did he use the same language to compare?

c 🎧 09 Listen again and tick the expression Emil uses to give a personal opinion.
1 Personally, I …
2 I'm not really very interested in …
3 It's very hard to say but …

d 🎧 09 Listen again. Which three words doesn't Emil know? How does he explain them?

e Do you agree with Emil's opinions?

> **EXPERT STRATEGY**
> • Listen carefully to the instructions.
> • Say what is similar and different about the photos. Don't just describe each one.
> • Give your personal opinion in the second part of the task.

Long turn

➤ EXPERT SPEAKING pages 179–180

9 Work in pairs. Read the strategy and follow the instructions below.

Student 1: Compare the photos above and say what you think is difficult about these jobs.

Student 2: Compare the photos on page 208 and say why you think dogs might be useful for this kind of work.

Task analysis

10 Discuss the questions about the task.
Did you:
1 compare the photos?
2 answer the second part of the task with your opinion/reaction?
3 speak for a full minute?

Discussion

11 What other jobs involve working with animals? Which ones would you most/least like to do? Why?

Listening (Paper 3 Part 2)

Before you listen

1 Read the instructions and gapped sentences in Exercise 2b. What do you think Jay Carter's experience of being in the Amazon rainforest was like?

Sentence completion

2a Decide what type of word is missing in each gap in Exercise 2b.
Question 1: a plural noun

b 🎧 10 Read the strategy and do the task.

*You will hear a man called Jay Carter talking about his time in the Amazon rainforest. For questions **1–10**, complete the sentences with a word or short phrase.*

Experiences in the rainforest

The purpose of Jay's trip to the Amazon was to write an article about the **(1)** _____ which live in the rainforest.

Jay was unprepared for the lack of **(2)** _____ in the rainforest.

Jay makes a comparison between the huge noisy insects in the rainforest and **(3)** _____ with wings.

Jay uses the word **(4)** _____ to describe his feelings when he first saw a jaguar.

Jay says that the average male jaguar has a territory of **(5)** _____ in size.

When he met the local forest people, Jay remembers being offered a very large **(6)** _____ to eat.

Jay says that the forest people have a feeling of **(7)** _____ for the jaguars.

Jay explains that in some areas, **(8)** _____ regard jaguars as a threat to their property.

Jay has heard that being in contact with animals such as **(9)** _____ is a potential health risk to jaguars.

The **(10)** _____ that Jay is now involved in are intended to raise awareness of the threats to the survival of jaguars.

EXPERT STRATEGY

- Read the sentences and decide what kind of information is missing.
- Listen and complete the sentences with a word, number or short phrase from the recording. The sentences are in the same order as the information on the recording.
- Write no more than three words. Only use words from the recording.
- Check your answers during the second listening. Don't leave any blanks.
- Check your spelling and grammar.

Task analysis

3 Compare and discuss your answers. If they were wrong, what was the reason?

Use of English 1 (Paper 1 Part 2)

Lead-in 1 Do you think the statements are *True* (T) or *False* (F)? (Your teacher has the answers.)
   1 Cats don't see colours as clearly as people do.
   2 A dog's sense of smell is much better than a person's.
   3 Elephants have long memories.
   4 Crickets can tell us the temperature.
   5 Cows lie down before a storm.

Open cloze

➤ EXPERT STRATEGIES page 175

2a Read the title of the article in Exercise 2c. What connection do you think it has with animals?

 b Read the article quickly and answer the questions. Ignore the gaps at this stage.
   1 How do some animals change their behaviour before an earthquake?
   2 What use have the Chinese made of animals?
   3 How can animals' behaviour be explained scientifically?

 c Read the strategy on page 31 and do the task. Use the Help notes for support with certain items.

➤ **HELP**

1 This question tests verb forms. What verb form is correct here?

3 This is another question testing verb forms. Were the animals restless before the reports were made or at the same time?

5 This city has been mentioned before. Which article is used to show this?

For questions **1–8**, read the text below and think of the word which best fits each gap. Use only **one** word in each gap. There is an example at the beginning (0).

Predicting earthquakes

It has long (0) *been* known that some animals behave differently before an earthquake. People (1) ___ seen fish jump out of water onto dry land and mice appear dazed before quakes.
In December 1974, Chinese scientists began (2) ___ receive reports of snakes coming out of hibernation and freezing to death before a series of minor tremors. The following month, reports were received from the city of Haicheng of cattle and horses which (3) ___ become restless and were much (4) ___ frightened to enter the buildings which sheltered them at night. As a result, city leaders evacuated (5) ___ entire city. Soon after, a major earthquake struck and countless lives were saved.
(6) ___ then, China has suffered a number of major quakes, which they were not as prepared (7) ___ . Nevertheless, the Chinese have demonstrated that earthquakes do not always strike without warning. (8) ___ is a fact that some animals are very sensitive to magnetic fields and therefore may be able to detect the seismic activity which comes before an earthquake.

Task analysis 3 Which questions in the task test:
   1 articles?
   2 auxiliary verbs?
   3 'verb + verb' patterns?

Language development 2

-ing forms and infinitives

➤ **EXPERT GRAMMAR** pages 187–188

1a Read the information. Then find examples of some of the structures in the article on page 45.

> **A** After a main verb we can use:
> - an *-ing* form: *I like walking. I heard a man shouting.*
> - a *to*-infinitive: *I wanted **to see** her.*
> - an infinitive (without *to*): *Let me help!*
>   *That **makes** me **feel** better.*
>   *Did anyone **see** John leave?*
> **B** The *-ing* form is used after prepositions.
> *I'm thinking **of getting** a new job.*
> *Nadia is keen **on learning** new things.*
> **C** The *-ing* form can also be used in some fixed expressions.
> *The family **spent** a lot of **time arguing**.*
> *It's always **worth asking** for a discount.*
> **D** The infinitive can be used after:
> - some adjectives: *She's **eager to learn**.*
> - some nouns: *It was **my decision to leave**.*

b Discuss the questions.
1 What causes a solar eclipse?
2 Have you ever seen a solar eclipse?

c Complete the notes about a solar eclipse. Use the correct form of the verbs in brackets.

> - Many creatures wanted **(1)** ___ (settle down) to sleep.
> - Other animals, like owls, had problems **(2)** ___ (sleep) and woke up.
> - I saw a bat suddenly **(3)** ___ (fly) out of a tree.
> - I couldn't help **(4)** ___ (notice) a cold breeze.
> - Scientists were interested in **(5)** ___ (solve) the mysteries of the sun.
> - Spectators saw the sky gradually **(6)** ___ (go) dark. I regretted **(7)** ___ (not record) it.
> - The experience was awesome – it made us all **(8)** ___ (feel) very small!
> - I found it hard **(9)** ___ (talk) for a few minutes.
> - A lot of people made the decision **(10)** ___ (not drive) during the eclipse.

2a The verbs *stop, try, remember* can be followed by an *-ing* form or a *to*-infinitive. Look at the sentence pairs below. What is the difference in meaning?
1 a He remembered to wear protective glasses.
  b He remembered wearing protective glasses.
2 a She tried using a camcorder to record the event.
  b She tried to use a camcorder to record the event.
3 a He stopped to look at the bright lights.
  b He stopped looking at the bright lights.

b Choose the correct answers.
1 He stopped at the shop *to buy / buying* a pint of milk.
2 I tried *to get / getting* eggs but they didn't have any.
3 Lucy stopped *to drink / drinking* coffee ages ago.
4 Please remember *to post / posting* the letter.
5 I remember *to call / calling* Mike yesterday.
6 Try *to add / adding* some salt. It might taste better.

3a Look at the photo in Exercise 3b. Have you heard of this natural phenomenon?

b Read about a couple's trip to see the Northern Lights. Then complete the blog entry with *to, on, from, for, of* or *in* and the correct form of the verbs in brackets.

> ⊙ **Browsing blogs**
>
>
>
> **Northern Lights in the skies above Scotland**
>
> The possibility **(1)** _____ (see) the Northern Lights was Laura's main reason for visiting the Shetland Islands. She had been looking forward **(2)** _____ (go) there for ages. I was more interested **(3)** _____ (get) some rest and fresh air.
>
> When we arrived, Laura had a headache, so I insisted **(4)** _____ (put up) the tent myself. She apologised **(5)** _____ (not help) and decided **(6)** _____ (go) for a walk. I didn't object **(7)** _____ (her/go) as I'm not very keen **(8)** _____ (walk) and I thought it might help her headache. And anyway, I can rarely prevent **(9)** _____ (her/do) what she wants to do!
>
> Soon, it got very dark. I decided to look for Laura. I was afraid **(10)** _____ (get) lost but I needn't have worried – suddenly, there were curtains of red, green and white light everywhere. It was the Northern Lights!

4a Complete the sentences so they are true for you.
1 When I'm on holiday, I enjoy …
2 My greatest ambition in life is …
3 The country I'd most like to visit …

b Compare and discuss your answers.

Use of English 2 (Paper 1 Part 1)

Lead-in

1 Read the title of the article in Exercise 2b and look at the photo. Have you heard of Groundhog Day?

Multiple-choice cloze

➤ EXPERT STRATEGIES page 175

2a Read the title and text quickly and answer the questions. Ignore the gaps at this stage.
  1 What happens on Groundhog Day?
  2 Why has it become better known in recent years?

b Do the task. Use the Help notes for support with certain items.

Punxsutawney Phil

> **HELP**

1 Only one of these adjectives can combine with *weather* to mean 'bad'.

4 Remember that *camera* is a countable noun.

*For questions **1–8**, read the text below and decide which answer (**A**, **B**, **C** or **D**) best fits each gap. There is an example at the beginning (**0**).*

| Home 🏠 | Previous ‹ | Next › | Search 🔍 |

Groundhog Day

According to a popular US tradition, the groundhog, a small furry animal, (0) _B_ of its winter sleep on 2 February. If the sky is clear, he sees his shadow. This means there are going to be six more weeks of (1) ___ weather and he returns to his hole. If the day is cloudy and he can't see his shadow, it means there will be an (2) ___ spring and he stays above ground. Each year reporters (3) ___ in Punxsutawney, Pennsylvania, at dawn and a large (4) ___ of cameras are focused on the burrow of a groundhog called Punxsutawney Phil.

In 1993, the Hollywood film *Groundhog Day* (5) ___ Phil into a major celebrity and the following February, over 30,000 people (6) ___ in Punxsutawney. Unfortunately, (7) ___ the large crowds were hoping for a prediction of good weather, Phil saw his shadow and returned to his hole, so everyone knew that winter was going to (8) ___ for a few more weeks.

0	A gets out	B comes out	C gets up	D comes up
1	A own	B severe	C ill	D rude
2	A advanced	B ahead	C early	D immature
3	A gather	B group	C crowd	D combine
4	A quantity	B number	C total	D sum
5	A got	B became	C took	D turned
6	A turned up	B called off	C came on	D looked over
7	A despite	B although	C still	D otherwise
8	A exist	B rest	C last	D hold

Task analysis

3a Which questions in the task test:
  1 phrasal verbs?
  2 linking words?

b Which adjective + noun collocations in the text link to either weather or the seasons? Make a note of the words you want to remember in your vocabulary notebook.

Language development 3

Nouns and adjectives: The weather

1 Discuss the questions.

1 What's the weather like in your country at different times of the year?

2 What kind of weather do you like best?

2a Write the nouns in the box in the correct column. Use a dictionary if necessary.

breeze   downpour   drizzle   gale   gust   hail
hurricane   lightning   shower   thunder

Rain	Wind	Storm

b Read the statements about extreme weather and choose the correct answers.

Fascinating weather facts

1 When *thunder / lightning* strikes the earth, its temperature is hotter than the surface of the sun.

2 In the Antarctic, *gales / gusts* of wind can reach speeds of over 320 kilometres per hour.

3 In some parts of the world, *hail / drizzle* can damage crops and kill animals.

4 *Hurricanes / Downpours* are whirling storms that can create giant waves up to eight metres high.

5 Snow and hail are both frozen water, but *snow / hail* doesn't fall in thunderstorms.

3a Match the adjectives (1–11) with the nouns (a–g). More than one answer may be possible.

1	torrential	a	breeze
2	tropical	b	shower
3	gentle	c	downpour
4	heavy	d	thunder
5	high	e	rain
6	light	f	wind
7	loud	g	storm
8	strong		
9	hard		
10	pouring		
11	chilly		

b Complete the sentences with adjectives from Exercise 3a. More than one answer may be possible.

1 Because of the _____ winds, all flights have been cancelled.

2 We're soaked. We got caught in a _____ shower.

3 We sat in the garden and enjoyed the _____ spring breeze.

4 The storm's nearly over. The thunder's not as _____ as it was.

5 The rain's quite _____ . Let's stay indoors.

6 The wind always turns a little _____ in autumn.

7 In the tropics, you usually get _____ rain during a storm.

4a Weather adjectives can also be used to describe people or things. Match the adjectives (1–5) with the nouns (a–e).

1	stormy	a	smile
2	heated	b	manner
3	icy	c	discussion
4	sunny	d	relationship
5	breezy	e	stare

b Can you guess what the phrases in Exercise 4a mean? Use a dictionary to help you.

5 What kind of weather do you think would be most appropriate for:

1 a romantic encounter?

2 a quarrel with your best friend?

3 a long car journey?

4 a holiday in the mountains?

5 a trip in a sailing boat?

Overview

4A
- **Reading and Use of English:** Multiple choice (Part 5)
- **Language development:** Narrative forms; Time conjunctions
- **Writing:** Article (Part 2)

4B
- **Speaking:** Vocabulary: Sports; Collaborative task (Part 3)
- **Listening:** Multiple matching (Part 3)
- **Language development:** Quantity; Determiners; Adjectives often confused; -ing and -ed adjectives; Phrasal verbs with *take*
- **Reading and Use of English:** Key word transformations (Part 4); Multiple-choice cloze (Part 1)

Lead-in

1 Discuss the questions.

1 The photos show people in challenging situations. Which situations would be the hardest/easiest for you? The most satisfying? The most interesting?

2 What's the most challenging situation you've faced in your school, college or working life?

Reading (Paper 1 Part 5)

Before you read

1 Look at the title of the article and the introductory paragraph. Write down at least three questions you would like to know about Lewis Pugh.
How does he prepare for this?

Skimming

2 Skim the text to find out if your questions from Exercise 1 were answered.

Multiple choice

➤ EXPERT STRATEGIES pages 175–176

3 Do the task. Use the Help notes for support with certain items.

You are going to read an article about a man who welcomes a challenge. For questions 1–6, choose the answer (A, B, C or D) which you think fits best according to the text.

1 As a child, Pugh's ambition was to be
A a sailor.
B a lawyer.
C a swimmer.
D an explorer.

2 Why did Pugh make travel a priority?
A to improve his knowledge of the seas
B to achieve things never done before
C to find out how far it was possible for him to swim
D to swim amongst the world's most dangerous animals

3 What was so extraordinary about Pugh's achievement in 2005?
A He broke the record for the fastest cold water swim.
B He swam in absolutely dreadful weather conditions.
C He was the first person to swim so near both the North and South Poles.
D He is the only human ever to dare to swim near polar bears in the Arctic.

4 What is so unusual about Pugh?
A He is able to warm himself up when he needs to.
B He is able to put on weight before an important swim.
C He has the kind of skin which can tolerate extreme cold.
D He has trained his body not to be affected by freezing water.

5 What motivates Pugh to do what he does?
A his determination to do what seems impossible
B his love of competitive swimming
C his obsession with any form of sport
D his fascination with the Polar regions

6 What do we learn about Pugh from the last paragraph?
A He no longer feels the need to beat world records.
B He is putting all his energy into saving the environment.
C He feels he has achieved all he wants to as a swimmer.
D He is not prepared to say what he might be doing next.

➤ **HELP**

1 What were Pugh's childhood dreams?

2 What does *collect 'firsts'* in the second paragraph mean?

3 He did two extraordinary things that year. What were they?

Task analysis

4 Compare and give reasons for your answers.
1 Which part of the text helped you to answer each question?
2 Which parallel words or phrases helped you identify the correct answers?

5 What do the underlined phrasal verbs in the text mean?

Discussion

6 Discuss the questions.
1 What have *you* taken to like a duck to water?
2 Have you ever put yourself through something really difficult? Are you glad you did?

In at the deep end

Lewis Pugh wants to conquer some of the most inhospitable, dangerous places in the world in his own unique way – by swimming through them.

Brought up on a diet of stories about Ernest Shackleton, Captain Cook and Sir Edmund Hillary, Lewis Pugh's childhood dreams were filled with his heroes' ground-breaking expeditions to the Poles, Australia and Mount Everest. The son of a Royal Navy officer, Pugh was 17 before he learned to swim but he took to it literally like a duck to water and from then on the future law student decided he would combine his passion for adventure with his other love: swimming. Just one month after his first lesson, Pugh decided to do something normally reserved for experienced athletes: the five-mile crossing from Robben Island to Cape Town in water of 16 degrees Centigrade.

Twenty years ago, a large chunk of the world's waters had still not been swum, so Pugh decided that, at the same time as studying maritime law, he'd spend as much time as he could going around the world to collect 'firsts'. Some of these achievements are impressive because of their distance, like the longest cold water swim (204 kilometres down Norway's longest fjord). Others would make anyone tremble with fear: swimming round the southernmost tip of Africa in shark-infested waters. But for Pugh, each challenge has to be greater than the last.

In August 2005 Pugh made worldwide headlines when, ignoring the threat of polar bears, he broke the world record for the most northern swim, as he plunged into the near-frozen waters of the Arctic near the North Pole and swam for a kilometre. Four months later, he went on to do the same for the most southern part of the Antarctic. This time there were icebergs around, the water was at freezing point and it was snowing.

'The first dive in Antarctica was an unforgettable experience. You get a terrible headache and your breathing speeds up until you can't control it. Then the skin gets terribly burned. After five or ten minutes, you start losing the feeling in your fingers and toes,' says Pugh, known as 'the Polar Bear' because of his ability to swim in temperatures which, physiologically, should be impossible. Like the seals and polar bears that live in these freezing conditions, Pugh has to insulate his body by putting on 15 kilos before a swim in order to up his fat levels. However, it is his unique ability to raise his core body temperature by as much as two degrees in anticipation of the water by the power of his mind that has made him a medical phenomenon.

It is incredible enough that anyone would choose to put themselves through the experiences he does, especially as, to raise the game, he wears only swimming trunks, a cap and goggles. So what drives him? 'Sometimes we set boundaries for ourselves in life or, even worse, we allow others to do so. In many cases, these boundaries are just in our mind and need to be pushed away. If you get frightened of sharks and things like that, it will paralyse you. You have to do maths problems or think about something else, otherwise you will fail.' He insists that everyone, however ordinary, is capable of extraordinary things if you can do this.

Swimming down the Thames in London might seem a little tame in comparison, until you realise that this was the full length of the river – 325 km in 21 days – in a heatwave. He used this as a publicity opportunity for a concern very close to his heart: to educate passers-by about ways of preventing global warming. He remains tight-lipped about future plans. 'It may be that I'll quit the aquatic world for a change,' he told us. 'But trust me: no matter what I do, it'll be something that no one has ever seen before.'

Language development 1

Narrative forms

> EXPERT GRAMMAR page 188

1a Read the first sentence of a story. How do you think it continues?

> I was unlocking my front door when I heard a noise inside the house.

b Read the next part of the story. Does it continue the way you thought it would?

> I closed the door again quickly and ran out into the street. Then I tried to call the police but my phone wasn't working because I'd been talking to people all day and the battery had run down.

c Underline the different past verb forms in the story.

d Match the uses below (1–4) with the verb forms you underlined in Exercise 1c. Then complete the table with the uses and examples from the story.

1 an action in progress at a point in the past
2 a single action which happened before a point in the past
3 an action or event at a particular point in the past
4 an action which continued up to a particular point in the past

Form	Use	Example
Past simple	_____	_____, _____, _____, _____
Past continuous (*was/were* + *-ing*)	_____	_____, _____
Past perfect simple (*had* + past participle)	_____	_____
Past perfect continuous (*had been* + *-ing*)	_____	_____

```
The battery had              I tried to call the
run down (3)                    police (1)              now
     ↓                             ↓                     ↓
_____
     (4)                           (2)
  ᴧᴧᴧᴧᴧᴧᴧᴧᴧᴧᴧᴧ              ᴧᴧᴧᴧᴧᴧᴧᴧᴧᴧᴧᴧ
 I'd been talking to           My mobile phone
  people all day                wasn't working
```

e Now complete the rest of the story with the correct form of the verbs in brackets. More than one answer may be possible.

> I **(1)** ____ (run) down the street to a payphone but someone **(2)** ____ (talk) on the phone. I think she **(3)** ____ (argue). After I **(4)** ____ (wait) for about ten minutes, she **(5)** ____ (come) out. I could see from her eyes that she **(6)** ____ (cry).
> A police officer **(7)** ____ (arrive) and I **(8)** ____ (tell) him what **(9)** ____ (happen). But then, while I **(10)** ____ (talk) to him, a friend of mine **(11)** ____ (come) out of my house. He **(12)** ____ (carry) balloons. Then I realised what **(13)** ____ (go on). Of course! It **(14)** ____ (be) my birthday and my friends **(15)** ____ (wait) in the house to give me a surprise birthday party!
> When I **(16)** ____ (go) into the house, everyone **(17)** ____ (laugh) and they **(18)** ____ (start) to sing *Happy Birthday*. I **(19)** ____ (feel) really stupid about the way I **(20)** ____ (react)!

Time conjunctions

A *as*, *while*
- a longer action happening 'around' a shorter action
  ***As/While** I was watching a horror film, I heard a noise outside.*
- two longer actions happening at the same time
  ***As/While** I was working, my brother was sitting on the beach.*

B *when*
- a short action in the middle of a longer action
  *I was watching a horror film **when** I heard a noise outside.*
- a short action immediately before another short action
  ***When** he crossed the line, everybody cheered.*

C *before*, *after*
- *Before* always goes with the second action in a sequence.
  ***Before** we left, I filled up/had filled up with petrol.* (first: *I filled up*; second: *we left*)
  *I filled up/had filled up with petrol **before** we left.*
- *After* always goes with the first action in the sequence.
  ***After** I filled up/had filled up with petrol, we left.* (first: *I filled up*; second: *we left*)
  *We left **after** I filled up/had filled up with petrol.*

D *as soon as*
- *As soon as* means 'immediately after'.
  ***As soon as** he went/had gone outside, it started raining.*
  *It started raining **as soon as** he went/had gone outside.*

E *by the time*
- *By the time* means 'before'.
  ***By the time** the police arrived, the robbers had run away.*
  *The robbers had run away **by the time** the police arrived.*

2 Read the information above and choose the correct answer (A, B, C or D).
1 ___ Joe arrived at the cinema, the film had finished.
  A While B As soon as C By the time D As
2 ___ we were sitting in a traffic jam, our plane was taking off.
  A As soon as B While C After D By the time
3 ___ I phoned Sara, she said she had been ill.
  A While B Before C When D By the time
4 She fell asleep ___ she was reading her book.
  A as soon as B before C by the time D while

5 ___ I turned on the TV, the programme had ended.
  A While B As soon as C By the time D After
6 Mechanics had checked the cars ___ the race started.
  A before B while C as D after
7 The police searched us ___ we arrived.
  A when B by the time C while D before
8 I felt so relieved ___ I found my missing purse.
  A while B before C by the time D after

3a Complete the sentences so they are true for you. Use the past simple, past continuous or past perfect simple/continuous.
1 When I left school, I …
2 I was … when I saw …
3 I had been … when I …
4 I had … but I …
5 When I heard the news about … , I …

b Compare your sentences from Exercise 3a with other students.

4 Join the sentence pairs. Use the time conjunctions in brackets and make any other changes necessary. You may need to change the order of the sentences.
1 I heard the news. Then I phoned my sister. (as soon as)
  As soon as I had heard the news, I phoned my sister.
2 I went to see a friend. Then I went home. (after)
3 I waited for around an hour. Then he eventually arrived. (by the time)
4 The boss resigned. Then the business collapsed. (when)
5 I was gardening for hours. Then she phoned me. (when)
6 His owner was talking. At the same time, the dog ran into the road. (while)
7 The plane left. Then we got to the airport. (by the time)
8 I never ate caviar. Then I went to Russia. (before)

5 Write a short story using the pictures. Use narrative forms and time conjunctions.

Writing (Paper 2 Part 2: Article)

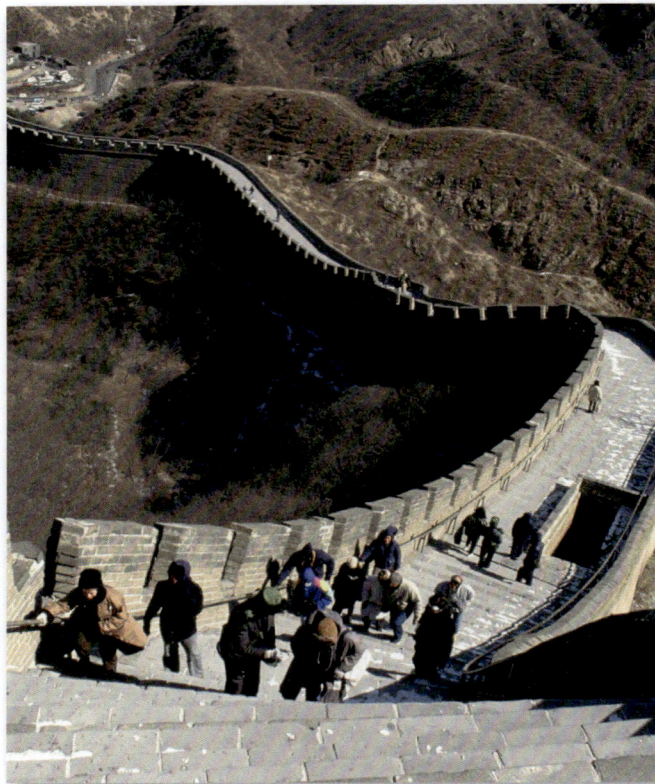

Lead-in **1a** Discuss the questions.

1 Decide on a good cause that requires money from charity (e.g. a community group, a hospital).
2 Think of an unusual personal challenge which would help raise money (e.g. a sponsored cycle ride across Cuba, a walk along the Great Wall of China).

b Imagine you took part in the challenge. Think about the experience and make some notes for an article (e.g. say why you did it, in what way it was challenging, how you felt).

Understand the task **2** Read the task and answer the questions.

1 What is the purpose of your piece of writing?
2 What points have you been asked to include?
3 What style will be suitable?
4 How will you have a positive effect on the reader?
5 What will make the reader think it's a well-written article?

You see this announcement on an English-language website.

Articles wanted

A charity event to remember

What is the most unusual way you've raised money for charity? How did you do it? What did you have to do? Was the event a success? Would you do it again?

Write us an article answering these questions.

We will publish the best articles on our website.

*Write your **article** in **140–190** words in an appropriate style.*

Plan your article

3a Make a paragraph plan using the questions in the task.
Paragraph 1: *What did you do? How did you do it?*
Paragraph 2: _____
Paragraph 3: _____
Paragraph 4: _____

b Match the follow-up questions (a–d) with the paragraphs in Exercise 3a and add them to your plan.
a How much did you raise?
b What was the experience like?
c How would it be different next time?
d Why did you decide to do it?

c Look at your notes in Exercise 1b and use them to answer the questions in your paragraph plan.

Language and content

4a Which of these opening sentences do you think would have a more positive effect on the reader? Why?

> **A** Last year I decided to cycle round Cuba. I did it for charity. I wanted to raise money for a local children's hospital.

> **B** So why was I mad enough to do a 90-kilometre walk in six days along the Great Wall of China?

b These sentences begin the last paragraph of the article. Which one do you prefer? Why?

> **A** In the end, I was pleased I finished the walk and raised so much money but I think next year I'll try and find some less challenging way of doing it.

> **B** It was OK in the end. I enjoyed the ride. I got the money I wanted but next year I'll do it differently.

c Look at the phrases in the table above right for giving an article 'colour'. Then make one sentence for each phrase in the table using the sentences in the box below. You can use the sentences more than once.

I had to walk 90 km in six days.
I walked along the Great Wall of China.
I had to cycle 400 km across Cuba.
It's not as flat as I thought – there are places which are quite hilly.
There were hundreds of high steps.
At first I was shocked, then I enjoyed it.
It was incredible.

Involving the reader	Adding a personal touch
Just imagine …	*Before I went, I thought … but I soon realised …*
Have you ever … (what/how) … ?	*When I … how/what …*
If the answer is … , you should …	*After a while I …*
How would you feel if … ?	*It was the … I had ever …*

Just imagine having to walk 90 km in six days.

d Choose some of the phrases in Exercise 4c and use them to write complete sentences for your own article.

Write your article

➤ EXPERT STRATEGIES pages 177–178

5 Now write your article using the ideas and some of the language above. You can use the title in the task or invent your own.

Check your article

➤ EXPERT WRITING page 201

6 Edit your work using this checklist. (There is a full checklist on page 198.)
Check your:
• paragraph plan. Are your paragraphs clearly organised?
• variety of verb forms and linking expressions.
• range of adjectives, adverbs and verbs. Will the article have a positive effect on the reader?
• number of words.

> **EXPERT LANGUAGE: Attitude adverbs**
> **Choose the correct answers.**
> 1 I was *absolutely / fairly* terrified when I realised how difficult it would be.
> 2 More *essentially / importantly*, it was something I enjoyed doing.
> 3 Not *amazingly / surprisingly*, it's a good way of raising money.
> 4 *Personally / Individually*, I've always had a fear of heights.
> 5 I don't remember *exactly / accurately* what the road sign said.
> 6 *Normally / Naturally*, everyone involved in the challenge was very proud.
> 7 *Luckily / Extraordinarily*, we found someone who knew the way.
> 8 The tent was cosy but *anxiously / worryingly* small for three people!

Speaking (Paper 4 Part 3)

A

B

Vocabulary: Sports

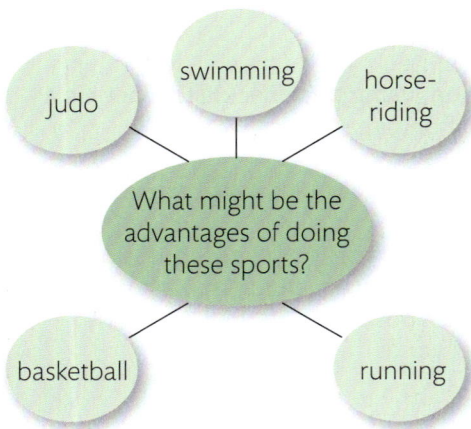

judo
swimming
horse-riding

What might be the advantages of doing these sports?

basketball
running

1 Look at the photos and the spidergram. Which of these sports do you/would you like to do? What might be the advantages of each?

2a Which sports do people do:
1 on a court?
2 on a track?
3 in a ring?
4 in a pool?
5 on a pitch?

b In which sports might you use:
1 a racket?
2 a bat?
3 trunks?
4 goggles?
5 a helmet?
6 spikes?

3a Match the sports in the photos and the spidergram in Exercise 1 with the verbs (1–3) they are used with.
1 do   2 play   3 go

b In which sports might you:
1 make a tackle?
2 hit a backhand?
3 win by two laps?
4 do the backstroke?

c Choose the correct answers.

Have you seen last night's football **(1)** *results / grades* in the paper this morning? There were a lot of important international **(2)** *plays / matches*. Brazil **(3)** *won / beat* France one-nil, Spain **(4)** *drew / lost* against Northern Ireland two-all and Russia **(5)** *hit / scored* four goals against Switzerland and **(6)** *won / beat* four-one. I saw some of the Northern Ireland–Spain **(7)** *game /competition* and I thought Spain were the better **(8)** *group / team*. They were one up at **(9)** *first half / half-time* but in the second half the **(10)** *referee / umpire* gave one of their players a red card, sent him off and gave Northern Ireland a **(11)** *penalty / shot*. Lafferty hit a brilliant **(12)** *shot / drive* into the corner of the net and later he headed in a second goal!

C

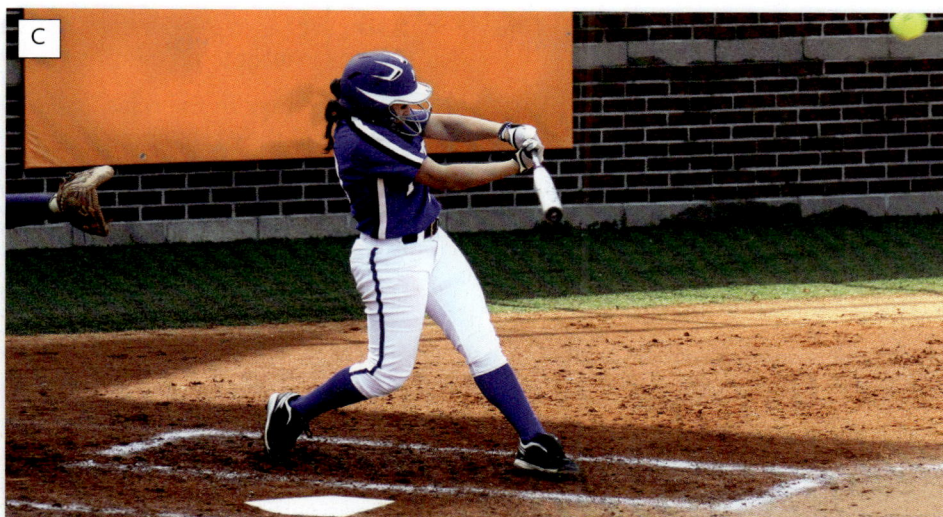

Collaborative task

> EXPERT STRATEGIES pages 179–180

4a 🎧 11 Look at the spidergram in Exercise 1 and listen to the interlocutor's instructions for the task. What are you required to do?

b 🎧 12 Listen to two candidates doing the first part of the task. Which points of view do you agree/disagree with? Why?

c 🎧 12 Listen again and tick the phrases the candidates use.

Starting a discussion	Why don't we start by … ? Let's begin with … Shall we … first? We could start with …
Interrupting	Sorry to interrupt, but … Yes, and as well as that, … Can I just say …
Involving the other person	So what would you say about … ? Don't you agree? What do you think about … ?

d 🎧 13 Now listen to the interlocutor's instructions for the second part of the task and the candidates' discussion. Which sport do they choose? Why?

5 Work in groups of three. Read the strategy and follow the instructions below.

> EXPERT SPEAKING page 208

EXPERT STRATEGY

• Talk to your partner, not the interlocutor.
• Take an active part in the discussion but involve your partner too.
• Talk about more than one option before making a decision or you will finish too quickly.

Student 1: You are the interlocutor. Turn to page 208 and give the instructions for the task. Remember: stop the first part of the discussion after two minutes and the second part after one minute.

Students 2 and 3: You are Candidates A and B. Follow the interlocutor's instructions.

Task analysis

6 Discuss the questions about Exercise 5.
1 Interlocutor: Did Candidates A and B listen and respond to each other? Did they both put forward ideas?
2 Candidates: Did you come to a conclusion? Did you run out of time or have too much time?

Listening (Paper 3 Part 3)

Before you listen

1 Discuss the questions.
   1 Do you think some sports are riskier than others?
   2 Think of as many extreme sports as you can. Why do you think people want to do them?

Multiple matching

> EXPERT STRATEGIES pages 178–179

2a Read the task in Exercise 2c. How many speakers will you hear? What will they talk about?

b Look at the reasons for taking up a sport (A–H) in Exercise 2c. Which sports do you think the speakers will mention? Have you ever taken up a sport for one of these reasons?

c 🎧 14 Read the strategy and do the task.

EXPERT STRATEGY

- Read the task and mark the key words in each option (A–H).
- The first time you listen, focus on each speaker's main point.
- Match the main points with the closest options and note down your answers.
- During the second listening, check that the statement matches exactly what the speaker says.

You will hear five short extracts in which people say why they took up a sport. For questions 1–5 choose from the list (A–H) the reason each speaker gives. Use the letters only once. There are three extra letters which you do not need to use.

A I was persuaded to do it by other people.	Speaker 1	1
B I needed to set myself a new challenge.	Speaker 2	2
C I did it to raise money for charity.	Speaker 3	3
D I wanted to give my family a surprise.	Speaker 4	4
E I needed to find a way to relax.	Speaker 5	5
F I wanted to prove to someone that I could do it.		
G I was advised to take more exercise.		
H I wanted to be able to join in with the children.		

Task analysis

3 Discuss these questions about the task. Listen again if necessary.
   1 How was the main point in each extract expressed?
      1 C: 'the whole point was to get people to give donations to a medical research organisation'
   2 Did you need to change any answers the second time you listened?

Vocabulary: Idiomatic expressions

4 Replace the words in *italics* in the sentences with the phrases in the box. All the phrases were in the recording. Make any other changes necessary.

(be) into (something)   fancy (something)   from the word 'go'
give (something) a go   sign up (for something)

---

   1 I really enjoyed playing tennis *from the moment I took it up.*
   2 My cousin has always been *keen on* snooker.
   3 Shall we *enrol* for the judo course on Fridays?
   4 Do you *like the idea of* joining the netball team?
   5 She has never tried diving but she is happy to *try it.*

Discussion

5 Discuss the questions.
   1 Do you fancy going scuba diving or doing parachute jumping? Why/Why not?
   2 What sports have you always been into from the word 'go'?
   3 Which sports would you like to give a go?
   4 Have you ever signed up for something and then given it up? If so, why?

Language development 2

Quantity

➤ **EXPERT GRAMMAR** pages 188–189

A **Countable nouns** have singular and plural forms.
*Pelé was **a** great **footballer**.*
*He was one of the greatest **footballers** of all time.*

B **Uncountable nouns** do not have a plural form.
*He has a lot of **confidence**.*

C Some nouns can be **countable or uncountable**, with a difference in the meaning.
*Football is **a sport** for everyone.* (countable: a particular sport)
***Sport** is big business these days.* (uncountable: sport in general)

1 Read the information above and decide whether each of these nouns is countable, uncountable or both. Use a dictionary if necessary.

1 spectator	fan	excitement
2 advice	fact	information
3 skiing	athletics	football
4 money	salary	coin
5 racket	equipment	glove
6 temperature	weather	sunshine
7 exercise	tracksuit	trainer

2 Correct the mistakes in the sentences.
1 Our trainer gives us good advices.
2 I've heard the results. The news are very bad.
3 People likes Lionel Messi.
4 Some footballers have long hairs.
5 It was a terrible weather, so the match was cancelled.
6 Ronaldo has very expensive furnitures in his house.
7 My shorts was very dirty after the match.
8 I had to do some hard works to beat the champion.
9 The national team stayed in a luxury accommodation.
10 I need informations about tickets.

Determiners

➤ **EXPERT GRAMMAR** page 189

A Use these words with **plural countable nouns**.
• *(a) few, fewer*
• *many, a great many, very many, not many*
*There were **a few people** at the match but **not many**.*
• *several*
***Several** players were injured.*
• *a small/good/large/great number of*
***A large number of fans** watch matches on Saturdays, but only **a small number** go on Wednesday evenings.*

B Use these words with **uncountable nouns**.
• *(very) little, not much*
*There wasn't **much interest** in the village cricket match.*
• *a good/great deal of, a small/large amount of*
*The club spent **a great deal of money** on their star player, so they only had **a small amount** left to improve facilities for spectators.*

C Use these words with **plural countable and uncountable nouns**.
• *a lot of, lots of, plenty of*
*There's been **a lot of improvement** in her tennis. She's got **a lot of fans**.*
• *no ... at all, none*
*He takes **no pride at all** in his appearance.*
• *a lack of*
*There's **a lack of honesty** in sport these days.*

3 Read the information above and choose the correct answers.

Camille Jenatzy

(1) *Many / Much* famous sportspeople get injured for unexpected reasons. For example, the English footballer Rio Ferdinand managed to injure himself by watching TV for (2) *a number of / a great deal of* hours with his leg on a coffee table. And after the cricketer Chris Lewis shaved his head, he spent too (3) *many / much* time in the sun and got sunstroke. But the worst accident occurred in 1913, when the racing driver Camille Jenatzy took (4) *several / a small amount of* friends hunting for boars. They didn't see (5) *no / any* boars, so the group went back to the house and had (6) *lots / too many* to eat and drink. Jenatzy was convinced they would soon have (7) *many / much* better luck and offered (8) *much / a lot of* money as a bet that they would be shooting in the next (9) *little / few* hours. After everyone had gone to bed, he crept outside, walked (10) *few / a few* metres away from the house and made (11) *a few / a little* sounds like a wild boar to wake up his friends. Unfortunately, his friends opened the window and shot him by mistake.

Use of English 1 (Paper 1 Part 4)

Lead-in

1 Look at three completed key word transformation questions. Match the questions (1–3) with the area of grammar (a–c) tested in each one.

1 Not many staff attended the meeting.
NUMBER
Only _a small number of_ staff attended the meeting.

2 He wasted no time looking for a new car.
SOON
He looked for a new car _as soon as he_ possibly could.

3 Sally moved here ten years ago.
LIVING
Sally _has been living here for_ ten years.

a time conjunctions
b determiners
c present perfect continuous + _since/for_

Key word transformations

➤ EXPERT STRATEGIES pages 175–176

2 Do the task. Use the Help notes for support with certain items.

For questions **1–6**, complete the second sentence so that it has a similar meaning to the first sentence, using the word given. **Do not change the word given.** You must use between **two** and **five** words, including the word given.

➤ **HELP**

1 You need four words. Will you need an adjective or a noun? (Remember that contractions count as two words.)
2 You will need an indefinite article.
4 Do you need a singular or plural verb?

1 The children were not very interested in what the guide said.
MUCH
There _____ among the children in what the guide said.

2 I think he's rather nice.
QUITE
I think he's _____ person.

3 She's worked very hard in the garden.
DEAL
She's done a _____ in the garden.

4 I don't know why golf is so popular.
PEOPLE
I don't know why _____ golf so much.

5 'This car's not mine,' said the old man.
BELONG
'This car _____ ,' said the old man.

6 There don't seem to be as many tourists around this year.
BE
There seem _____ tourists around this year.

Task analysis

3 Discuss the questions about the task.
1 Which questions test:
  a quantity expressions?
  b determiners?
  c verb forms?
2 Think of other examples using _quite_ (Question 2) and _deal_ (Question 3).

Use of English 2 (Paper 1 Part 1)

Lead-in

1 Discuss the questions.
1 In which sports is it easy to hurt yourself? Why do people take part?
2 Do you know any new sports that didn't use to exist?

Multiple-choice cloze

EXPERT STRATEGIES page 175

2a Read the title and text quickly and answer the questions. Ignore the gaps at this stage.
1 What is parkour?
2 What recent changes have there been?

b Do the task. Use the Help notes for support with certain items.

> *For questions **1–8**, read the text below and decide which answer (**A**, **B**, **C** or **D**) best fits each gap. There is an example at the beginning (**0**).*

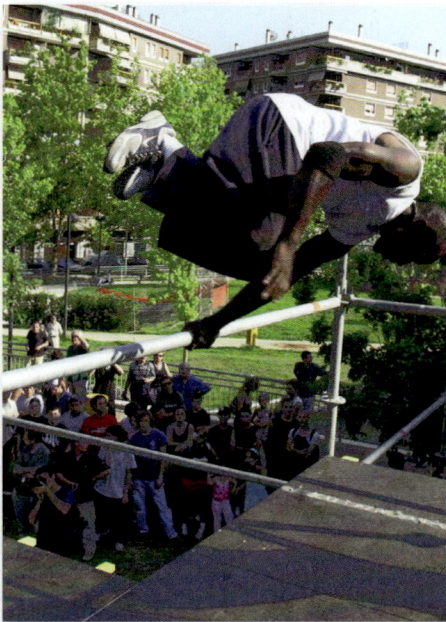

Home Previous Next Search

Parkour

Parkour (from the French *parcours*, meaning 'course') is an activity which (0) _C_ in towns. The aim is to get over, under or through (1) ___ obstacles like hedges, or man-made objects like buildings, in the fastest, most direct manner possible. The sport demands great agility and (2) ___ athletics, dance and acrobatics. Participants are expected to improvise their movements rather than rehearse them. However, in order not to cause themselves injury as they (3) ___ to run up walls or jump from rooftop to rooftop, they have to learn good jumping and landing techniques.

In the UK, the sport really (4) ___ after it was featured on television but it actually (5) ___ in the suburbs of Paris in 1988. In its (6) ___ days there were no tricks for their own sake but (7) ___ , when the sport became really popular, some participants started doing interesting things for show, like mid-air flips.

Of course, anyone interested in taking up the sport has to be young and athletic but (8) ___ all they need is a good pair of shoes!

0	A goes off	B gets up	C takes place	D comes about
1	A native	B natural	C usual	D accustomed
2	A jumbles	B ties	C combines	D fixes
3	A practise	B keep	C enjoy	D attempt
4	A got out	B took off	C turned on	D came out
5	A originated	B made	C derived	D resulted
6	A beforehand	B previous	C early	D preceding
7	A following	B later	C next	D presently
8	A alternatively	B instead	C however	D otherwise

> **HELP**
>
> 3 Which verb is followed by an infinitive?
> 6 You need an adjective that can mean 'near the beginning of a period' and combines with *days*.

Task analysis

3 Make a note of the verbs, phrasal verbs and adjective + noun collocations you want to remember in your vocabulary notebook.

Language development 3

Adjectives often confused

> A The **actual** origins of parkour were in the suburbs of
> Paris. ✓ (= real)
> The **current** origins of parkour were in the suburbs of
> Paris. ✗ (= present)
> B The sport demands **great** agility. ✓ (= a large amount
> of)
> The sport demands **big** agility. ✗ (= large in size)
> C In **ancient** times some sports were far more
> dangerous. ✓ (= many centuries ago)
> In **old** times some sports were far more dangerous.
> ✗ (= not young or new)

1 Choose the correct definitions for each pair
of words.

1 pleasant   a understanding other
                     people's problems
   sympathetic   b friendly, easy to talk to

2 sensitive   a understanding other
                     people's feelings
   sensible   b practical and able to
                     judge things well

3 nervous   a happy because
                     something
                     good is happening
   excited   b worried about
                     something that is
                     happening

4 usual   a having the normal
                     features of a group
   typical   b the same as what
                     happens most of the
                     time

2 Answer the questions about yourself.
1 Are you sensitive or sensible? Or both?
2 When do you get nervous? Excited?
3 Who's the most sympathetic person you know?

-ing and -ed adjectives

➤ EXPERT GRAMMAR page 189

3a Look at the sentences from the text on page 61.
What is the difference between -ing and -ed
adjectives?
1 Some participants started doing *interesting* things
for show.
2 Of course, anyone *interested* in taking up the sport
has to be young and athletic.

b Complete the sentences with adjectives formed
from the words in brackets.
1 Golf is so ___ (bore)!
2 The team felt ___ (disappoint) not to win the final.
3 Professional football looks glamorous but it's ___
(tire).
4 The crowd got ___ (annoy) because the game was
so bad.
5 I've never tried skiing. It looks ___ (terrify) to me.
6 The team captain is ___ (depress) about his injuries.
7 I'm not at all ___ (interest) in sport.
8 It was very ___ (amuse) when a dog ran onto the
field!

c Answer the questions about yourself.
1 What do you find interesting/amusing?
2 When was the last time you felt annoyed/
disappointed?
3 What's the most boring/terrifying thing you've
ever done?

Phrasal verbs with *take*

4 Find an example of a phrasal verb with *take* in
the text on page 61.

5 Replace the phrases in *italics* in the sentences
with a phrasal verb with *take* that includes a
particle from the box.

after off over to up

1 The darts player Bobby George *started a new
career in* acting after he was discovered by a film
producer during the World Darts Championship.
2 Andy Murray's tennis career *began to be successful*
after he played at Wimbledon.
3 The England football team improved enormously
after a new manager *became responsible*.
4 Damon Hill *did the same thing as* his father,
Graham Hill, and became a racing driver.
5 Although Sonny Liston was a great boxer, the
general public never really *felt a liking for* him as
they did Muhammad Ali.

6 For you, which is the best way to keep a record
of phrasal verbs: by topic, verb or particle? How
do you record a phrasal verb with more than one
meaning?

5 Discovery

Lead-in

1 Discuss the questions.
   1 Look at the photos. What benefits have these inventions and discoveries brought?
   2 How would our lives be different without them?
   3 When is progress not necessarily a good thing?

Reading (Paper 1 Part 7)

Before you read

1 Match the fields of science (1–6) with the definitions (a–f).

1 psychology
2 forensic science
3 genetics
4 linguistics
5 astronomy
6 archaeology

a the study of the stars and planets
b the study of ancient societies by examining what remains of their buildings, graves, etc.
c the study of how the mind works
d the study of language
e the study of the characteristics that living things pass on from one generation to the next
f the study of blood, hair, fingerprints, etc. to find out who is guilty of a crime

2 Look at the title of the article and the photo. What field of science do you think each book is about?

Multiple matching

> EXPERT STRATEGIES pages 175 and 177

3 Do the task. For the example question, the key words have been highlighted for you.

You are going to read four reviews of classic science books. For questions 1–10, choose from the reviews (A–D). The reviews may be chosen more than once.

Which review states that the book:

follows on from the author's earlier book?	0 C
includes a number of funny stories?	1
is interesting even for non-scientists to read?	2
would be a good gift choice for someone?	3
mentions a theory that has been disproved?	4
puts forward the author's own ideas about the subject?	5
discusses research carried out on newborns?	6
reflects the writer's wider educational aims?	7
explains the principles on which important ideas are based?	8
was intended to accompany a filmed documentary?	9
contains very interesting pictures?	10

Task analysis

4 Discuss the questions about the task.

1 Why is A not the answer to the example question although it refers to earlier books?
2 Which key words did you mark in the questions?
3 What related phrases or parts of sentences did you find in the text?

Home 🏠   Previous ◀   Next ▶   Search 🔍

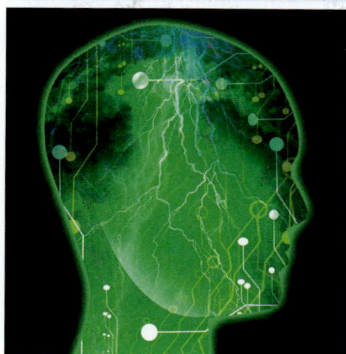

Four classic science books

Oliver Mansell reviews four books, all of which are must-reads for people who want to learn more about themselves.

A *In the Blood: God, Genes and Destiny*, by Steve Jones

This is the book for anyone who wants to understand the thinking behind theories of DNA. Did you know, for example, that whoever our parents may be, we are all united by 'the basic stuff of life', which contains our genes? And did you know that most of the population of the world may have descended from fewer than 100 people? Other discoveries like these are still being made almost every week, which is why genetics is at the forefront of 21st-century science. Before they'd heard of genes, people believed that family traits were carried in the blood. Today we know that they were wrong. Issues like these are among those discussed in this thrilling book by Professor Jones. As with his earlier books on other subjects, you will find it hard to put down.

B *The Human Face*, by Brian Bates with John Cleese

This fascinating book collects together the findings of various scientific studies concerning the human face. One of these has shown that 30 minutes after birth, when our eyes can hardly focus, we gaze at faces rather than anything else. And it seems that we continue to be fascinated with them all through life. There have been a number of psychological tests designed to investigate beauty but their conclusions only prove what the Ancient Greeks always knew: a beautiful face is one with regular features. So maybe this is not the book to buy if you want new facts but it does provide some fascinating insights into how faces have developed over the years and whether one can judge a person by their appearance alone. Although rather serious in places, the book is packed with eye-catching photos, making it an ideal birthday present even for the most reluctant student of science.

C *Brain Story*, by Susan Greenfield

When she was Director of the Royal Institution of Science, Susan Greenfield's main objective was to encourage the greater public understanding of scientific ideas. In this book, she introduces us to the inside of our heads and shows the kind of enthusiasm about the brain that other writers reserve for fine art or football. The idea of 'intelligence' worries her, however, because this suggests that a person's 'brain power' is pre-determined. She agrees with those who insist that the brain, which is capable of amazing things, is constantly developing, and gets better and better with age, providing you look after it. Although this book develops the ideas introduced in her previous one, *The Private Life of the Brain*, it clearly had television audiences in mind (there was a tie-in series on BBC 1) and as a consequence, it is rather shorter on detail, focusing instead on one or two interesting examples.

D *The Language Instinct*, by Steven Pinker

Where does our feeling for language come from? How do we learn to speak it so effortlessly? Why is it so hard for adults to learn a foreign language? Cleverly structured, with many amusing anecdotes, linguist Steven Pinker's book examines why we use language and where this ability comes from. His personal belief is that language is as instinctive to us as flying is to geese and that we use it to great effect in order to communicate. He illustrates his theory with examples of language taken from various sources, including children's conversations, pop culture and politicians' speeches. Pinker has packed his book full of original ideas; it does not make for light reading, but it will nonetheless appeal both to specialists and anyone who finds language and human beings fascinating in the widest sense.

Discussion   **5**   Discuss the questions.

1   Based on the reviews, which of these books would you most and least like to read? Why? What else would you like to know about the subject?

2   Which popular science books or TV science programmes have you found interesting?

Language development 1

Future forms ➤ GRAMMAR REFERENCE pages 189–190

1a Read the sentences. Guess who is talking to who and what the situation is.
1 I don't feel well. I think I'm going to be sick.
   A child talking to a parent, in a car. The child is feeling travel-sick.
2 I can't, I'm afraid. I'm taking my driving test tomorrow.
3 Did I tell you it doesn't work? I'm going to take it back to the shop.
4 I know what she's like. I'm sure she'll tell everyone, so don't tell her!
5 Hurry up! It starts at eight.
6 That bag looks heavy. I'll carry it for you.

b Underline the verb forms in Exercise 1a that are used to talk about the future.

c Match the uses (a–f) with the verb forms in the sentences (1–6) in Exercise 1a. Then complete the table below.
a planned, decided earlier (intention)
b unplanned, decided now (e.g. an offer, a promise)
c planned, definite arrangement (e.g. in a diary)
d prediction: we notice something in the present that will make something happen
e planned, fixed (e.g. a public timetable)
f prediction: we expect something to happen (it is our opinion or we have experience of it)

Form	Use	Example
Present continuous	(1) _____	(2) _____
Present simple	(3) _____	(4) _____
going to + infinitive	(5) _____	(6) _____
	(7) _____	(8) _____
will + infinitive	(9) _____	(10) _____
	(11) _____	(12) _____

Future time clauses

2a Read the information and answer the question.

> Use the present simple, not *will*, after time words and phrases that refer to the future (e.g. as *soon as, when, before, after*).

Which example is not correct?
1 I'll give her the message as soon as she arrives.
2 When everyone is on the coach, it will leave.
3 Are you going to have a drink before the show will start?
4 After we move offices, we'll start on the new project.

b Choose the correct answers.
1 He adapts quickly; I'm sure he *will be / is going to be* fine in his new job.
2 Sorry, I can't. *I'll visit / I'm going to visit* Tom in hospital tonight.
3 We'll call you as soon as *we get / we'll get* there.
4 It says here that the play *starts / is going to start* at seven.
5 You look tired. You rest, and *I'll cook / I'm going to cook* dinner tonight.
6 I'd love to come tomorrow but *I have / I'm having* lunch with my brother.
7 Have you heard the news? *Tara'll have / Tara's going to have* a baby.
8 Just before *you go / you'll go*, can you check this for me?

3a Underline the examples of the future continuous and the future perfect in the quote.

> 'I am confident that in 50 years' time we will have established a permanent base on Mars and that later this century, people will be having holidays in space.'
> (Martin Rees, astronomer)

b Read the information and answer the questions.

> A Future continuous: will/won't be + -ing
> People **will be having** holidays in space.
> B Future perfect: will/won't have + past participle
> We **will have established** a permanent base on Mars.

Which verb form refers to an action:
1 which will be complete by a point in the future?
2 which will still be in progress at a point in the future?

c Complete the predictions for the year 2100 with the correct form of the verbs in brackets. Use the future continuous or the future perfect.
1 We _____ (find) life on other planets before then.
2 We _____ (travel) around in aerial vehicles, like flying saucers.
3 Long before then, scientists _____ (discover) how to make fresh food last for years.
4 Many people _____ (live) in space, which will help with the overpopulation problem.
5 The internet _____ (take over) most teachers' jobs and _____ (provide) most of our entertainment.
6 Scientists and engineers _____ (make) parts of the body routinely. When we're sick, we _____ (go) to mechanics, not doctors!

4a Read the statements and decide which are very certain, fairly certain or not certain.
1 *I am confident that* in 50 years' time we will have established a permanent base on Mars.
2 *We may have* found life on other planets *but I doubt it.*
3 *I think it's quite likely that* scientists will be making blood.
4 *There could be* holidays in space.
5 *We should be* travelling in aerial vehicles.

b Use the expressions in *italics* in Exercise 4a to comment on the predictions in Exercise 3c.

c What things do you think will be possible in 100 years' time? Think about these questions.
1 What will we be eating?
2 What progress will have been made in medicine and technology?
3 What changes will have taken place in education and entertainment?

5a Complete the sentences so they are true for you. Think about your arrangements, plans, hopes and dreams.
1 At the weekend …
2 In the next few days …
3 For my next holiday …
4 On my birthday …
5 In the future I hope …
6 By this time next year …
7 Within the next ten years …

b Discuss your arrangements, plans, hopes and dreams from Exercise 5a with other students.

6 Correct the mistakes with future forms in this piece of student's writing.

> After I will finish the last year of university, I am definitely going to have a long holiday. I expect I am going with my friend, Luis, to a place where we will be doing lots of sport and relaxing in the sun to recover from all our hard work.
> But before that there is a lot of work. My exams will start on 15 June and they are lasting two weeks. The results will not have been here before the end of August, so I am having a long time to wait. For the next month, I will have studied for two hours every evening and I won't have gone out during the week.

Writing (Paper 2 Part 1: Essay)

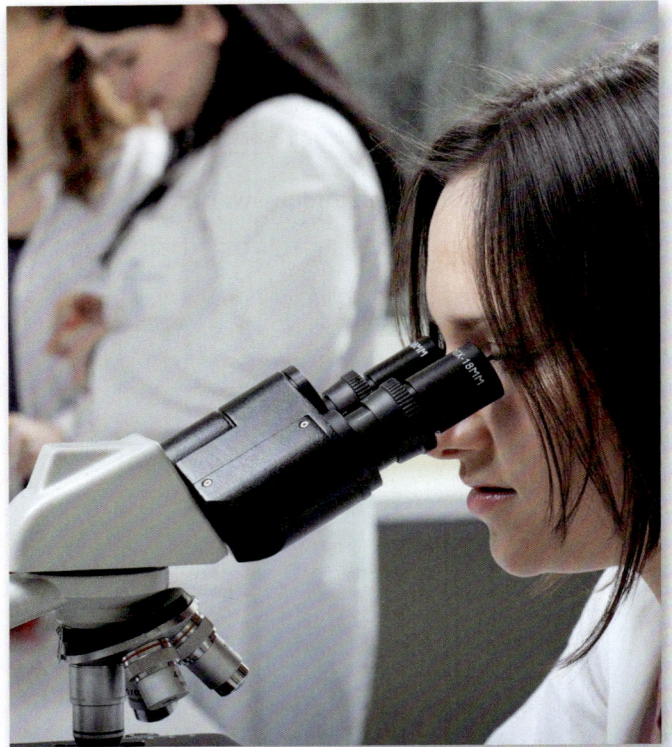

Lead-in **1** Discuss the questions and make notes.

1 In some Western countries science is not a very popular subject among the young. Why do you think this is?
2 How could science be made more appealing?

Understand the task **2** Read the task and answer the questions.

1 Which of these essay types are you being asked to write?
   a for and against
   b supporting an opinion
   c making a comparison
   d problem and solution
   e advantages and disadvantages
2 What must you remember when writing an essay? Check your answer on pages 177–178.

In your English class, you have recently had a discussion about science and young people. Now your English teacher has asked you to write an essay.

*Write an essay using **all** the notes and give reasons for your point of view.*

Science is very important in the 21st century. How do you think it could be made more appealing to young people?

Notes

Write about:

1 television programmes

2 interactive museums

3 _____ (your own idea)

*Write your **essay** in **140–190** words in an appropriate style.*

Plan your essay

3a Answer the questions.

1 Which of these ideas are possible for Note 3?
   a higher salaries for scientists
   b cutting back on arts subjects in education
   c different ways of teaching science
2 Did you think of other ideas in Exercise 1? Select the best idea for Note 3 for your essay.

b Look again at Notes 1–3 in the task. What would be your ideas for making science more appealing to young people? How would they work and why? Can you think of an example? Make notes.

c Complete the paragraph plan with the topics in the box. Remember that it is usually best to have four or five paragraphs.

> solution 1: television programmes
> solution 2: interactive museums
> solution 3: (your own idea)
> add why this is an important topic
> state the overall situation (a problem)

Paragraph 1: _____
Paragraph 2: _____
Paragraph 3: _____
Paragraph 4: _____
Paragraph 5: _____

d Look at the paragraph plan in Exercise 3c. Which paragraph(s) is/are:

a the introduction?
b the main body?
c the conclusion?

e Add your notes from Exercise 3b to your paragraph plan.

Language and content

4a A paragraph in an essay needs to open with a clear sentence (a topic sentence) which introduces the idea. Read a student's notes for topic sentences for this essay. Expand the notes to make complete sentences.

a another idea / set up interactive science museums / every town / parents / take children / weekends
b average scientist / not very well paid / children / not take up / science / career
c young people / love gadgets / at school / many / science / dull
d whatever / choose / vital / more young people / attract / science
e one way / lively television programmes / presented by celebrities

b Match the topic sentences (a–e) in Exercise 4a with the paragraphs (1–5) in Exercise 3c. Some sentences can go in more than one paragraph.

c Match the supporting sentence openings (1–5) with the topic sentences (a–e) in Exercise 4a. Then complete them with your own ideas.

1 The reason is that society's prosperity depends on …
2 They think it means working in …
3 This worrying attitude has led to fewer young people …
4 It's much better to teach children science by …
5 This is because we live in a celebrity culture and children …

d We often use modal verbs and conditional sentences when giving solutions. Complete the sentence openings with the correct form of the verbs in brackets. More than one answer may be possible. Then complete the sentences with your own ideas.

1 One way in which science _____ (make) more attractive …
2 Another idea _____ (be) to find more interesting ways …
3 If more teachers _____ (use) games in science classes …
4 If scientists in general _____ (be) better paid …

Write your essay

➤ EXPERT STRATEGIES pages 177–178

5 Now write your essay, using the ideas and some of the language above.

Check your essay

➤ EXPERT WRITING pages 199–200

6 What things will you check when you edit your work? Refer to the checklist on page 198.

> **EXPERT LANGUAGE: Avoiding over-generalisation**
> Make topic sentences from the jumbled words below. Use the words and phrases in the box to make them less generalised. Make any other changes/additions necessary.
>
> > can   for many people   generally speaking
> > in many cases/situations   might   often
> > on some occasions   one of   some people feel
> > it is sometimes/often said   tend to
>
> 1 than / more intelligent / women / men
>   *It is sometimes said that women tend to be more intelligent than men.*
> 2 harm / than / technology / more / good
> 3 pets / wonderful / dogs / make
> 4 should not / to school / allow / smartphones / take / children
> 5 in the world / to live / best place(s) / Canada
> 6 lie / truth / better / tell

Speaking (Paper 4 Parts 3 and 4)

Vocabulary: Technology

1 Look at the photos and the spidergram and discuss the questions.

1 All the items use computer technology. Which have you got/would you like to have? Why?
2 What are the benefits of each? Are there any disadvantages?
3 Which could you describe as a groundbreaking invention? A useful gadget? An important recent development? An unnecessary luxury?

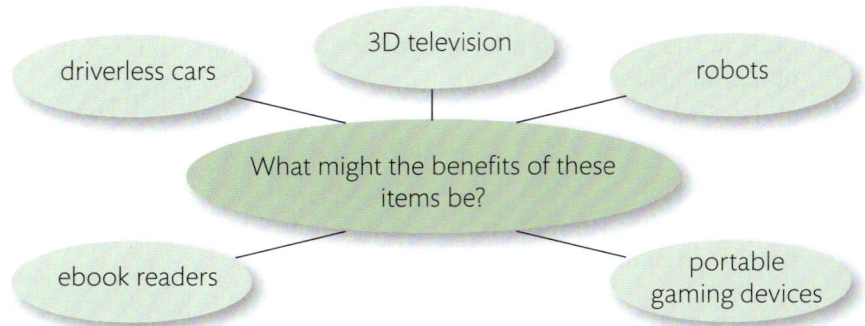

driverless cars — 3D television — robots

What might the benefits of these items be?

ebook readers — portable gaming devices

2a Verbs 1–8 are all actions you might perform on a computer. Match them with their definitions (a–h).

1	download	a	make a copy of your files
2	log on	b	keep for future use
3	click (on)	c	work from home and communicate online
4	cut and paste	d	copy from the internet
5	telework	e	make a computer system or network recognise you
6	back up	f	move to a different place
7	word process	g	perform an action by touching the mouse
8	store	h	produce a written document

b Which of the actions in Exercise 2a can you do using the equipment in the box? More than one answer may be possible.

digital camera   laptop/tablet   MP3 player   satnav   smartphone

c When would you use:

1 headphones?
2 a keyboard?
3 a mouse?
4 a webcam?
5 an external hard disk?

3 What do you use computer technology for (e.g. social networking)? What would your life be like without it?

Collaborative task

➤ **EXPERT STRATEGIES** pages 179–180

4a Look again at the spidergram in Exercise 1. Which piece of technology do you think is the most important? Why?

b 🎧 15 Look again at the spidergram in Exercise 1. Listen to the interlocutor's instructions for the first part of the task and a candidate's response and answer the questions.

1 Complete the sentences from the interlocutor's instructions.
  a Now, I'd like you to talk _____ minutes.
  b First you _____ task.
  c Now, talk to each other about _____ .
2 What does the candidate say to check he has understood?
  So, _____ ?

c 🎧 16 Listen to two candidates doing the task and number the items in the spidergram in the order in which they are mentioned. Do both candidates participate in the discussion?

d Do you agree with the candidates' points of view?

e 🎧 17 Now listen to the interlocutor's instructions for the second part of the task and the candidates' discussion. Which item do they choose? Why?

f 🎧 18 Listen again to both parts of the task and answer the questions.
1 What phrases do the candidates use to express
  a strong agreement?
  b tentative agreement?
2 Does it matter if the candidates don't completely agree?

Three-way discussion

➤ **EXPERT STRATEGIES** pages 179–180

5a Look at the questions the interlocutor might ask about modern technology in Part 4. Which ones do you think you would find easy or difficult to answer? Why?

1 Do you think social networking is a good thing? Why/Why not?
2 Do you think we are too dependent on electronic technology? Why/Why not?
3 Can you imagine life without smartphones? Why/Why not?
4 What do you think the biggest advantage is of technology for our health? Why?
5 What item of technology would you like someone to invent? Why?

> **EXPERT STRATEGY**
>
> Don't just answer questions with *yes* or *no*. Give your opinions, justify them and develop your ideas.

b 🎧 19 Listen to the two candidates' discussion in Part 4 and tick the questions in Exercise 5a the interlocutor asks. Did both candidates participate equally in the discussion? How does the interlocutor involve the other candidate?

6a Work in groups of three. Follow the instructions below.

Student 1: You are the interlocutor. Ask each candidate one question from Exercise 5a.

Students 2 and 3: You are Candidates A and B. Answer the interlocutor's questions and develop your ideas.

b Change roles and repeat the task in Exercise 6a.

Task analysis

7 Did you follow the advice in the Expert strategy?

Listening (Paper 3 Part 2)

Before you listen

1 Look at the picture. Do you think this is a typical modern family? Which of the items in the picture are important to you and your family? What are they used for?

Sentence completion

➤ EXPERT STRATEGIES pages 178–179

2 🎧 20 Do the task.

You will hear a journalist called Nina Cooke talking about the impact that technology has had on her family. For questions 1–10, complete the sentences with a word or short phrase.

Technology and me

Of all her domestic chores, (1) _____ is the one that Nina dislikes most.

Nina has no intention of ever buying (2) _____ online.

Nina still buys a newspaper because of the (3) _____ provided.

Nina believes the convenience of (4) _____ has saved her money.

Nina is impressed by the (5) _____ at which teenagers communicate by text.

Nina worries about potential (6) _____ when her son is absorbed in his music.

The (7) _____ she has gained now the family all own MP3s makes Nina happy.

Nina praises the (8) _____ facility on the computer, which allows even young children to work on their own.

The possible implications of the amount of (9) _____ required by schools concerns Nina.

YouTube has given access to videos of favourite bands from the (10) _____ for Nina's husband.

Task analysis

3 Compare and discuss your answers to Exercise 2.

Vocabulary: Collocations

4 Complete the text with the correct form of these verbs from the listening text.

book   catch up   pay   save   take   try

With most people now (1) _____ the computer very much for granted, it is possible to do many things online, from (2) _____ bills to (3) _____ holidays. This can (4) _____ a lot of time if you are busy, and a lot of money too. Now that many people have laptops, they are also able to (5) _____ on their emails and the news while they are travelling to work. However, although it is convenient to shop online, many people still prefer to go shopping for clothes as they want to (6) _____ them on and see what they look like before they buy.

Discussion

5 Make a list of three appliances or gadgets that you think are essential to your life, and three that you consider an unnecessary luxury.

Use of English 1 (Paper 1 Part 4)

Lead-in

1 Look at three completed key word transformation questions. Correct the mistakes in the answers and say what language area is tested in each question.

1 I can't speak Mandarin Chinese.
   HOW
   I don't know *how speak* Mandarin Chinese.
2 Nobody helped her clean the house last week.
   HERSELF
   She *by herself cleaned the house* last week.
3 Jane decided to wait and only hand in her work at the last minute.
   PUT
   Jane decided to *put up handing in* her work until the last minute.

Key word transformations

➤ **EXPERT STRATEGIES** pages 175–176

2 Do the task.

*For questions **1–6**, complete the second sentence so that it has a similar meaning to the first sentence, using the word given. **Do not change the word given.** You must use between **two** and **five** words, including the word given.*

1 I don't live with anyone else in this house.
   OWN
   I live _____ in this house.

2 It won't help if Tania goes to see the manager.
   POINT
   There's _____ to see the manager.

3 He loves her and she loves him very much.
   EACH
   They _____ very much.

4 It was only after she left that I realised that she was famous.
   WASN'T
   It _____ that I realised that she was famous.

5 Unfortunately, nobody would paint the room for me.
   MYSELF
   I _____ , unfortunately.

6 Caroline was too tired to work anymore, so she stopped.
   CARRY
   Caroline _____ anymore because she was too tired.

Task analysis

3 Discuss the questions about the task.

1 Which question(s) test:
   a phrasal verbs?
   b reflexives?
   c time clauses?
   d noun phrases?
2 If you had wrong answers, what made them incorrect? For example, did you use too many words?

Language development 2

Reflexives

1a Read the information and find examples of the language in the exercises on page 73.

A Reflexive pronouns
- when the subject and object of a transitive verb are the same
  *He **hurt himself** when he fell off the chair.*
  (Compare: *He hurt his sister when he bumped into her.*)
- to mean 'without the help of others'
  *I repaired the television **myself**.*
- with *enjoy*, when there is no direct object
  *They enjoyed **themselves** at the party.*
- with *by*, to mean 'alone'
  *She went to the cinema **by herself**.*

B *own*
- to mean 'without the help of others'
  *I repaired the television **on my own**.*
- to mean 'alone'
  *She went to the cinema **on her own**.*
- to mean 'belonging to no other person'
  *I wish I had my (very) **own** room.*
  *I saw it with **my own** eyes.*

C *each other/one another*
  when each of two or more does something to the other:
  *They talked to **each other/one another**. They talked to **themselves**.*

b Tick the correct sentences. Correct the mistakes in the wrong ones.
1 I used to live for my own.
2 My printer turns itself off.
3 Can you help myself?
4 Robots can't talk to each one another.
5 This was her very own invention.
6 Have you enjoyed you?
7 He found himself in trouble.
8 Relax yourself!
9 I built the model my own.
10 Clare and Rob met themselves last year.

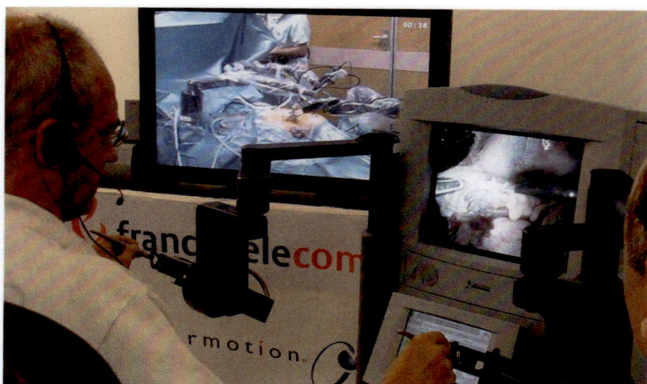

c Complete the article with reflexives and object pronouns (*me, them,* etc.).

ROBOTS

Robots are not new. As long ago as 400 BCE, the philosopher and mathematician Archytus built a wooden bird that could fly on its (1) _____ . And in the 17th century, Johann Müller created both an iron fly and an artificial eagle that could take to the air by (2) _____ . These days robots are everywhere but I sometimes ask (3) _____ whether they are a good thing. There are even robot dogs that we can have as pets but I can't imagine buying one (4) _____ . For a start, I can't believe we'd ever manage to communicate with (5) _____ , unlike real animals. I suppose there is some point in having a robot helping (6) _____ in our daily lives – like doing the household chores that some people can't do (7) _____ or doing a mechanical job in a factory – but I wouldn't want a robot carrying out a delicate operation on (8) _____ in hospital, would you? I'd rather the surgeons did it (9) _____ !

2 Discuss the questions.
1 What things do you prefer to do yourself?
2 Do you like being on your own?
3 Do your friends ever argue with each other?

Structures with question words

A question word + *to*-infinitive
*He didn't know **what to do**.*
B question word + clause
*They never found out **why it had happened**.*
*Do you know **how to download** these files?*

3a Read the information above. Then complete the second sentence so that it has a similar meaning to the first sentence, using the word given.
1 Mike can't use a camcorder. **how**
   Mike doesn't _____ a camcorder.
2 When you've done the things I want you to do, you can go out. **what**
   You can go out when _____ want you to do.
3 We don't know the right places to find the information. **where**
   We aren't sure _____ the information.
4 I'm not sure which person I should believe. **who**
   I don't _____ believe.

b Complete the sentences so they are true for you.
1 Next year I have no idea what …
2 I wish I could decide where …
3 It would be useful if I knew how to …

Use of English 2 (Paper 1 Part 3)

Lead-in

1 Do you know who discovered:
1 penicillin?   2 gravity?
3 the water displacement principle?

Word formation

➤ EXPERT STRATEGIES pages 175–176

2a Read the title and text below quickly and complete this summary.

> Alexander Fleming discovered (1) _____ by accident, when he found that (2) _____ was killing the (3) _____ he was growing. He didn't think it was an (4) _____ discovery.

b Do the task. Use the Help notes for support with certain items.

For questions 1–8, read the text below. Use the word given in capitals at the end of some of the lines to form a word that fits in the gap in the same line. There is an example at the beginning (0).

The discovery of penicillin (1928)

One of the most amazing advances ever made in medicine began with an	
(0) *unexpected* event. Sir Alexander Fleming, a Scottish bacteriologist, had	EXPECT
been conducting an (1) _____ looking into new ways of killing germs, when	INVESTIGATE
he came upon something puzzling in his laboratory.	
Some mould had (2) _____ landed on one of the dishes and, for some	ACCIDENT
(3) _____ reason, had killed the bacteria he was growing. At first he was	KNOW
(4) _____ by his discovery and grew more of the mould, giving it the name	DELIGHT
'penicillin'. However, his (5) _____ wore off when he decided that penicillin	EXCITE
would only really be (6) _____ as an antiseptic against certain skin	EFFECT
(7) _____ and soon lost interest as he believed that antiseptics often did	INFECT
more harm than good. It wasn't until ten years later that two other scientists	
managed to isolate the substance that killed the bacteria, and	
(8) _____ began to save people's lives with it. In 1945 Fleming and the two	SUCCESS
others were awarded the Nobel Prize in Medicine.	

> **HELP**
>
> 2 Do you need an adjective or an adverb?
>
> 7 Do you need a singular or plural noun?

3a Read the text quickly. Why was 'Lucy's baby' so important?

b Do the task. Use the Help notes for support with certain items.

For questions 1–8, read the text below. Use the word given in capitals at the end of some of the lines to form a word that fits in the gap in the same line. There is an example at the beginning (0).

'Lucy' (1974) and 'Lucy's baby' (2006)

The 3.3-million-year-old remains of a human-like child were (0) *originally*	ORIGIN
found in a block of sandstone in 2000 but it took over five years of (1) _____	CARE
work to free the bones. Judging from the (2) _____ of her teeth, the infant was	LONG
probably about three years old when she died. According to (3) _____ working	RESEARCH
in this area, these remains were (4) _____ because of their completeness and	USUAL
this gave them a great opportunity to study the (5) _____ of one of our distant	DEVELOP
ancestors. Earlier discoveries, such as the 3.2 million-year-old fossil of an	
adult female known as 'Lucy', were still regarded as highly significant but their	
remains were less well preserved. Since the species has a (6) _____ of ape-like	MIX
and human-like qualities, scientists said that the findings told us a lot about	
our early ancestors. However, their conclusions came in for (7) _____ from	CRITICISE
some people. They said there was (8) _____ evidence to regard the remains	SUFFICIENT
as the missing link between apes and humans.	

> **HELP**
>
> 5 Is the suffix -ment or -ance?
>
> 8 Do you need a positive or negative word?

Language development 3

Forming nouns

1 Look at the examples of nouns formed from verbs. Then add nouns from the texts on page 75 to the table.

-ment	-ure	-ance	-ence
achievement equipment amusement _____ _____	failure departure pleasure _____	assistance appearance performance	presence existence correspondence _____

-tion/-sion	-y	-er	-or
decision organisation _____ _____	delivery recovery _____	explorer employer _____	sailor supervisor _____

2a Do the quiz. Guess the answers if you don't know.

Explorers' quiz

1 Who reached the South Pole first?
  A Captain Robert Scott
  B Roald Amundsen
2 Who discovered Hawaii?
  A the Polynesians
  B Captain Cook
3 Who sailed round Africa first?
  A Magellan
  B Vasco da Gama
  C the Phoenicians
4 Who attempted to cross the Gibson Desert in Western Australia in 1874?
  A Alfred Gibson
  B Dr Livingstone

b Read the sentences and check your answers to Exercise 2a. Then complete the sentences with nouns formed from the verbs in brackets.
  1 Norwegian Roald Amundsen reached the South Pole in 1911, with the ____ (assist) of a determined team and through brilliant ____ (organise).
  2 The Polynesians discovered Hawaii in 400 CE, 900 years before the Europeans knew of its ____ (exist). Making such a journey by canoe was a remarkable ____ (achieve).
  3 The Phoenicians were the first ____ (sail) to travel round Africa. They completed their journey in the seventh century BCE, without the technical ___ (equip) which is available today.
  4 The Gibson Desert is named after the ____ (explore) Alfred Gibson, who died after his ____ (fail) to reach a camp in search of help.

3a Complete the table with nouns formed from the adjectives in the box.

~~able~~   ~~dark~~   equal   generous   ill   kind   lonely
~~long~~   popular   real   sad   strong   true   wide

-ness	-th	-ity
darkness	length	ability

b Complete the sentences with nouns formed from the words in brackets.
  1 The ____ (popular) of travelogues has increased recently.
  2 The best travelogues have always been ____ (describe) of cultures which are new to the writer.
  3 *The Hai-lu*, a Chinese traveller's account of the West, was written in the 18th century by the writer Hsieh Ch'ing-kao, who had the ____ (able) to write vividly about Europe from a Chinese point of view. Its ____ (important) has been widely recognised.
  4 In the 14th century, Moroccan writer Ibn Buttuta spent 29 years travelling and making ____ (observe) about Africa, Asia and Europe. We can only imagine the ____ (lonely) he must have felt at times.

Phrasal verbs with *come*

4a Read this sentence from the text on page 75 and choose the correct definition for the phrasal verb in *italics*.

Their conclusions *came in for* criticism from some people.

  A gave   B asked for   C received

b Match the phrasal verbs (1–7) with their definitions (a–g).
  1 come across
  2 come off
  3 come up
  4 come round
  5 come up with
  6 come out
  7 come about

  a visit (somebody) at home
  b find by chance
  c happen
  d succeed
  e get discovered
  f get mentioned
  g have an idea for something

c Complete the sentences with the correct form of the phrasal verbs in Exercise 4b.
  1 Did anything important ____ at the meeting?
  2 Tania ____ last night but you weren't in.
  3 I'm sure the truth will ____ one day.
  4 We ____ some old school photos the other day.
  5 How did the accident ____ ?
  6 Jackson's attempt to break the record didn't ____ .
  7 Has anybody ____ any new ideas?

Overview

6A
- ➤ **Reading and Use of English:** Multiple matching (Part 7)
- ➤ **Language development:** Relative clauses
- ➤ **Writing:** Review (Part 2)

6B
- ➤ **Speaking:** Vocabulary: Art and entertainment; Long turn (Part 2)
- ➤ **Listening:** Multiple choice (Part 1)
- ➤ **Language development:** Adjective/Noun + preposition; *be/get used to* + *-ing*; Word formation: Verb + noun collocations
- ➤ **Reading and Use of English:** Open cloze (Part 2); Word formation (Part 3)

Lead-in

1 Discuss the questions.
  1 Which of the following are especially important to you? Why?
    · music · books · cinema · dancing · theatre
  2 Do governments have a responsibility to support and develop the arts or should this be left to private enterprise?

Reading (Paper 1 Part 7)

Before you read

1 Look at the title and introductory paragraph of the article and answer the questions.

1 Which of the types of music in the box do you associate with 'easy listening' and which with 'youthful rebellion'? Add any other types you can think of.

country   disco   folk   heavy metal   hip hop   jazz   R&B   rap
reggae   rock   salsa   swing

2 What types of music do you associate with the instruments in the box? (For example, the trumpet and saxophone are played in jazz bands.) Add any other instruments you can think of.

accordion   acoustic guitar   banjo   clarinet   electric guitar   flute
harmonica   harp   keyboard   piano   saxophone   sitar
tabla drums   trumpet   violin   xylophone

Skimming

2 Skim the text to find out what kind of music genre each person is known for.

Multiple matching

3 Do the task. Use the Help notes for support with certain items.

➤ EXPERT STRATEGIES pages 175 and 177

You are going to read an article about young musicians who are well known for music that was popular in their parents' or grandparents' day. For questions **1–10**, choose from the people (**A–D**). The people may be chosen more than once.

Which musician:

is globally very successful?	1
has a celebrity following?	2
has had a wide and varied experience of performing live?	3
likes to dress up when doing a show?	4
admits to not being fashionable with younger fans?	5
plays music which is a mixture of different genres?	6
was trained as a classical musician?	7
uses music as a political message?	8
receives a mixed reaction from music lovers?	9
wanted to offer an alternative to the usual music on offer?	10

➤ **HELP**

1 Find a word which means the same as 'global'.

2 Celebrities might include famous actors and models.

3 What is an idiomatic way to say 'performing live'?

Task analysis

4 Compare and give reasons for your answers.

Feels nothing like teen spirit

The albums chart is filled with some of the least offensive music ever made and rock critics are wondering whatever happened to youthful rebellion, as embodied by punk rock. The stars of easy listening see things differently.

A When Jamie Cullum was a teenager, music was his hobby and he worked his way through college doing every kind of gig possible – weddings, cruise liners, parties – and playing in every band going from heavy metal to freestyle hip hop. Backed by experienced professionals on double bass and drums, the charismatic vocalist and pianist brings a contemporary approach to jazz. 'What I'm doing isn't pure jazz. Pop, rock, dance, hip hop – everything gets thrown together.' He covers heroes of his own generation like Coldplay and Radiohead, as well as those of the past by doing jazzy new interpretations of their songs but also writes songs of his own with modern themes in old styles. A gifted but self-taught performer, Cullum provokes extremes of love and loathing amongst record buyers and jazz purists.

B Michael Bublé has gone from strength to strength since he achieved over a million worldwide sales for his first album of old dance band favourites from the 1930s and 40s. He discovered swing through his Italian grandfather. 'While I was growing up, this music would be everywhere. Of course, I heard modern stuff too but there wasn't enough melody for me. Swing is all about rhythm. When I was growing up, kids weren't given any choice, so this was my rebellion. I like rap, pop and R&B but for too long there's only been room for that and nothing else.'

C At the age of 19, Katie Melua spent most of the year at number one in the charts. Her music is not easily categorised but she laughs at the idea that she is conservative. 'If everyone else was doing jazz, blues and folk in the charts, then you could accuse me of this. But everyone's doing R&B and hip hop.' Haven't some of her contemporaries accused her of being a little unexciting? 'OK, it happens not to be hip and cool but I'm not suddenly going to get an electric guitar out just to attract the kids. Perhaps my music appeals to an older generation because I myself listen to artists such as Ella Fitzgerald, Bob Dylan and Eva Cassidy. When I heard Cassidy's *Over the Rainbow*, it opened my eyes because it sounded old-fashioned but also fresh and new.' So would she ever consider using her fame to write a song about the wrongs of the world, as Dylan did? 'I already have. This kind of protest can be a powerful tool with young people and it's been neglected in the current popular charts.'

D Being in a band which does cover versions of old songs is rarely cool or glamorous but Marcella Puppini includes supermodel Kate Moss amongst her famous fans. Marcella met the other two 'Puppini Sisters' at the Royal College of Music, where they followed a traditional course in singing and learnt to play various instruments, including the piano, saxophone, violin, harp and accordion. All accomplished musicians, in 2004 they decided to turn the clock back 60 years to form a three-part harmony group. As well as creating up-to-date interpretations of favourites from the 1940s, they also translate 'modern' songs and reinterpret them in the 1940s style. Helped by the present vogue for all things retro, they have achieved a cult following in the coolest, trendiest clubs and festivals in the UK, wearing clothes and make-up in keeping with the songs they sing.

Discussion

5 Discuss the questions.

1 Do you agree that contemporary music is not 'rebellious'? Should it be?
2 Do you like singers to write their own songs or do you prefer them to do covers?
3 What kind of music do you like?

Language development 1

The Rolling Stones

Bob Marley

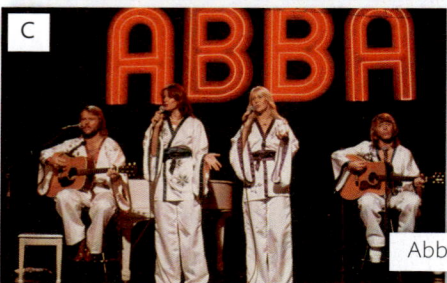

Abba

The Sex Pistols

Gladys Knight and the Pips

Snoop Dogg

Defining and non-defining relative clauses

➤ **EXPERT GRAMMAR** pages 190–191

1a These artists in the photos belong to different genres in the history of popular music. Match the genres (1–6) with the photos (A–F).

1 rock
2 disco
3 punk
4 reggae
5 hip hop
6 soul

b Discuss the questions.
1 Can you think of any other artists for each genre? Any other genres?
2 Have you heard the music of the people in the photos?

2a Read about the history of popular music and answer the questions.

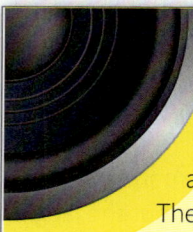

The bands which dominated Western popular music in the 1960s were the Beatles and the Rolling Stones, although *the one singer who had the most influence* was probably the 'protest' singer Bob Dylan. In the 1970s and 80s popular music moved in different directions. There were singers like Elton John, *whose piano-based pop songs were hugely* popular, the reggae artist, Bob Marley, *who had a huge hit with 'No woman, no cry'*, and there was highly polished disco music. In reaction, punk bands *and the records they made* were crude and aggressively anti-establishment. In the 1990s and the 2000s, *decades in which 'boy bands' and 'girl bands' became popular*, music fashion was heavily influenced by hip hop, *which was an Afro–American musical movement* from New York *that first emerged in the 1970s*.

1 When were these genres popular: reggae, punk, hip hop?
2 Where did hip hop develop?

b Read the information. Then look at the clauses in *italics* in the text in Exercise 2a and add examples for each point in the box.

> A **Defining relative clauses** add essential information.
> 1 _____
> 2 _____
> 3 _____
> Use *who* or *that* for people, *which* or *that* for objects, *whose* for possession and *where* for places.
> In defining relative clauses, the relative pronoun can be omitted when the clause defines the object of the clause.
> 4 _____
>
> B **Non-defining relative clauses** add extra, non-essential information and are separated by commas.
> 1 _____
> 2 _____
> 3 _____
> 4 _____
> Use *who* for people, *which* for objects, *whose* for possession and *where* for places. Do not use *that* in non-defining relative clauses.

3 Complete the sentences with relative pronouns and add commas where necessary. Show where two different pronouns could be used and where the pronoun could be omitted.

1 The singer Katy Perry _____ real name is Katheryn Hudson grew up in a strict religious family. Katy __ heard very little pop music as a child started her career in gospel music.

2 *The X Factor* is a British television programme ____ members of the public ____ are would-be singers are given the opportunity to present their talents. It is the programme in ____ the popular British girl band Little Mix first appeared.

3 The rock band Snow Patrol was formed in 1994 in Scotland ____ two of its original members were studying at the time. Both of them were born in Ireland so it's not surprising that the band ____ they admire most is the Irish rock band U2.

4 Shakira ____ means 'grateful' in Arabic was born in Colombia ____ she grew up among the Lebanese and Italian communities. Her song *Hips Don't Lie* reached number one in almost every country in ____ it was sold.

5 Justin Timberlake was one of several singers ____ were first discovered on the popular TV show *The Mickey Mouse Club* ____ first began in the 1950s. Other Club singers ____ went on to become famous were Britney Spears and Christina Aguilera.

6 Oasis ____ major musical influence was the Beatles was one of several bands in the 1990s to ____ the media gave the label 'Britpop'. One drummer they had was Zak Starkey ____ father, Ringo Starr, was drummer for the Beatles.

4 Join the sentences with relative clauses. Add commas where necessary.

1 I saw a poster. It was advertising a gig for a new rock band.

2 I phoned the box office. It was in London.

3 There was an answering machine. It was telling me to call another number.

4 I spoke to a man on the other number. He told me there were only expensive seats left.

5 I booked two tickets. They cost 100 euros each.

6 I paid by credit card. This is a very convenient way to pay.

7 On the day, we went to the theatre. It overlooks the River Thames in London.

8 We couldn't get into the theatre. It had been closed because of technical problems.

9 I went home with my friend. She was very disappointed.

10 Next day I phoned the theatre. They were very helpful and offered replacement tickets.

5 Expand the sentences about the Latin American dance music salsa by adding the extra information in brackets. Use relative clauses and add commas where necessary.

1 Salsa is a mixture of Spanish Caribbean rhythms and styles. (*Salsa* means 'sauce' in Spanish.)

2 The salsa band La Sonora Carruseles was formed in Colombia in 1995. (Their songs are played in salsa dance clubs everywhere.)

3 The singer Gloria Estefan uses salsa rhythms in many of her songs. (She was born in Cuba but now lives in the USA.)

4 The Puerto Rican American Víctor Manuelle is often thought of as a romantic salsa singer. (His career began when he was discovered by salsa superstar Gilberto Santa Rosa.)

5 The album *Travesía* was a huge success with Manuelle's fans. (On it, he improvises vocals and lyrics within a salsa tune.)

Reduced relative clauses

Some relative clauses can be reduced to participle clauses.

A **A present participle clause** (*-ing*) can replace:
  • a relative clause in the present or past continuous.
    *The woman **singing** that song is a famous actress.*
    (*The woman **who is singing** ...*)
    *The car **going** round the corner was the new BMW.* (*The car **which was going** ...*)
  • a relative clause describing a permanent state.
    *The people **living** in that house work in the theatre.*
    (*The people **who live** ...*)
    *The flat **belonging** to my brother was the nicest.*
    (*The flat **which belonged** ...*)

B **A past participle clause** can replace a passive relative clause.
    *All TVs **sold** in this shop have a one-year guarantee.*
    (*All TVs **which are sold** ...*)
    *The video **released** last week has sold a million.*
    (*The video **that was released** ...*)

---

6 Read the information above. Then join sentences 1, 3, 5 and 7 in Exercise 4 with reduced relative clauses.

7 Make notes about a time when you went to see a musical event. Write pairs of sentences like the ones in Exercise 4. Then talk about the event, using defining, non-defining and reduced relative clauses.

Writing (Paper 2 Part 2: Review)

Lead-in

1 Discuss the questions.

1 How do you decide which singers and bands to see?
2 Do you read reviews of live performances? Do you follow their advice?

2 Read the task and answer the questions.

1 What is the purpose of the review?
2 How many parts are there to the question?
3 Which of these are you being asked for in each part?
   • an opinion
   • an anecdote
   • facts
   • a description
   • an explanation
4 What style will you use: neutral, formal or informal?

You have seen this announcement in your college English-language magazine.

Music reviews wanted
Have you been to a great music concert recently?

Write us a review of the concert, telling us about the band or singer and their performance. Say whether you would recommend seeing them perform live. We will publish the best reviews next month.

*Write your **review** in **140–190** words in an appropriate style.*

Plan your review

3 Complete the paragraph plan with the topics in the box.

brief description of the person/band and concert
what you didn't like
conclusion
attention-grabbing introduction
what you liked
recommendation

Paragraph 1: _____
Paragraph 2: _____
Paragraph 3: _____
Paragraph 4: _____
Paragraph 5: _____

Language and content

4a Choose the best opening paragraph.

> My favourite singer is Beyoncé. She's very good.

> What a performer! Beyoncé's spectacular concert will get you on your feet dancing.

b Choose the best closing paragraph.

> Throughout the concert, Beyoncé showed why she is the new queen of pop. Get tickets if you can.

> I think you will like the concert. I did.

c Choose some sentences from the table to complete about your favourite singer, musician or band.

Catching the reader's attention (paragraph 1)	Have you seen/heard … ? I have to tell you about my favourite singer/musician/band … Without doubt, they give/they've made one of the best …
Describing the performers (paragraph 2)	He/She is/They are … who/whose … On stage/On disc … Since he/she/they decided to …
Saying what you like (paragraph 3)	What an incredible … ! Both … and … As the show started …/The first track on the CD … … are/were amazing. The set began with …
Saying what you don't like (paragraph 4)	The only thing I'm not/I wasn't really happy about was … My only reservation is/was … I must admit that …
Conclusion/ Recommendation (paragraph 5)	Judging from this CD/show, he/she/they will be one of the best … Overall, if you like … , you'll love/you should … Although some of … he/she is/they're still a great … You really must/should buy it/try and catch one of their shows.

Write your review

> EXPERT STRATEGIES pages 177–178

5 Now write your review using the ideas and some of the language above.

Check your review

> EXPERT WRITING page 205

6 Edit your work using this checklist. Check your:
- plan. Have you covered everything?
- style. Is it lively and interesting?
- language. Is it varied and interesting?

EXPERT LANGUAGE: Avoiding repetition

a Read the text. What do the words in *italics* refer to?

We Will Rock You

Good musicals make sure **(1)** *their* audience feel good when **(2)** *they* leave the theatre. In **(3)** *this* amateur production, the acting and singing are wonderful. The actors hit **(4)** *their* notes with gusto and give **(5)** *the show* all **(6)** *they*'ve got. The youngest **(7)** *ones* are the best. You won't know **(8)** *their* names but **(9)** *they*'re as good as any professional. However, **(10)** *these* are the plus points. The plot is less than satisfactory. **(11)** *It* can't be taken seriously and **(12)** *this* is the reason we don't really care about the characters or what happens to **(13)** *them*.

b Rewrite the sentences, changing the underlined words to avoid repetition.

1 I like *The Bodyguard* and *Les Misérables*. <u>The Bodyguard and Les Misérables</u> are both musicals.
2 *The Bodyguard* is on at the Adelphi. <u>The Adelphi</u> is a lovely theatre. We've been <u>to the Adelphi</u>.
3 I'd love to see *The Lion King* but I can't afford to see <u>The Lion King</u>.
4 Can you get me tickets for Friday? I've got a day off <u>on Friday</u>.
5 These seats are quite near the stage but the <u>seats</u> over there are nearer.

Speaking (Paper 4 Part 2)

Vocabulary: Art and entertainment

1a Look at the photos, which show two kinds of art, and answer the questions.

1 Which one shows modern art and which one shows classical art?
2 Do you go to art galleries and art exhibitions?

b Choose the correct answers.

1 I'm very *interested / keen* on landscape painting.
2 I *can't see the point / couldn't care less* of abstract painting.
3 I thought his portraits were *fascinating / fascinated*.
4 Those sketches really *appeal / interest* to me.
5 This watercolour is nothing *special / wonderful*.
6 I *absolutely / completely* adore her drawings.
7 She's really *into / onto* sculpture in a big way.

c Divide the words in the box into two groups: those with the stress on the first syllable and those with the stress on the second syllable. Then use the words to talk about a work of art you know.

amusing   awful   boring   brilliant   depressing   dreadful   enjoyable
exciting   moving   powerful   shocking

2a What do we call someone who:

1 paints?
2 makes sculptures?
3 dances?
4 produces a TV programme?
5 writes a review?

b What do these people do?

1 a choreographer
2 a comedian

3 Match the kinds of TV programmes in the box with the extracts from a TV listings page (1–7) below.

chat show   current affairs   documentary   quiz show
reality show   sitcom   soap opera

1	17.30	**Pointless** – Four pairs of new contestants. Alexander Armstrong asks the questions.
2	19.00	**EastEnders** – Alfie wants the truth from Roxy.
3	20.00	**Panorama** – A new investigation into teenage crime.
4	21.00	**Mrs Brown's Boys** – Another hilarious episode about the Brown family.
5	21.30	**Celebrity Big Brother** – Which celebrity will you vote out of the house tonight?
6	22.15	**Question Time** – Five public figures answer your questions on politics.
7	23.00	**Graham Norton** talks to Cate Blanchett and JayZ.

4 Decide which word in each group is the odd one out and why.

1 audience, front row, interval, viewers, stage
2 adverts, switch on, channel, final act
3 rehearsals, cartoon, performance, clap/boo, reviews
4 turn off, box office, screen, remote control, live programme
5 horror, thriller, trailer, comedy, sci-fi

5 Look at the photos again. Which of the two kinds of art do you prefer?

Sample answer

6a 🎧 21 Listen and complete the sentence from the interlocutor's instructions.

I'd like you to compare the photographs and say why _____ .

b 🎧 22 Listen to two candidates doing the task and answer the questions.

1 Does the man give enough time to both parts of the task?
2 Does he make full use of the one minute?

c 🎧 23 Listen to the first candidate's response again and tick the phrases he uses to speculate about the photos.

1 It could be/might be ...
2 It can't be ...
3 It must have/must have had ...
4 I get the impression that ...

d 🎧 23 Listen again and complete the man's opinion.

Well, I think classical art is **(1)** __ modern art. In the first photo, my guess is that the people know what **(2)** __ but if you want, you can **(3)** __ why they were painted. In my opinion, the people who like modern art like it because **(4)** __ .

7 🎧 24 Now listen to the second candidate's response again and complete the interlocutor's instructions and the woman's opinion.

Interlocutor: Anna, do you think that **(1)** __ classical art or modern art?

Candidate: Modern art, **(2)** __ . Classical art is **(3)** __ , I think. There's no doubt that young people like modern art because the artists **(4)** __ .

Long turn

➤ EXPERT STRATEGIES pages 179–180

8 Work in pairs. Do Task 1 below. Then turn to page 209 and follow the instructions for Task 2.

➤ EXPERT SPEAKING page 209

EXPERT STRATEGY

When the interlocutor asks you about the other candidate's photos, just give a brief response to the question (maximum 30 seconds).

Task 1

Look at the photos on page 84.

Student A, compare the photos and say which type of art you think is more interesting.

Student B, listen to Student A without interrupting. Stop him/her after one minute and say briefly whether you think young people prefer classical or modern art.

Task analysis

9 Discuss the questions about the task.

1 Did you follow the strategies on pages 179–180?
2 What language did you use to compare, speculate and give your opinion?

Listening (Paper 3 Part 1)

Before you listen

1 Look at the task in Exercise 2. The extracts are not related. What kind of information does each question (1–8) require? Mark the key words.

Multiple choice

> EXPERT STRATEGIES page 178

2 🎧 25 Read the strategy and do the task. For the first question, the key words have been highlighted for you.

EXPERT STRATEGY

- Read each question carefully and highlight who is speaking and what information you are listening for.
- Focus on the speaker's main idea – you don't need to understand every word.
- Choose one of the options after listening the first time.
- Check your answer during the second listening. Make sure the other options are wrong.
- Guess the answer if necessary.

You will hear people talking in eight different situations. For questions 1–8, choose the best answer (A, B or C).

1 You overhear a woman talking on her phone. What is the purpose of her call?
A to thank a friend who's done something for her
B to ask a friend for information about an event
C to invite a friend to something she's organising

2 You hear part of an arts programme on the radio. What is the speaker talking about?
A a film
B a stage play
C a novel

3 You hear an extract from a radio play. Where is this scene taking place?
A in a restaurant
B in a hotel reception
C in a motorway café

4 You overhear two teenagers discussing a film they have just seen. How does the boy feel about it?
A uninterested in the storyline
B disappointed by the acting
C unimpressed by the photography

5 You overhear two people talking. Who are they talking about?
A a close friend
B a colleague
C a relation

6 You overhear a man talking about an art exhibition. What does he criticise?
A the way it is laid out
B the information available to visitors
C the quality of the works of art on show

7 You hear two people discussing a band's new album. What do they agree on?
A how original it is
B how enjoyable it is
C how exciting it is

8 You hear two people talking about the difficulty of getting cinema tickets. What does the man think the cinema should do for older people?
A allow them to book in advance
B reduce prices on seats during the day
C reserve a number of seats for them

Task analysis

3 🎧 25 Compare and discuss your answers. Then listen again and note down the words that helped you choose each answer.

1 B: So do they give the exact dates?

Use of English 1 (Paper 1 Part 2)

Lead-in

1 Discuss the questions.

1 Look at the photo from the Edinburgh Festival in Scotland. What kinds of event do you prefer? Why?
2 Do you like going to cultural events? Why/Why not?

Open cloze

➤ EXPERT STRATEGIES page 175

2a Read the title and text quickly. Are these statements *True* (T) or *False* (F)?

1 The Fringe is separate from the main International Festival.
2 Performances are carefully selected for the Fringe.
3 Comedy is becoming more popular.

b Do the task. Use the Help notes for support with certain items.

*For questions **1–8**, read the text below and think of the word which best fits each gap. Use only **one** word in each gap. There is an example at the beginning (**0**).*

The Edinburgh Festival

If you are interested (**0**) *in* the arts, Edinburgh in August is the place to be. Apart from the main International Festival, (**1**) ___ is what is called 'The Fringe', offering 2,700 different shows in over 270 venues throughout the city, many of (**2**) ___ are free.

Visitors are often surprised (**3**) ___ the range of shows on offer. This includes comedy, cutting-edge theatre, dance, children's shows and music. As there is no selection committee, (**4**) ___ kind of event is possible and the quality varies.

While many high-profile performers take part, the vast majority (**5**) ___ a mixture of unknown professionals, actors and students, who use the festival as a way of bringing their talents (**6**) ___ an audience for the first time. Indeed, many well-known comics first appeared there (**7**) ___ student productions.

In recent years many new audiences have been drawn almost exclusively to stand-up comics and some regular visitors are disappointed (**8**) ___ this trend. However, as comedy is very much in fashion, they will have to get used to it.

➤ **HELP**

2 This is a relative clause.
3 Which prepositions collocate with *surprised*?
5 Do you need a singular or plural verb?

Task analysis

3 Discuss the questions about the task.

1 Which questions test:
   a adjectives + prepositions?   b verbs + prepositions?   c verb forms?
2 Which questions did you find the most difficult? Why?

4 Make a note of the word + preposition collocations you want to remember. You can record them by main word (A), by preposition (B) or by example sentence (C).

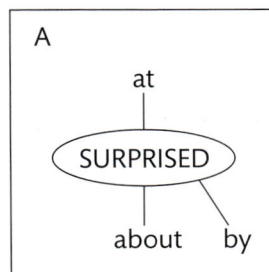

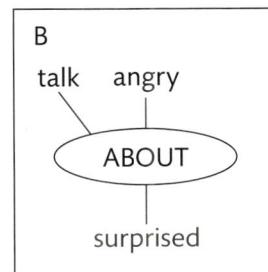

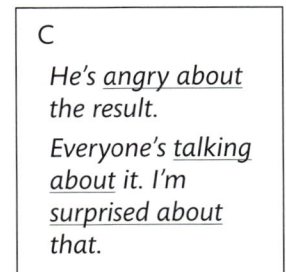

A

at

(SURPRISED)

about   by

B

talk   angry

(ABOUT)

surprised

C

He's angry about the result.

Everyone's talking about it. I'm surprised about that.

Language development 2

Adjective/Noun + preposition

➤ **EXPERT GRAMMAR** page 191

> A Adjective + preposition
> I'm **tired of** walking around this exhibition.
> It's **unusual for** him to be late.
>
> B Noun + preposition
> **Congratulations on** an excellent performance!
> I have no **doubt about** the artist's talents.
>
> C Some adjectives and nouns go with different prepositions, with a change in meaning.
> He's **good at** acting. (= He is skilful.)
> Relaxation is **good for** you. (= It benefits you.)
> That's very **good of** you. (= You are kind and thoughtful.)
> My sister's **good with** children. (= She deals with them well.)

1a Read the information above and choose the correct answers.

1 What was the result *for / on / of* the competition?
2 Audiences often feel sorry *for / by / with* the good guy!
3 I have a lot of respect *of / in / for* the artist's talents.
4 There's no comparison *of / with / between* those two comedians.
5 I'm puzzled *by / of / in* what the play meant.
6 Moira always gets involved *on / in / of* discussions about art.
7 I have difficulty *for / in / by* understanding modern dance.
8 Your ideas are quite similar *in / of / to* mine.
9 Ellie was annoyed *with / on / in* her husband for forgetting the tickets.
10 That comedian's got no hope *from / to / of* getting an award.

b Complete the article with prepositions.

> ### Carlos Acosta
>
> Carlos Acosta's background is unusual (1) ___ a great ballet star. As a boy from a very poor family in Cuba, he mixed with some rough kids and had a huge natural talent (2) ___ street dancing. It was only after strong encouragement (3) ___ his father that he enrolled in ballet school.
> As a dancer, Acosta became famous (4) ___ his perfect control and has always been capable (5) ___ powerful jumps that hang in the air. He also showed how good he was (6) ___ choreography when he was responsible (7) ___ the dance drama *Tocororo*, which combined classical discipline with lively Cuban music. Acosta has had great success (8) ___ his career, particularly since joining the Royal Ballet in London in 1998. His relationship (9) ___ them has always been strong and everyone interested (10) ___ ballet was excited (11) ___ the news that he would be choreographing and starring in *Don Quixote* for the Royal Ballet, the first full-length ballet he had choreographed. They knew that if the critics were right (12) ___ how this production would turn out, they were in for a treat.

2 Answer the questions about yourself.
1 What are you shocked by/keen on/bad at?
2 Who are you impressed by/scared of/worried about?
3 What are you puzzled by/excited by/tired of?
4 Who are you sorry for/annoyed with/similar to?

be/get used to + -ing

> I'm **used to eating** spicy food. (= accustomed to it)
> I'm **not used to eating** spicy food. (= it's new and strange for me)
> I can't **get used to driving** on the left. (= can't get accustomed to, it's difficult)
> I left home last year. I had to **get used to living** alone.
> Compare: I **used to watch** TV a lot when I was younger but I don't now.

3 Read the information above and complete the sentences. Choose the correct answers and then complete the gaps with the correct form of the verbs in brackets.

1 He *used / is used / get used* to _____ (live) in Hollywood but he moved to Cannes in July.
2 It took him a long time to *used / be used / get used* to ____ (live) in France.
3 Katie got tired quickly. She *didn't used / wasn't used / didn't get used* to ____ (film) so early.
4 If you want to be an actor, you'll have to *used / be used / get used* to ____ (hear) criticism of your work.
5 Newspapers *weren't use / didn't use / couldn't get used* to ____ (print) such awful stories.
6 These days we *aren't used / don't used / can't get used* to ____ (watch) films in black and white.
7 When he became famous, he had to *be used / get used / used* to people ____ (stare) at him.
8 I'm exhausted. I *don't used / didn't use / 'm not used* to ____ (go) round art galleries.

4 What things do you have to *get used to* when you:
1 get married?
2 go travelling?
3 start work?
4 change college?
5 go on a diet?

Use of English 2 (Paper 1 Part 3)

Lead-in   **1**   Who is your favourite comedian? Who did you use to like?

Word formation   **2a**   What advice would you give someone doing the word formation task below? Check your answer with the strategies on page 176.

➤ EXPERT STRATEGIES pages 175–176

   b   Do the task. Use the Help notes for support with certain items.

For questions 1–8, read the text below. Use the word given in capitals at the end of some of the lines to form a word that fits in the gap in the same line. There is an example at the beginning (0).

The perfect comedy face

Ricky Gervais is a highly (0) *inventive* British comedian, who rose to fame when he wrote and acted in a funny TV mock-documentary series called *The Office*. In it, Gervais causes great (1) _____ as the boss of a paper supply company, whose (2) _____ high opinion of his managerial skills and his sense of humour is not shared by his group of (3) _____ .

INVENT
EMBARRASS
FANTASY
EMPLOY

Now, having analysed the facial characteristics of 20 top comedians, scientists have surprised many by coming to the (4) _____ that the perfect comedy face must be (5) _____ soft and feminine, with a small forehead, wide nose, large lips and high cheekbones. They say we should not (6) _____ the importance of how comedians come across when we first see them. Their (7) _____ to appear agreeable and obliging puts us at our ease and encourages us to relax; in fact, the ideal image has an incredible (8) _____ to Ricky Gervais!

CONCLUDE
ATTRACT
ESTIMATE
ABLE
SIMILAR

➤ HELP

2 What suffix do you need?

6 Do you need a suffix or a prefix?

3   Do the task. Use the Help notes for support with certain items.

For questions 1–8, read the text below. Use the word given in capitals at the end of some of the lines to form a word that fits in the gap in the same line. There is an example at the beginning (0).

A serious actress

Penélope Cruz's career in movies has been (0) *extraordinarily* successful, although she feels she has always had to struggle for (1) _____ as an actress because of her looks. As she says, 'Once you are seen as (2) _____ , you get called "the pretty woman" and no one takes you seriously.' Nevertheless, in the best films she has made in her native Spain, she managed to play some well-rounded, (3) _____ characters that people could identify with. In 2000, Cruz was (4) _____ to resist the call of Hollywood and early on appeared in one or two (5) _____ films there, such as *All the Pretty Horses*. Now she is an international performer who appears in both Spanish and English-language films and many regard her (6) _____ in *Pirates of the Caribbean* as one of her best later English-language films. In it, she plays a dangerous pirate who not only looks good but also has great (7) _____ of character. Not just a talented actress, Cruz gives generously to charitable (8) _____ and has spent a lot of time as a volunteer in Uganda.

EXTRAORDINARY
RECOGNISE
GLAMOUR
BELIEVE
ABLE
DISAPPOINT
PERFORM
STRONG
ORGANISE

➤ HELP

One word requires a prefix. You have to make four nouns.

Task analysis   **4**   Which questions did you find the most difficult? Why?

Discussion   **5**   Discuss the questions.
     1 Have you ever acted on stage? If so, what part did you play?
     2 Which male or female actor do you most admire?

Language development 3

Word formation

1a Discuss the questions.

1 What are events like the one in the photo called?
2 What is their purpose?

b Complete the article with words formed from the nouns in brackets.

I think awards ceremonies make good television
(1) _____ (entertainer). Every year MTV gives awards to talented (2) _____ (music) and (3) _____ (song) and the fans get the chance to see some of their heroes perform. In Hollywood, the Academy Awards gives over 20 Oscars, including one to the best film (4) _____ (direction) and the best film (5) _____ (acting) and the show is watched by millions around the world. I also enjoy theatre and television awards, where they give an award to the person they consider the best
(6) _____ (drama) and even one to the person who the public votes as best television news
(7) _____ (presentation). However, the ceremonies I like most are when gifted (8) _____ (comedy) get awards, which is not (9) _____ (surprise), really, as most of them are good live (10) _____ (performance) and some of their speeches can be very funny.

2a Find three adjectives with negative prefixes in the articles on page 89 and write them in the correct place in the table.

un-	in-	dis-
unpleasant	inconvenient	dissatisfied
im-	il-	
impossible	illegal	

b Choose the correct negative prefix for each of the adjectives in the box. Then write them in the correct place in the table in Exercise 2a.

experienced   fair   fit   honest   literate   logical
loyal   patient   polite   practical   satisfactory
secure   tidy

c Choose an adjective from Exercise 2b to describe:
1 a child who never puts his things away.
2 a man who can't cook or change a tyre on a car.
3 a good student who feels her homework is not good enough.
4 homework which is not good enough.
5 someone who can't read or write.
6 a graduate who has just started in her first job.
7 a man who is exhausted after running for a bus.

d Answer the questions.
1 Are you ever impatient, impolite or unfair?
2 What's the most illogical or impractical thing you've ever done?
3 Is your room untidy?

Verb + noun collocations

say	*tell*
anything/something (to someone)	someone
	the time
a few words	the truth/a lie
yes/no	a joke/a story/a secret
a prayer	someone's fortune
hello	**talk**
your name	sense/nonsense/rubbish
speak	business/sport/politics
a language	
your mind	

3a Read the information above and correct the mistakes in the sentences.
1 The teacher spoke us a horror story.
2 I can't stand it when artists say politics.
3 We all talked a prayer together.
4 My little sister is just learning to say the time.
5 My brother talks three languages.
6 Tell hello to Rosie for me.
7 Mike said the police what he had seen.
8 Don't trust him. He's always speaking lies.

b Complete the email with the correct form of *say*, *tell*, *speak* or *talk*.

Why don't we go to Spain together – for a holiday, perhaps? I (1) ____ a little Spanish and it would be fun. Please (2) ____ yes but don't (3) ____ anything to Jason – he'll be very jealous! I like Jason but sometimes he (4) ____ a lot of rubbish! Last week he (5) ____ me that he had seen the musical *Le Cirque d'hiver Bouglione* in Paris but I knew he was (6) ____ one of his lies again – he's never been to France! I didn't (7) ____ anything to him at the time because I was in a hurry but when I get the chance, I'll (8) ____ my mind and (9) ____ him exactly what I think about him and his lies.
OK, I've got to go now. Hope you can come!

7 In fashion

Lead-in

1 Discuss the questions.

1 Look at the photos. How have fashions changed over the last 25 years in your country in these areas?
a food and how we eat it   b clothes and dress codes
2 Read the quote. What do you think it means? Do you agree with it?

'There's never a new fashion but it's old.' (Geoffrey Chaucer, 1342–1400)

91

Reading (Paper 1 Part 5)

Before you read

1 Look at the title and introductory sentence of the article and think of three things you would like to know about the fashion for competitive eating.

Skimming

2 Skim the article to find the answers to your questions from Exercise 1.

Multiple choice

3 Do the task. Use the Help notes for support with certain items.

➤ EXPERT STRATEGY pages 175–176

You are going to read an article about a competitive eater. For questions 1–6, choose the answer (A, B, C or D) which you think fits best according to the text.

1 What does the writer find surprising about Sonya?
A her nickname
B her appearance
C her determination
D her attitude to men

2 Why did Sonya first get involved in competitive eating contests?
A She was keen to take up a challenge.
B She wanted to find a way of leaving her job.
C She heard about it through her work at a fast food restaurant.
D She needed to earn some money to finance her eating habits.

3 *That many* in line 19 refers to
A calories.
B minutes.
C crab cakes.
D competitions.

4 Taking part in eating competitions
A has been proved to be harmful for your general health.
B can be dangerous if the food is not swallowed properly.
C means that there is no point in taking any kind of exercise.
D does not appear to have affected the weight of most competitors.

5 What does the writer say about the fashion for competitive eating?
A It has always been very popular in the US.
B It is widely accepted as a sport these days.
C It does not have a following in other countries.
D There are uncomfortable moral issues involved.

6 The choice of the word *straight-faced* in line 38 emphasises that
A Sonya is convinced that competitive eating is a sport.
B Sonya is trying very hard not to laugh out loud.
C the writer thinks that Sonya is not telling him the truth.
D the writer can't believe that Sonya takes competitive eating seriously.

➤ **HELP**

1 *Unlikely* is a similar word to *surprising* in this context. What does the writer find unlikely?

2 Where did Sonya first hear about the competition? What was her reason for entering it?

Home   Previous   Next   Search

The craze for competitive eating

Crab cakes, hot dogs and chicken wings. We meet Sonya Thomas – the woman who has taken the male world of competitive eating by storm – and watch her in action.

When you first see Sonya Thomas, you wonder whether she might be blown away by the breeze. Yet she is a tough nut. Unlikely as it may seem, this tiny woman, who weighs no more than 46 kilos, is a top-ranked competitive eater, holding over 40 eating records, including 162 chicken wings in 12 minutes and 52 eggs in five minutes. Known as 'the Black Widow' (after the female spider which destroys the males of the species), she routinely humiliates hulking men three times her size as she wolfs down her food, leaving them watching her in bewilderment, unable to keep up. There's something about being paid to eat large quantities of (usually fast) food in a short time period that speaks volumes about consumerist values in 21st-century western society. And yet Sonya was born and raised in South Korea. After emigrating to the US, she took a job at Burger King but it wasn't until she saw the World Hot Dog Eating Championship on television that she finally found a channel for the competitiveness that had always been part of her nature. Sonya signed up for the competition straightaway and ended up breaking the record for the fastest-eating female.

In the competition I saw, she was trying to break her own record for eating 40 highly calorific crab cakes in 12 minutes and I wondered how anyone, let alone a slightly built woman, can put away that many in one sitting. The competition is, without question, the most disgusting thing I have ever seen and I heard someone in the crowd mutter, 'What the hell are these people doing to themselves?' It's a good question. At that competition, Sonia would consume around 11,000 calories in her quest for the $1,500 first prize, and put on around four and a half kilos in the process. But despite this, her policy of undereating – only one meal every day – and regular running or walking enables her to keep very slim. The same cannot be said for the majority of contestants, who tend to be absolutely huge! And while it is true that there has been no conclusive evidence that competitive eating causes health problems, there have been instances in Japan of people choking while speed-eating and ending up in intensive care, which is why paramedics are always on hand during competitions and why competitive eating is no longer shown on television in that country.

line 19

Watching these competitions, you don't have to be unduly sensitive to find yourself thinking that the amount of food consumed here would represent the difference between life and death for a substantial number of people in the world's poorest countries. I discovered that this so-called sport dates back decades, to events held at country fairs, where the idea was simply to dispose of left-over food. However, unlike Japan, which has been a stronghold of the competition since the 1990s, it has only taken off in a big way in the US fairly recently. The US holds around 150 eating events a year and there are those who are convinced that it will get bigger, even becoming part of the Olympics. The majority of people that I spoke to, though, regarded it as a sign of the decay of society and an example of stupidity rather than sport.

Despite that, Sonya still hopes that one day in the future she will be thought of in the same way as an international sports star. She also tells me – completely straight-faced – that she studies video footage of her rivals' performances for clues to improve her technique, and claims that even if there were no money involved, she would still compete, both for the sheer joy of winning and the opportunity to become a celebrity.

line 38

Discussion   4   Discuss the questions.

1 How much effect do you think what you eat has on your health?
2 What kind of fast food do you like?
3 In what ways can people become celebrities in your country?

Language development 1

Permission and necessity: Present

➤ **EXPERT GRAMMAR** pages 191–193

1a Look at these comments made in a restaurant. Which ones are more likely to be made by a waiter (W) and which ones by a customer (C)?

1 Children under 12 *are allowed to* use the play area.
2 You *don't have to* give them a tip.
3 I'm afraid you *can't* sit there – it's reserved.
4 You *are not allowed to* bring your own food into the restaurant area.
5 Excuse me, Sir, children under 12 *mustn't* use the play area.
6 Steve, you *are not supposed to* use your mobile phone here. Turn it off.
7 I'm sorry, but you *have to* wear a tie to eat here.
8 I *must* try one of the desserts – they look delicious.
9 You *can* choose any table on this side, Madam.
10 I think we *are supposed to* leave a tip.

b Write the words and phrases in *italics* in Exercise 1a in the correct place in the table.

Giving permission	(1) _____
	(2) _____
Expressing prohibition	(3) _____
	(4) _____
	(5) _____
	(6) _____
Expressing obligation	(7) _____ (the speaker feels it's necessary)
	(8) _____ (the rules or situation make it necessary)
	(9) _____ (the rules or situation make it necessary)
Expressing lack of necessity	(10) _____

2a Complete the sentences with the correct form of the words in brackets. You may need to make the verb negative.

1 They're very busy at the weekend, so we _____ (must/book) a table.
2 It's a formal dinner. You _____ (can/wear) jeans.
3 Of course she _____ (allow/come) in – she's a club member.
4 I think we _____ (suppose/wait) for a waiter to show us to our table.
5 You _____ (have to/have) a starter if you don't want one.
6 You _____ (must/bring) your own food to this restaurant!
7 Children _____ (not/allow/play) in this area.
8 You _____ (can/pay) by cash, cheque or credit card.

b Talk about the rules in a café or restaurant that you know.

Permission and necessity: Past

3a Read the extract from an email about a new restaurant and answer the questions.
  1 Was it necessary to wear a suit?
  2 What was the worst thing about the restaurant?

We went to that new restaurant yesterday. It's very big, so *we didn't have to book a table.* John wore a suit because he thought it would be very formal, but in fact, it wasn't, so *he needn't have dressed so smartly.* Of course, *the children couldn't play in the restaurant* but *they were allowed to use the play area* outside. The meal was very expensive though – *we had to pay by credit card* because we didn't have enough money with us. And worst of all, *I wasn't allowed to use my phone* to call a taxi! I had to go outside!

b Write the sentences in *italics* from the email in Exercise 3a in the correct place in the table.

Meaning	Example
It was permitted.	(1) _____
It was prohibited.	(2) _____
	(3) _____
It was necessary.	(4) _____
It wasn't necessary.	(5) _____
It was done but it wasn't necessary.	(6) _____

4a Choose the correct answers.

When I was a student, I worked as a waiter during the holidays. The best thing was that I (1) *needn't have paid / didn't have to pay* for my meals, as they were all free. We (2) *were allowed to / had to* eat as much as we wanted during breaks but the work was tiring because we (3) *could / had to* work long hours. And although customers (4) *had to / could* give us tips, we (5) *couldn't have kept / couldn't keep* the money – we (6) *had to / were allowed to* share it with the other staff. I was nervous when I started because they said that sometimes I would (7) *need to have cooked / have to cook* the food but I (8) *couldn't worry / needn't have worried* because I (9) *was allowed to / didn't have to* cook at all while I worked there.

b Talk about the rules about food and eating your family had when you were a child.

Advice and recommendations

5 Correct the mistakes in the sentences.
  1 You ought complain about that soup – it's cold.
  2 You shouldn't having a dessert if you're full up.
  3 If you don't like pasta, you'd better to have a pizza.
  4 You must have try that new restaurant in Castle Street.

6 Replace the words in *italics* in the email with the correct form of the words in the box. Make any other changes necessary. You can use the words more than once.

can   had better   have to   must

Dear Melanie,

Thanks for agreeing to look after our house while we're away. Just a few things to remember:

Be careful with the front door lock. (1) *It's necessary to* pull the handle up before turning the key. But (2) *it's very important not to* force the key or it'll break!

Please feed the cat twice a day. You (3) *are allowed to* give him anything from the bottom shelf.

(4) *It's not necessary for you to* pay us to use the phone and you (5) *are permitted to* use the computer. (6) *We strongly recommend you* try the local restaurant. (7) *It's a good idea to* book though.

Have fun,

Louise

7 Complete the sentences so they are true for you.
  1 This year I really must … but I mustn't …
  2 At college/work we have to … but we don't have to …
  3 When I was younger, I could … but I wasn't allowed to … . I had to … but I didn't have to …

Writing (Paper 2 Part 2: Report)

Lead-in **1** Discuss the questions.

1 What are the best places to eat out in your area? Why?
2 What recent trends are there in the kinds of eating place available? Are you happy with the range?

Understand the task **2** Read the task and answer the questions.

1 How many parts are there to the task?
2 Decide how personal or formal your style should be. Remember the task type and who you are reporting to.
3 What will make the reader think it is a good report?

> Your English teacher has asked you to write a report on where people can eat out in your area. You should include the views of visitors and local people, comment on any recent trends and dissatisfaction and make a recommendation.
>
> Write your **report** in **140–190** words.

Plan your report **3a** Make notes under these headings. Then choose the two most important points under each heading.

Range of eating places	Recent trends/ dissatisfaction	Comment/ recommendation
cafés popular with young mothers	*higher prices*	*too little for vegetarians*

b Match the pieces of advice (a–g) with the paragraphs (1–4). Some can go with more than one paragraph.

a Focus on a maximum of two points.
b State the purpose of the report.
c Give a clear summary of the situation.
d Describe how you got the information.
e Only give relevant information.
f Make a comment and a suggestion.
g Give the facts briefly and clearly without strong opinions.

1 **Paragraph 1:** Introducing the report
2 **Paragraph 2:** Stating the range of eating places
3 **Paragraph 3:** Recent trends/Dissatisfaction
4 **Paragraph 4:** Comment/Recommendation

c Match your notes in Exercise 3a with the paragraphs in Exercise 3b.

d Choose the best heading for the report.

A   B   C

Strengths and weaknesses   *Good places to eat*   *Local eating places*

Language and content

EXPERT LANGUAGE: Passive report structures

a **Complete the second sentence so that it has a similar meaning to the first sentence.**

1 The principal is thought to be in favour of extending the lunch break.
It is thought _____ .

2 About 20 students are expected to take part in the research.
It is expected _____ .

3 Many of the residents are reported to have written a letter of protest.
It is reported _____ .

4 Some of the shopkeepers are also said not to be happy.
It is said _____ .

b **Complete the second sentence so that it has a similar meaning to the first sentence, using *supposed to*.**

1 People say that food is getting more and more expensive.
Food _____ .

2 People say that we are eating out less than we used to.
We _____ .

3 People say that cooking should be something we do, not watch on TV.
Cooking _____ .

4 People say that pubs and cafés are taking business away from restaurants.
Pubs and cafés _____ .

Write your report

➤ EXPERT STRATEGIES pages 177–178

Check your report

➤ EXPERT WRITING page 204

4a Complete these possible topic sentences for each paragraph.

1 **Paragraph 1:** This report describes …
2 **Paragraph 2:** There are a number of …
3 **Paragraph 3:** It was reported that in recent years …
4 **Paragraph 4:** The main area of concern …

b Study the sentence openings in the table. Then match each opening with endings 1–10 below, to make complete sentences.

Introduction	*The main aim/purpose of this report is to …* *To prepare for this report, …*
Reporting findings	*We are fortunate to have …* *These are very popular with …* *Since they want to …* *A cause of dissatisfaction was that …* *As a consequence,/Consequently, …* *It was commented upon by …*
Concluding and making recommendations	*All things considered, …* *It is recommended that …*

1 … people are not going out as often as they used to.
2 … a number of people we spoke to that few restaurants offer vegetarian dishes.
3 … restaurants are made aware of this view.
4 … office workers at lunchtime.
5 … we spoke to both tourists and local people.
6 … the findings were mainly positive.
7 … several good-quality gastro pubs in the area.
8 … prices had gone up dramatically recently.
9 … give an overview of the town's eating facilities.
10 … increase their business, fast food restaurants are staying open longer.

c Choose the correct answers to complete the advice.

Use *active / passive* verb forms in a report to make it *more / less* formal and *more / less* personal.

5 Now write your report using the ideas and some of the language above. Avoid copying whole phrases from the task. Use passive forms where appropriate.

6 Edit your work using this checklist.

1 Is the information relevant? (Have I included everything, but not too much?)
2 Is the style clear and neutral?
3 Does the report feel balanced? (Are different viewpoints presented fairly?)

Speaking (Paper 4 Part 2)

Vocabulary: Clothes

1 Look at the photos on page 99. How would you describe the differences in how the people are dressed (e.g. *scruffy, fashionable*)?

2 When do people wear these things?

flip-flops   fur coat   high heels   jumper   open-neck shirt   parka
pyjamas   sandals   shorts   slippers   tracksuit   trainers
trouser suit   vest top

3 In which situations would you:
1 dress down?
2 dress up?
3 get changed?
4 try something on?
5 tuck something in?
6 hang something up?
7 get a bigger size?
8 get something taken in?

4 Which clothes do you associate with these styles and fabrics? Write some examples for each of the words in the box.

bootleg   cashmere   chunky   cotton   denim   moleskin
roll-neck   suede   three-quarter length

5a The table shows the usual order of adjectives describing clothes. Complete it with the words in the box.

~~checked~~   elegant   fitted   ~~French~~   Italian   ~~khaki~~   ~~linen~~   navy
old-fashioned   patterned   short-sleeved   silk   straight   striped
tight   viscose   woollen

opinion	size/ shape	colour	pattern	origin	material
elegant	*fitted*	*khaki*	*checked*	*French*	*linen*

b Describe what the people in the photos on page 99 are wearing. Use the words above and your own words. Then add your own words to the table.

6a Look around your classroom. What styles and colours seem to be most popular in your group?

b What kinds of clothes are you comfortable wearing?

Why are the people dressed in this way?

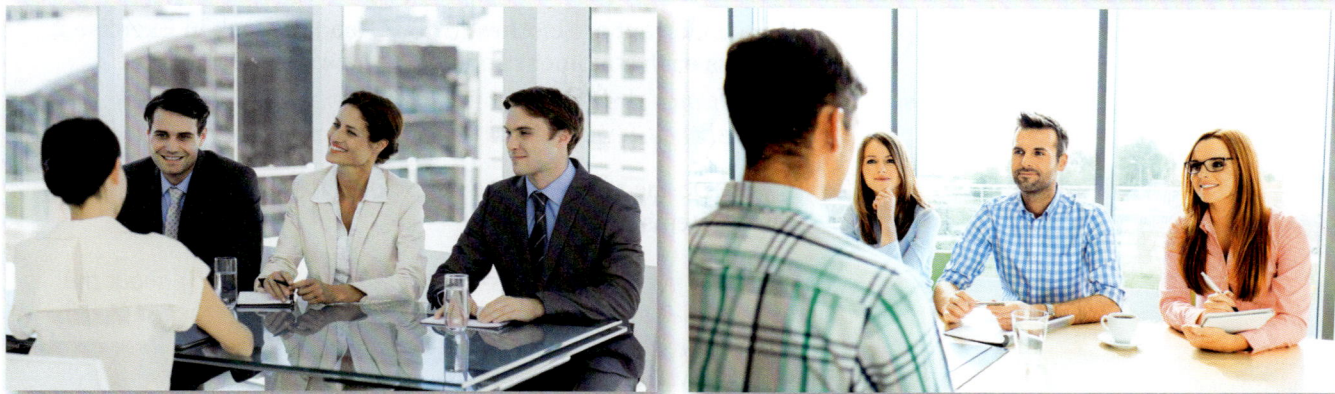

Sample answer

7a 🎧 26 Look at the photos and listen to two candidates doing the first part of a Part 2 task. Answer the questions.
1 What do the candidates have to do?
2 Who gave the better answer? In what way was it better?

b 🎧 27 Listen to the first part of the recording again and tick the phrase the woman uses to check she has understood the question.
1 Sorry, I'm not quite sure what you mean.
2 To be honest, I'm not 100 percent clear. Do you mean ... ?
3 You mean you want me to ... ?
4 So you want me to ... ?

Long turn

➤ EXPERT STRATEGIES pages 179–180

8a Work in groups of three. Follow the instructions below.

➤ EXPERT SPEAKING pages 209–210

Task 1

Student 1: You are the interlocutor. Turn to page 209 and follow the instructions for Task 1.

Students 2 and 3: You are Candidates A and B. Look at the photos above and follow the interlocutor's instructions. Candidate A, pretend you don't really understand the task and ask the interlocutor to repeat the instructions.

b Work in the same groups. Follow the instructions below.

Task 2

Student 2: You are the interlocutor. Turn to page 210 and follow the instructions for Task 2.

Students 1 and 3: You are Candidates A and B. Look at the photos on page 210 and follow the interlocutor's instructions. Candidate B, pretend you don't understand the question and ask the interlocutor to repeat it.

Task analysis

9 Discuss the questions about the two tasks.
1 Were you able to keep going without too many hesitations and paraphrase when necessary?
2 Were you reasonably accurate? Could you be understood easily?
3 Did you complete the task according to the instructions?

Listening (Paper 3 Part 3)

Before you listen

1 How important are clothes to you? Read the task in Exercise 2. Discuss each statement and decide how true it is for you.

I sometimes dress to look smart. It depends what I'm doing. For instance, I have to look reasonably well turned-out at work.

Multiple matching

➤ EXPERT STRATEGIES pages 178–179

2 🎧 28 Do the task. Use the Help notes for support with certain items.

You will hear five short extracts in which people are talking about the clothes they like to wear. For questions **1–5** choose from the list (**A–H**) what each speaker says. Use the letters only once. There are three extra letters which you do not need to use.

A	I can't afford new clothes.	Speaker 1	1
B	I buy good-quality clothes.	Speaker 2	2
C	I don't care what I wear.	Speaker 3	3
D	I choose clothes that are easy to look after.	Speaker 4	4
E	I wear fashionable clothes.	Speaker 5	5
F	It's important that my clothes are clean.		
G	I dress to look smart.		
H	My priority is to be comfortable.		

➤ **HELP**

Speaker 1 How does she feel about wearing casual clothes?

Speaker 2 Listen to the last sentence for what he says is important to him.

Task analysis

3 🎧 28 Compare and give reasons for your answers. Listen again to check.
1 What phrases helped you choose your answers?
2 Did you need to change any answers the second time you listened?

Discussion

4 Discuss the questions.
1 What kinds of clothes are best to buy as an investment?
2 Speaker 5 says that she isn't a fashion victim. What does she mean? Why do you think people become fashion victims?
3 Do you ever buy clothes in sales or charity shops? What is the best bargain you have had?
4 What is it 'cool' to wear these days in your country if you are a young person?

Language development 2

Speculation and deduction

Use	Present: modal + infinitive	Past: modal + *have* + past participle
must: certainty (we are sure it's true)	*The light's on. Ken **must be** at home.*	*Helen's late. She **must have missed** the train.* *He **must have been** going to work. That's why he was in a hurry.*
can't/couldn't: certainty (we are sure it's not true)	*Jamie **can't/couldn't be** in the library. It's closed.*	*It **can't/couldn't have rained/been** raining. The roads are dry.*
may/might/could: possibility (we are less sure)	*Sally **may/might/could be** at home – I don't know.* *They **may/might/could be** watching us.*	*She **may/might/could have left** already. I'll check.* *The train **may have been** delayed. Who knows?*

A

B

C

1a Look at the first two columns in the table above and correct the mistakes in the sentences.

1 Marlie's in her pyjamas. She can be going to bed.
2 It mustn't be his jacket – it's too small.
3 That might be Kate. I recognise that voice.
4 I think that's John's case, so he couldn't be here.
5 She's decided not to buy those shoes. She could not have enough money.
6 Mike must work in a clothes shop – he knows nothing about fashion!

b Look at the pictures and make guesses about the owner of each bag.
A must belong to a woman. She might be ...

2 Look at the third column in the table above. Complete the conversations with modals from the table and the correct form of the verbs in the box.

be   buy   cost   go   have   leave   steal

1
A: Have you seen my make-up box in the bedroom?
B: No, you _____ it there. I've just tidied up and I didn't see it.
2
A: What happened to Sarah's necklace?
B: Nobody knows, but it _____ .
3
A: Those shoes are so elegant! They _____ you a lot of money.
B: Not really – I got them in a sale.
4
A: Why is Mark looking so suntanned?
B: He _____ to the beach yesterday or else he _____ a sunlamp!
5
A: I saw Frank at the gym this morning.
B: Oh. So his illness _____ very serious!
6
A: Jane's nose looks completely different.
B: She _____ plastic surgery!

3 Complete the sentences about yourself and the class. Speculate using modals.
1 The teacher looks ... He/She ...
2 The classroom feels ... It ...
3 The student next to me seems ... He/She ...

Use of English 1 (Paper 1 Part 4)

Lead-in

1a Look at two completed key word transformation questions. In what way has the candidate not followed good exam strategy in each one?

1 I'm sure Sue was pleased when she saw the coat you bought her.
   BEEN
   Sue *must be pleased* when she saw the coat you bought her.

2 I'd love to go to the cinema tonight but I've got to do the ironing.
   WISH
   I *wish I could go with you to* the cinema tonight but I've got to do the ironing.

b Read the strategies on page 176 and check your answers to Exercise 1a.

Key word transformations

➤ **EXPERT STRATEGIES** pags 175–176

2 Do the task. Use the Help notes for support with certain items.

*For questions **1–6**, complete the second sentence so that it has a similar meaning to the first sentence, using the word given. **Do not change the word given.** You must use between two and five words, including the word given.*

1 I'm sure Tom's tired because he's yawning a lot.
   MUST
   Tom _____ because he's yawning a lot.

2 I'm hungry because the last time I ate was five hours ago.
   FOR
   I'm hungry because I _____ five hours.

3 He's so relaxed – I'm sure he's just got back from holiday.
   BEEN
   He's so relaxed – he _____ holiday.

4 I'm not fit enough to go in for a marathon.
   TOO
   I'm _____ go in for a marathon.

5 It was possible that he was having a shower, which is why he couldn't hear the bell.
   MAY
   He _____ shower, which is why he couldn't hear the bell.

6 I'm sure she hasn't left because her coat's still here.
   HAVE
   She _____ because her coat's still here.

➤ **HELP**

1 You need to use a modal. Is it in the present or the past?
2 Be careful. You need to change the verb form.
5 Infinitive or *have* + past participle?

Task analysis

3 Discuss the questions about the task.

1 Which questions test modals of speculation and deduction? Which modals are in the present and which are in the past?
2 What do the other questions test?

Use of English 2 (Paper 1 Part 1)

Lead-in

1 Discuss the questions.

1 In what way do you think hairstyles can make a statement about someone's character?
2 Which hairstyles do you find annoying or fun?

Multiple-choice cloze

➤ EXPERT STRATEGIES page 175

2a Read the title and text in Exercise 2b quickly and answer the questions. Ignore the gaps at this stage.

1 Why do people change their hairstyles?
2 How have hairstyles in the UK changed since the 1960s?

b Do the task. Use the Help notes for support with certain items.

For questions 1–8, read the text below and decide which answer (A, B, C or D) best fits each gap. There is an example at the beginning (0).

Hairstyles

Hairstyles tend to (0) *C* statements about what people are like. They are sometimes used to give the (1) ___ that we are different from others. Alternatively, we can choose a particular hairstyle in the (2) ___ that people will think we are fashionable.

In the UK in the early 1960s, the Beatles' hairstyle was copied by boys who, on the whole, wanted and (3) ___ to shock their parents. Later, middle-class 'hippies' let their hair grow long to (4) ___ their commitment to an alternative lifestyle. In the 1970s, 'skinheads' shaved their heads and (5) ___ to represent the working class; for those who felt themselves part of a multicultural society, dreadlocks were (6) ___ fashion.

Recently, fashion icons such as the footballer David Beckham have (7) ___ a huge influence on men's hairstyles. In fact, one consequence of the Beckham phenomenon is that young men now spend as much time and money (8) ___ their appearance as young women do.

0	A do	B cause	C make	D give
1	A thought	B meaning	C design	D impression
2	A proposal	B hope	C wish	D suggestion
3	A required	B expected	C supposed	D assumed
4	A explain	B create	C perform	D show
5	A allowed	B admitted	C claimed	D said
6	A in	B with	C at	D by
7	A showed	B had	C made	D put
8	A for	B about	C on	D of

➤ **HELP**

3 In this context the verb means 'believe that it is likely'.
8 Which preposition comes after *spend*?

Task analysis

3 Which questions test preposition + noun collocations?

Discussion

4 Discuss the questions.

1 When you buy something new to wear, do you care what other people think?
2 Would you consider completely changing your image (e.g. through a new hairstyle, different clothes or tattoos)?
3 What do you think of people who are always changing their image?

Language development 3

Prepositional phrases

1a Look at the examples of prepositional phrases from the text on page 103 and complete them without looking back at the text. Then look back and check your answers.

> A *We can choose a particular hairstyle ___ the hope that people will think we are fashionable.*
> B *The Beatles' hairstyle was copied by boys, who, ___ the whole, wanted to shock their parents.*
> C *Dreadlocks were ___ fashion.*

b Choose the correct answers.

> ### ◉ Browsing blogs
>
> Before I was sent to Milan to write an article about Fashion Week, I hadn't realised that it was a place where you are expected to look good **(1)** *at all times / at the moment*. So, when I arrived in scruffy jeans and with my hair all over the place, people stared at me as if they were **(2)** *in danger of / in favour of* contracting some dreadful disease. Things went **(3)** *from time to time / from bad to worse*. When I got to my hotel, **(4)** *at least / at first* the receptionist assumed I had walked in **(5)** *by mistake / by the way* and **(6)** *to my surprise / to my advantage*, asked the porter to give me directions. When she realised I was a guest, she apologised but **(7)** *by that time / by heart* I was **(8)** *in a very loud voice / in an extremely bad mood*.
> However, I had learnt my lesson. **(9)** *From time to time / From then on* every morning **(10)** *without fail / without notice* I would spend hours in front of the mirror making sure I looked good before I went out.

c Cross out the word in each group that cannot be used with the preposition in bold.
  1 **on:** sight / purpose / the beginning
  2 **for:** fun / conclusion / a change / nothing
  3 **in:** uniform / the end / luck / time to time / conclusion / fashion
  4 **out of:** date / fashion / sight / purpose / breath

d Replace the words in *italics* in the sentences with a prepositional phrase from Exercise 1c.
  1 Ellen didn't turn up, so *finally* I decided to go in by myself.
  2 My clothes were no longer *a popular style*.
  3 The doorman said my pass was *no longer valid*.
  4 I'm sorry, I didn't do it *deliberately*.
  5 Please be honest with me *in contrast with your usual behaviour*.
  6 You're *fortunate* today – I've found your wallet.

Verbs with similar meanings

2a Look at the examples from the text on page 103 and choose the correct verbs.

> A *Hairstyles tend to **make / do** statements about what people are like.*
> B *Young men now **buy / spend** as much time and money on their appearance as young women do.*

b Complete the phrases with *make* or *do*.
  1 ___ your hair   7 ___ a difference
  2 ___ friends   8 ___ a job
  3 ___ a suggestion   9 ___ an excuse
  4 ___ a course   10 ___ something for a living
  5 ___ the washing-up   11 ___ a profit
  6 ___ a phone call   12 ___ a good impression

c Complete the text below with the phrases in the box.

> a lot of money on it   an Armani suit   feel so good   in cash   it would be comfortable   to show my friends   trying it on

> I've just bought **(1)** _____ . I spent **(2)** _____ and paid **(3)** _____ , not by credit card. I was looking forward to **(4)** _____ in the shop and I hoped **(5)** _____ but I wasn't expecting it to **(6)** _____ . And, of course, it looks great – I can't wait **(7)** _____ !

d Choose the correct answers.
  1 That fashion company's profits didn't *raise / rise* at all last year.
  2 It all started when Johnson *became / grew* the director.
  3 It soon emerged that he *earned / won* $20 million a year.
  4 Their reputation was badly *damaged / injured* by the scandal.
  5 He was forced to *retire / resign* and look for another post.
  6 But the company's wounds have still not *cured / healed*.

e Complete the text with appropriate verbs in the correct form.

> After I **(1)** _____ from work at 60, I decided to **(2)** _____ some money on a day at Royal Ascot, the most popular horse race meeting in the UK. I didn't **(3)** _____ to get a ticket for the Royal Enclosure but I **(4)** _____ the decision that I would **(5)** _____ my best to look good. So I **(6)** _____ a dress from a London store and paid a designer to **(7)** _____ me a hat. On the day, my hat **(8)** _____ such a great impression that I was invited to the Royal Enclosure and met the Queen!

Lead-in

1 Discuss the questions.

1 Look at the photos. Which important things in life do they illustrate? Which are the most important for you? Do you think you devote the right amount of time to each?

2 Read the quote. What do you think it means? Which is better: to go alone or to wait for the other?

> 'The man who goes alone can start today. But he who travels with another must wait until that other is ready.' (Henry David Thoreau 1817–1862)

Reading (Paper 1 Part 6)

Before you read   1   Where or how do people usually make new friends in your country (e.g. in a club, at work, online, through friends or family)?

Skimming   2a   Read the title and introduction to the article and answer the questions.
     1   Where did this couple first meet? How do you think it happened?
     2   What do you think the title means?

     b   Skim the text to see if your answers in Exercise 2a were right. Ignore the gaps at this stage.

Gapped text   3   Do the task. Use the Help notes for support with certain items.

➤ EXPERT STRATEGIES pages 175–177

> *You are going to read an article about a couple's first meeting. Six sentences have been removed from the article. Choose from the sentences (**A–G**) the one which fits each gap (**1–6**). There is one extra sentence which you do not need to use.*

     A   So I really had met my Mr Right on an underground train.

     B   Wendy's heart was pounding as she stepped onto the platform, clutching the scrap of paper.

     C   This came as a shock to Wendy, who told him it was out of the question.

     D   As Wendy explains, 'I know it seems ridiculous but it never occurred to me to refuse.'

     E   Fortunately, Wendy saw the funny side of it and they started going out together.

     F   Seeing this, Dennis suddenly felt irritated and gave the man's briefcase a kick.

     G   It was Dennis, who had noticed Wendy as soon as she got on but was trying not to make it too obvious that he found her attractive.

➤ **HELP**

Gap 1 Which of the gapped sentences explains who the man sitting opposite was?

Gap 2 Which of the gapped sentences mentions the sleeping businessman?

Gap 3 Which of the gapped sentences explains where Wendy was at the time?

Task analysis   4   Compare and give reasons for your answers.

Discussion   5   Discuss the questions.
     1   What is your reaction to the way Wendy and Dennis met? Do you think this is a true story?
     2   Do you believe that everyone has one 'soul mate' who is just right for them?
     3   Which of these things do you think is most important in a successful relationship?
       a appearance   **b** shared interests   **c** age   **d** education
       e sense of humour

Vocabulary   6a   What preposition is used in these phrases? How do they translate into your language?
     1   go out ___ someone
     2   get on ___ someone
     3   fall in love ___ someone

Home 🏠   Previous ❮   Next ❯   Search 🔍

Meant to be

Five minutes later, and Wendy would never have met Dennis on the tube. Wendy Hatton, 39, and her husband Dennis, 32, live in London. She works in publishing and he is a scientist.

On 18 October, Dennis and Wendy celebrated their second wedding anniversary – three years to the day after they first met on a crowded underground train in London. However, it was only a chance in a million that they got to know each other at all. Wendy had intended to get a taxi home that night but seeing the long queue, she changed her mind and got the tube instead. It was a decision that was to change her life. She remembers: 'The train was packed. There was only one seat free – next to a businessman in a smart suit who had dropped off to sleep. As I pulled out my book, I caught the eye of the man sitting opposite, who gave me a little nod. [1] 'Late night trains are horrible enough without strange men staring at you,' he says. Wendy smiled briefly and got on with her reading but she could feel herself blushing.

Meanwhile, the businessman's head was slowly moving towards Wendy's shoulder as he fell into a deeper sleep. Suddenly, to her horror, it was resting on her arm. Wendy was very embarrassed but didn't know what to do. [2] It woke him up, and Wendy smiled her appreciation.

As Wendy reached her stop and got to her feet, Dennis pushed a note into her hand with his phone number on it. To this day, he doesn't know what made him do something so totally out of character but he felt he couldn't just let her disappear into the night. [3] She hadn't gone far before she felt a tap on her shoulder. 'I'm sorry,' said Dennis, who had run after her. 'I honestly don't make a habit of chatting up women on trains but would you come for a coffee with me?'

[4] There was, however, nowhere open at that time of night, so they ended up going back to Wendy's flat for a drink. As she recalls: 'He was so non-threatening that I felt instantly comfortable with him.' They sat and talked for hours, both realising they had met someone special. When Dennis left, he asked Wendy to phone him.

Five minutes later, on his way home in a taxi, he rang her. 'I was worried that I might never see you again,' he said, and started to explain. When he'd scribbled down his mobile number on that scrap of paper in the train, he'd been feeling very flustered. Suddenly, the horrible truth had just hit him: he hadn't given her the right number! He could never remember his own number and, without thinking, he'd written down the number of his ex-girlfriend! [5] They got on so well that two weeks later, realising they were made for each other, Dennis proposed.

'To me, it seemed too soon to be thinking of anything like that,' said Wendy. 'But later that night Dennis had a bad fall – he slipped on some wet stairs at home and knocked himself out. At the hospital they found my number on a slip of paper in his wallet and called me. I dashed straight round. It was when I saw him lying there on that hospital trolley that it really hit me: I had fallen in love with him. [6] Fate must have been on my side when I decided against getting that taxi, because there's no way we'd have met at any other time.'

They got married the following year. Wendy is still stunned by her good fortune.

b The text contains a lot of vivid words and phrases. Find the ones that have these meanings.

1 extremely full (paragraph 2)
2 fell asleep (paragraph 2)
3 stood up (paragraph 4)
4 wrote in a hurry (paragraph 6)
5 confused and nervous (paragraph 6)
6 go somewhere very quickly (paragraph 7)

Language development 1

Reported speech

➤ EXPERT GRAMMAR pages 193–194

1a Read the sentences and discuss the questions.

> Irene, who is British, first met her Romanian husband, Ilie, while she was on holiday in Bucharest. They now live in Bucharest.

1 Do you think it's a good idea to marry someone from a different country? Would you do it? Do you know anyone who has?
2 Would you be happy to live in his/her country?

b Read Irene's blog and answer the questions.
1 How did she meet her husband?
2 Is she happy?

◉ Browsing blogs

I was staring at a painting in the National Museum of Art, when this amazingly attractive man came up and asked me if I liked the painting. I replied that I'd seen it before in a book I have at home. He then said he'd been looking at me for the last few minutes and that he found me very attractive. I was embarrassed and told him to leave me alone. I said I didn't talk to strange men in art galleries. He asked me what the matter was and explained that he was just trying to be friendly. Then he smiled and asked me to join him for a coffee. I don't know why but I said I would, and that was the beginning of our romance. Somebody asked me last week if I regret marrying a foreigner and living abroad and I replied, 'Certainly not!' and that I'm the happiest I've ever been in my life.

c Complete the table with the exact words each person used.

Direct speech	Reported speech
Present simple	Past simple
(1) 'I _____ to strange men.'	She said she didn't talk to strange men.
Present continuous	Past continuous
(2) 'I _____ to be friendly.'	He said he was just trying to be friendly.
Present perfect (continuous)	Past perfect (continuous)
(3) 'I _____ the painting before .'	She replied that she'd seen the painting before.
(4) 'I _____ at you.'	He said he'd been looking at me.
Imperative	*tell/ask* + object + *to*-infinitive
(5) '_____ alone.'	I told him to leave me alone.
(6) '_____ for a coffee.'	He asked me to join him for a coffee.
Yes/No question	*if/whether*
(7) '_____ the painting?'	He asked me if/whether I liked the painting.
Wh- question	
(8) 'What _____ the matter?'	He asked me what the matter was.
No tense change	
(9) '_____ marrying a foreigner?'	They asked me if I regret marrying a foreigner.
(10) 'I _____ the happiest I _____ .'	I replied that I'm the happiest I've ever been.

d Answer the questions about reported speech.
1 Why is there no tense change in examples 9 and 10?
2 What does the past simple usually change to in reported speech?
3 What do these words and expressions usually change to?

today tomorrow yesterday last week next month
this here come bring

2 Read the conversation and complete the text below.
Tim: Hi Sarah, it's Tim. What are you doing tonight?
Sarah: You're nosy! Anyway, I'm studying.
Tim: That's boring – come out for a meal instead.
Sarah: Well, I've nearly finished, I suppose. Which restaurant do you have in mind?
Tim: That new Indian one. I went there last week – it's great.
Sarah: OK then. Can you pick me up?
Tim: Sure. I'll be there at seven.
Sarah: Great. I must be back early though.

Tim took me out last night – he called and asked me (1) _____ doing, so I said that I (2) _____ . He said (3) _____ boring and asked me (4) _____ for a meal instead. I replied that I (5) _____ finished and asked him which restaurant (6) _____ in mind. He told me that he (7) _____ to the new Indian restaurant the previous week and that it (8) _____ great. I asked him (9) _____ up and he said he (10) _____ there at seven. I said I (11) _____ back early.

3a Work in pairs. Tell each other about a person, place or pet that is important to you. As you listen, ask each other questions and make notes.
b Report your conversations to the rest of the group.

Reporting verbs

4a Look again at the conversation in Exercise 2 and complete the sentences with the verbs in the box.

accused agreed explained invited suggested

1 Sarah _____ Tim of being nosy.
2 Tim _____ Sarah to go out for a meal.
3 She _____ to go out for a meal.
4 Tim _____ going to the new Indian restaurant.
5 He _____ that he'd been there before.

b Write the verbs in Exercise 4a in the correct place in the table.

Verb + *to*-infinitive	
Verb + object + *to*-infinitive	
Verb + *-ing*	
Verb (+ object) + prep + *-ing*	
Verb (+ object) + *that* + clause	

c Now write the verbs in the box in the correct place in the table in Exercise 4b. Some verbs may go in more than one category.

admit advise apologise decide deny insist
offer recommend refuse remind warn

5 Report what the people say using a reporting verb from Exercise 4.
1 'You shouldn't get married yet,' Jane's father told her.
Jane's father _____ .
2 'I started the argument,' Nadia said.
Nadia _____ .
3 'I don't care what you say, I want to talk to the manager!' Paul said.
Paul _____ .
4 'Don't go out with Mike – he's not nice,' Adela told her sister.
Adela _____ .
5 'I'm sorry if I hurt your feelings,' Nick told his girlfriend.
Nick _____ .
6 'Why don't we stay in this weekend?' Mark said.
Mark _____ .
7 'I'll carry that bag for you,' Marta said to her mother.
Marta _____ .
8 'No, I won't help him!' Carol said.
Carol _____ .

6 Complete the sentences so they are true for you.
1 Once I had to apologise …
2 … asked me if …
3 … persuaded me …
4 My friend and I have decided …

7 Use the prompts to write complete sentences.
1 sometimes people / suggest / marriage / old-fashioned idea
2 parents often / persuade / children / get married
3 some people / insist / get married / while / still teenagers
4 one couple / admit / get married / for financial reasons
5 some women / decide / not / change their surname

Writing (Paper 2 Part 1: Essay)

Lead-in 1 Discuss the questions.
1 Would you prefer to live alone or with someone else? Why?
2 What are the advantages and disadvantages of each? Make notes.

Understand the task 2 Read the task below and answer the questions.
1 Will you just give your opinion or will you compare the advantages and disadvantages?
2 What style will you use?

> In your English class you have recently had a discussion about relationships. Now your teacher has asked you to write an essay.
>
> Write an essay using all the notes and give reasons for your point of view.
>
> > Is it better to live alone or with someone else?
> >
> > Notes
> >
> > Write about:
> >
> > 1 independence
> >
> > 2 money
> >
> > 3 _____ (your own idea)
>
> Write your **essay** in **140–190** words in an appropriate style.

Plan your essay 3a Look at your notes from Exercise 1 and discuss ideas for Note 3.

b Look at a possible paragraph plan for the essay. (Note: essays of this length are normally between four and five paragraphs but there is no fixed number.) Which of your points would you include in each paragraph?

Paragraph 1: Introduction:	general statement/rhetorical question; qualifying the argument
Paragraphs 2/3: Advantages:	opening statement → advantage 1 → reason (→ specific example)
	advantage 2 → reason (→ specific example)
Paragraphs 3/4: Disadvantages:	opening statement → disadvantage 1 → reason (→ specific example)
	disadvantage 2 → reason (→ specific example)
Paragraphs 4 or 5: Conclusion:	summing up/balancing the argument/overall point of view

Language and content 4a Choose the best statement for the essay from each pair below.

A
1 On balance, despite the various advantages, it would be difficult to live alone.
2 Fine, yes, there are good things about it but overall, no, not really.

B
1 I think it's better to live alone.
2 Nowadays more people are deciding to live by themselves.

C
1 I like being with my mates, don't you?
2 Most people would find it lonely and miss the friendship.

D
1 There is nobody to tell us what to do.
2 We make the decisions, no one else.

b Match the statements you chose in Exercise 4a (A–D) with the paragraphs in Exercise 3b.

c Write the headings in the box in the correct place in the table. Then choose some sentence openings to complete for your essay.

General introduction
The first part of the argument
Another reason
The second part of the argument
Conclusion

(1) _____	In the first place, …
	The main advantage is that (you are free to) …
	For one thing, (there is no one else to …)
	First of all, I'd like to say that …
	The first point I'd like to make is …
(2) _____	Then there is …
	What's more, …
	Another major advantage/disadvantage is that …
	Last but not least, …
(3) _____	Many people think that …
	Some people say/claim that …
	Why do some people believe … ?
	However, if that is the case, then why … ?
	I'd like to begin by …
(4) _____	To sum up, there are arguments …
	However, in my view, …
	It is clear that …
(5) _____	On the other hand, …
	In contrast, …
	However, not everyone …

EXPERT LANGUAGE: Linking expressions

Choose the correct answers.

1 Flatmates often don't get on very well at first. *In addition / In fact*, they can have a lot of arguments.

2 Flats in my city are very expensive for one person. *In addition / In other words*, I like sharing.

3 Most people share household tasks. *For instance / That is to say*, they take it in turns to wash up.

4 I haven't got room for a flatmate. *Moreover / For example*, I like living on my own.

5 I think that house would be too expensive. *Similarly / Besides*, it's a long way from the centre.

6 He's a nice guy to live with. *Nevertheless / What's more*, he needs to help out more.

7 The flat's on the fifth floor and there's no lift. *Because of this / Even so*, we decided to rent it.

8 It's not very big. *Even so / On the other hand*, it's right in the centre.

Write your essay

➤ EXPERT STRATEGIES pages 177–178

5 Now write your essay, using the ideas and some of the language above.

Check your essay

➤ EXPERT WRITING pages 199–200

6 Which of the statements are true about your essay?
1 I have answered the question.
2 The sentences and organisation are clear and logical.
3 Arguments are followed by reasons (and examples).
4 Both sides of the argument are given equal treatment.
5 It is clear what I think by the end.
6 The style is consistent and semi-formal.
7 I have checked: length, grammar, spelling, punctuation and linking expressions.

Speaking (Paper 4 Part 1)

Kristen Stewart (actor)

Ronaldinho (footballer)

Taylor Swift (singer)

Colin Farrell (actor)

Claudia Schiffer (model)

Ryan Gosling (actor)

Vocabulary: Free-time activities

1a Look at the photos. Which person do you think does the following?

1 makes jam
2 juggles
3 knits
4 sings karaoke
5 collects insects
6 does line dancing

b Turn to page 210 and check your answers to Exercise 1a. Are you surprised? Why do you think they have these hobbies?

2a Match a verb from box A with a leisure activity from box B. Then match the collocations with the pictures.

A

collect   do   go   learn   make   play

B

amateur dramatics   how to draw   models   Monopoly   rare coins
waterskiing

b Cross out the activity in each group that cannot be used with the verb in bold.

1 **do** (a bit of/some) gardening / darts / yoga / drawing
2 **collect** autographs / old sports cars / pool / stamps

c What other free-time activities go with the verbs in Exercise 2a?

3a One of these words/phrases is stressed on a different syllable from the others. Which is it?

backgammon bird-watching dominoes folk dancing paragliding
photography rock-climbing scuba diving train spotting windsurfing

b Which of the activities in Exercises 1a and 2a is the most:

1 relaxing?
2 exciting?
3 time-consuming?
4 expensive?
5 unusual?
6 dangerous?
7 energetic?
8 rewarding?
9 popular in your country?

4 Discuss the questions.

1 Which free-time activity are you most keen on?
2 Is there any free-time activity which:
   a helps you unwind?
   b you dabble in?
   c you are obsessed with?
   d you would like to take up?
3 What is your favourite board game?

Sample answer

5a In Part 1 of the exam you may be asked questions about these topics. Try to think of some questions for each topic and make notes about your answers.

1 likes and dislikes (e.g. your free-time activities)
2 special occasions (e.g. birthdays)
3 media (e.g. watching TV)

   1 *'What's your favourite film?' 'The one I like most right now is ...'*

b Practise asking each other your questions from Exercise 5a.

6a 🎧 29 Listen to the Part 1 conversation between the interlocutor and two candidates and answer the questions.

1 What topics does each candidate talk about?
2 Do you think they made a good first impression?

b 🎧 29 Listen again. Which two words don't the candidates know? How do they describe them?

Conversation

▶ EXPERT STRATEGIES pages 179–180

7 Work in groups of three. Take turns to be the interlocutor (asking the questions), the assessor (listening to and assessing the candidate) and the candidate. Follow the instructions below.

Interlocutor: Ask some of your questions from Exercise 5a. Don't repeat questions already asked.
Assessor: Make notes on the candidate's performance.
Candidate: Answer the questions. Try to follow the Expert strategies on page 180.

Task analysis

8 Discuss the questions about the task.

1 How well did you each do?
2 Did you give full answers?
3 Were any answers too short or too long?
4 Did you have to think of different ways of saying things?
5 What would you do differently next time?

Listening (Paper 3 Part 4)

Multiple choice

> EXPERT STRATEGIES pages 178–179

1 🎧 30 Do the task. Use the Help notes for support with certain items.

You will hear a radio interview with a journalist called Simon, who is talking about the psychology of hobbies. For questions 1–7, choose the best answer (A, B or C).

1 According to Simon, what can you learn by knowing about people's hobbies?
   A what kind of job they have
   B what kind of person they are
   C what kind of skills they have

2 What do celebrities' hobbies often have in common?
   A They take place outdoors.
   B They are connected with music.
   C They involve being part of a group.

3 On film sets, the most popular way for actors to spend their time is
   A playing competitive board games.
   B helping each other with crosswords.
   C doing creative activities by themselves.

4 What is unusual about the Dalai Lama?
   A He loves old movies.
   B He collects vintage cars.
   C He is always mending things.

5 What does Bill Wyman get most pleasure from?
   A collecting antique jewellery
   B writing archaeological books
   C looking for items of historic interest

6 Simon says that the hobbies of world leaders are often
   A dangerous.
   B obsessive.
   C embarrassing.

7 What does Simon say about ordinary people who are fanatical about their hobbies?
   A They are usually a little strange.
   B Luckily, they are the exception.
   C It can be hard for others to put up with them.

> **HELP**

2 Listen for the expression *in the fresh air*. What does it mean?

4 What have all the Dalai Lama's hobbies got in common?

6 What does *take over their lives* mean?

Task analysis

2 🎧 30 Compare and give reasons for your answers. Listen again to check.

Discussion

3 Discuss the questions.
   1 Tell each other about your free-time activities. What interesting experiences have you had?
   2 What do your own hobbies tell people about your personality?

Use of English 1 (Paper 1 Part 2)

Lead-in 1 Discuss the questions.
1 Why do people go fishing?
2 Have you been fishing? What do/don't you like about it?
3 Is fishing popular in your country?

Open cloze 2a Read the title and article quickly and answer the questions.
➤ EXPERT STRATEGIES page 175
1 What type of fishing is 'angling'?
2 How is angling changing in the UK?

b Do the task. Use the Help notes for support with certain items.

*For questions 1–8, read the text below and think of the word which best fits each gap. Use only **one** word in each gap. There is an example at the beginning (0).*

Angling

Angling (fishing with worms or artificial flies, using a rod, line and hook) is (0) <u>one</u> of the most popular outdoor pursuits in the UK, with between two and four million people taking part (1) ___ a regular basis. For a father, (2) ___ able to spend some 'quality' time with his son must be a big attraction but (3) ___ else would anyone want to spend hours in the wind and rain, standing waist-high in water in the hope of catching a fish? If they (4) ___ , they would probably throw it back anyway!

Until recently, 98 percent (5) ___ all anglers have been male. (6) ___ , a few years ago the Environmental Agency made a decision to try and attract more female participants to the sport. They appear to have succeeded (7) ___ their aim, since more and more women are now using angling (8) ___ an effective way of relaxing.

➤ **HELP**

2 Which auxiliary is needed here? What form is it in?

7 Which preposition combines with *succeed*?

Task analysis 3 Which questions test:
1 verb forms?
2 verb + preposition collocations?

Discussion 4 Discuss the questions.
1 Some people say fishing for fun is cruel. Do you agree?
2 Why do you think fishing is generally less popular with women?

Language development 2

Expressing ability

A Present: *can*
Can is more common than *be able to* in the present.
Can you play tennis? No, I can't.
Can also expresses future ability if we are deciding now about the future.
I *can* play tennis tomorrow if you want.

B Past: *could, was/were able to*
Use *could* for general past ability.
Could you play chess when you were a child?
Use *was able to*, not *could*, for ability in a specific situation.
I *was* finally *able to* finish my model plane last weekend.
Use *wasn't able to* or *couldn't* for both general and specific ability.
I *couldn't/wasn't able to* beat Tom at squash yesterday.

C Future/Perfect tenses, infinitive: *be able to*
Can has no infinitive or past participle, so we use *be able to*.
I *will be able to* play more tennis in the summer.
Has he ever *been able to* finish a marathon?
I *might be able to* go hiking next weekend.

D Other ways of expressing ability
I *know how to* play chess. (I have learnt the skill.)
I *succeeded in* beating my sister last week. (suggests some difficulty)
I *managed to* beat my brother as well. (suggests a lot of difficulty)

1a Read the information above and choose the correct answers. Both options may be correct in some sentences.
1 I *can / manage to* play the piano quite well.
2 Last week I *was able to / could* get away for a few days.
3 I *could / have been able to* ride a bike from a very early age.
4 When I was at school, I *couldn't / wasn't able to* draw very well.
5 In the last month I *have managed to / knew how to* get some outdoor exercise every weekend.
6 Once the exams are over, I *will be able to / can* spend more time on my favourite hobby.
7 I *could / managed to* beat my father at chess eventually but it wasn't easy.
8 I was very pleased when I finally *managed to find / succeeded in finding* a salsa class.

b Work in pairs. Which of the sentences in Exercise 1a are true for you and your partner?

2 Complete the sentences with the correct forms of the words in brackets.
1 If Paul doesn't get some help, he _____ (able/finish) that model.
2 How do you _____ (manage/stay) so slim?
3 After five years Nico has _____ (succeed/pass) his driving test.
4 I'm afraid I _____ (can/come) to the party on Saturday night.
5 After making three big mistakes, Tara realised she _____ (could/win) the match.
6 We _____ (know/play) chess. Can you teach us?
7 Sergio _____ (able/stay) ahead at the end, so he lost the race.
8 I _____ (could/swim) until I was 12 but then I learnt very quickly.

3 Complete the sentences with the verbs in brackets and *can, could, be able to, succeed* or *manage* in the correct form. There may be more than one possibility.

I've been making models all my life. When I was nine, I had my first Lego® set – you know, those plastic pieces which you (1) ___ (use) to make machines – and everyone was amazed that I (2) _____ (put together) cars that moved.
Later I (3) _____ (build) a larger car which (4) _____ (reach) quite high speeds. I also built a radio-controlled machine that looked like a plane but, unfortunately, it (5) _____ (not/fly).
Now I make radio-controlled robot machines that battle with other machines. Last year I entered Victor, my warrior robot, into two international competitions and we (6) _____ (win) them both. I hope I (7) _____ (carry on) making machines for many years to come.

Use of English 2 (Paper 1 Part 4)

Lead-in

1 Look at three completed key word transformation questions. Which question tests:

a verb/adjective/noun + preposition collocations?

b prepositional phrases?

c phrasal verbs?

1 I am here as a representative of the government.

BEHALF

I am here *on behalf of* the government.

2 They employ extra staff at weekends.

ON

Extra staff *are taken on* at weekends.

3 Prices have gone up sharply again.

INCREASE

There has been *a sharp increase in* prices.

Key word transformations

➤ EXPERT STRATEGIES pages 175–176

2a Look at the task. What language point does each question test?

b Do the task. Use the Help notes for support with certain items.

*For questions **1–6**, complete the second sentence so that it has a similar meaning to the first sentence, using the word given. **Do not change the word given.** You must use between **two** and **five** words, including the word given.*

1 Phil knows how to cheat successfully at chess.

AWAY

Phil knows how to _____ at chess.

2 I'll take my MP3 player because we might want to listen to music.

CASE

I'll take my MP3 player _____ listen to music.

3 There probably won't be any more customers today.

UNLIKELY

It _____ be any more customers today.

4 They had to cancel the outdoor exhibition because of the bad weather.

CALLED

The outdoor exhibition _____ because of the bad weather.

5 I failed to persuade Tom to take up stamp collecting.

SUCCEED

I _____ Tom to take up stamp collecting.

6 We found it difficult to write the story.

TROUBLE

We _____ the story.

➤ **HELP**

4 You need a phrasal verb in the passive.

6 Which form of the verb goes with *trouble*?

Task analysis

3 Discuss the questions.

1 Did you 'over-transform' (add words which are not necessary) any of the sentences?

2 Compare and discuss your answers. Which question did you find the most difficult? Why?

Language development 3

Phrasal verbs with *get*

1a Read the posts (1–3) and match them with the pictures (A–C).

---

1 Emily

I didn't *get off* to a very good start with the BodyCombat® classes because my shoes were too heavy and not very comfortable. Also, I had to miss a couple of sessions and found it difficult to *get back* into the routine. But everything's fine now and the trainer says I'm *getting on* really well.

2 Keira

Hi, guys! I just have to tell you what I've been *getting up to*. Remember last time I was *getting over* the death of my pet rat and my dad wouldn't let me have another pet? Well, I managed to *get round* him in the end – it took me two weeks and I had to promise to do better at school – and he's bought me a bearded dragon to look after! How cool is that?!

3 Jack

I love singing in the choir. We *get together* early Friday evening, which means I have to *get off* work a couple of hours early. When I get there, we usually chat for a bit before we *get down* to serious rehearsals. I know I'm not a very good singer but I *get by*.

A

B

C

b Look at the phrasal verbs in *italics* in Exercise 1a and decide if these statements are *True* (T) or *False* (F) according to the texts.

1 Emily's BodyCombat® classes began badly. *T*
2 It was hard to start doing the BodyCombat® classes again.
3 Emily is making good progress in her classes.
4 Keira is saying what she's been doing recently.
5 She forgot to mention the death of her pet.
6 She eventually persuaded her father to buy her a new pet.
7 Jack's choir meets on a Friday evening.
8 Unfortunately, he can't leave work early.
9 They only rehearse seriously after a chat.
10 He doesn't really sing well enough to be in the choir.

c What do you think of how the people spend their free time?

2 Choose the correct paraphrase (A or B) for each sentence.

1 It takes ages to get through to the complaints department.
  A Contacting the complaints department takes a long time.
  B Travelling to the complaints department takes a long time.
2 This weather's getting me down.
  A The weather's making me happy.
  B The weather's making me unhappy.
3 To his surprise, he got away with a fine.
  A He thought his punishment would be smaller.
  B He thought his punishment would be bigger.
4 He always manages to get his ideas across.
  A He is a good communicator.
  B He gets his ideas mixed up.
5 I get along very well with my sister.
  A My sister and I have a good relationship.
  B My sister and I often go out together.
6 They got behind with their work.
  A They lost their work.
  B They didn't do as much work as they should have done.

3a Complete the questions with phrasal verbs from Exercises 1a and 2 in the correct form.

1 How often do you _____ with friends from your previous school/job?
2 What kind of things _____ you _____ ? What do you do to cheer yourself up again?
3 Have you ever done anything wrong and _____ it?
4 How well do you _____ with your parents?
5 How much money do you need to _____ ?
6 What will you be _____ this weekend?
7 What time do you _____ lessons today?

b Work in pairs. Take turns to ask your partner the questions in Exercise 3a.

Overview

9A
> **Reading and Use of English:** Multiple matching (Part 7)
> **Language development:** Conditionals
> **Writing:** Article (Part 2)

9B
> **Speaking:** Vocabulary: Shopping; Collaborative task and discussion (Parts 3 and 4)
> **Listening:** Multiple choice (Part 1)
> **Language development:** Subject–verb agreement; *it/there*; Money and banks; Forming verbs
> **Reading and Use of English:** Open cloze (Part 2); Word formation (Part 3)

Lead-in

1 Discuss the questions.
   1 What are the benefits and drawbacks of the consumer society?
   2 Read the statement. How far do you agree with it?
   The people who do all the work don't get their fair share of the profits.

Reading (Paper 1 Part 7)

Shelter   age UK Love later life   OXFAM   WWF

Before you read

1 a Which of these charities would you be most and least likely to give to? Why?

- the homeless
- medical research
- the elderly
- children
- animals

- the environment
- the developing world
- disaster relief
- the disabled

b Do you think helping the needy should be the responsibility of individuals or of the government?

Multiple matching

➤ EXPERT STRATEGIES pages 175 and 177

2 Do the task. Remember to read the questions carefully before you scan the texts to find the information.

You are going to read an article in which five people talk about contributing to charity. For questions 1–10, choose from the people (A–E). The people may be chosen more than once.

Which person

admires the efforts made to raise funds for charity?	1
thinks some people support charities out of self-interest?	2
believes that giving money directly to individuals in need is not the best solution?	3
resents feeling pressured into giving money?	4
suspects that some charities don't make the best use of their money?	5
has mixed feelings about giving to street collectors?	6
contributes to society in non-financial ways?	7
is impressed by the general public's generosity after a disaster?	8
prefers to support less 'fashionable' charities?	9
admits they have given money out of a feeling of guilt?	10

Task analysis

3 Compare and give reasons for your answers.

Discussion

4 Which person in the article do you agree and disagree with most?

Vocabulary: Informal expressions

5 Match the definitions with the underlined words and phrases in the article.

1 help
2 admire
3 emotional
4 makes you realise

5 give money
6 very embarrassed
7 on the street
8 deliberately do something

Could you spare some change, please?

What motivates you to give or deny money to people in need? We hit the streets of Manchester to find out your views.

A Tom (30)

'Whenever I see a fundraising event on TV to raise money for an earthquake or whatever, I always feel <u>moved</u> by the number of people – especially the worse-off – who <u>make donations</u>. I do think the TV coverage helps – it really <u>brings it all home to you</u>. Of course, it's not only about giving money, although obviously that is a key part of it; I've often wished that I had medical or engineering skills to offer so that I could go out there and help the relief effort. I'm more unwilling, though, to just give money to people on the streets because I don't think this helps solve the problem long-term and in fact could encourage more people to sleep <u>rough</u>.'

B Yvette (26)

'I can never pass anyone in the street holding a collection tin without asking myself whether or not I should give. I sometimes feel reluctant if it's for medical research or the homeless – isn't that what I pay my taxes for, after all? But on the other hand, if everyone gave just a little, then we wouldn't have all these problems. I read somewhere that the average person only gives one percent of what they earn to charity, which means they spend 99 percent on themselves! However, I do worry that some organisations have become so big that they are, perhaps, spending too much on bureaucracy instead of sending it directly to those in need.'

C Jeanette (57)

'I really <u>applaud</u> those people who actively do something for good causes, such as car boot sales or sponsored walks. Sometimes I think about taking part in something like that but thinking is as far as I get! To tell the truth, I think that most of us need to have a personal reason for getting involved, such as knowing someone who has a certain disease or something. I do give money to charity collectors on the street whenever I have change but if I'm honest, that's because I feel <u>ashamed</u> walking on past them when it's cold or the rain is pouring down.'

D Graham (45)

'I get really annoyed with the charity collectors who stand outside shops and swoop on you, asking you for money for this cause and that cause, trying to make you feel guilty if you say no. I also disapprove of all those junk letters you get – you know, with photos of starving children or animals in pain or whatever. I feel that they are almost trying to exploit you – it's a kind of emotional blackmail. It's up to me, after all, who I donate money to and I actually <u>make a point of</u> giving to organisations that get less publicity rather than the trendy ones that are linked to celebrities.'

E Laura (35)

'I wouldn't have any money at all if I gave money to every charity collector on every street corner! That's why I don't do it. And I've stopped giving myself a hard time about it because I do feel that I <u>do my fair share</u> for the community in other ways. I donate blood three times a year and I work as a volunteer in a retirement home. I also give our old clothes and toys to the local charity shop. I think that there are those who only give money to charity to ease their conscience rather than really wanting to help those they are giving it to. The same goes for those celebrities who get a lot of publicity because they are associated with a charity. Who benefits more: the celebrity or the charity?'

Language development 1

Zero, first, second and third conditionals

➤ EXPERT GRAMMAR pages 194–195

1a Read the extract. Would you give your money away like Warren Buffet?

Warren Buffet gives his money away!

Warren Buffet, one of the world's richest men, has pledged to give away 99 percent of his wealth to charitable foundations during his lifetime or at death. He has already donated to a number of organisations, with most of the money going to the Bill and Melinda Gates Foundation.

b Read the statements below and answer the questions.
1 Is Jake as rich as Warren Buffet?
2 Is it possible that Scarlett will give money to a street musician tonight?
3 Does Keith give money to charity?
4 Did Libby give money to an animal sanctuary?

Jake:	If I had Warren Buffet's money, I'd leave most of it to my children.
Scarlett:	If I see a street musician on my way home tonight, I'll probably give him or her something.
Keith:	If someone from a charity comes to my door, I nearly always give them money.
Libby:	If I had been the old lady, I wouldn't have left my fortune to my cat but I would have given a large sum to an animal sanctuary.

c Complete the Example column in the table with the statements in Exercise 1b.

Use	Example	Form
Zero conditional: always true (*if* = *when*)		
First conditional: possible and likely		
Second conditional: unlikely or imaginary		
Third conditional: unreal in the past		

d Now complete the Form column in the table in Exercise 1c with 1–4.

1 *if* + past simple + *would*
2 *if* + past perfect + *would have* + past participle
3 *if/when* + present simple + present simple
4 *if* + present simple + *will*

2a Use the prompts to write questions with *if* about the present or future. Choose conditionals based on how likely you think the situation is.

1 you / win / a lot of money / what / you / spend it on?
2 a classmate / ask / lend / small amount of money / what / you / do?
3 a classmate / ask / lend / large amount of money / what / you / do?
4 what / you / do / you / need / change for a vending machine?
5 you / find / a lot of money / what / you / do?
6 what / you / do / you / lose / wallet or purse?
7 what / you / say / you / receive / a present you / not like?
8 what / you / buy / you / go / shopping this weekend?

b Ask each other the questions in Exercise 2a.

3 Write sentences with *if* to make a story.

1 James forgot to set his alarm, so he overslept.
If James had remembered to set his alarm, he wouldn't have overslept.
2 Because he was late for work, he got the sack.
3 He couldn't find another job, so he started his own business.
4 The business was a great success because it was such a good idea.
5 James worked very hard and became a millionaire.
6 So he became very rich because he didn't set his alarm!

Mixed conditionals

4a Choose the correct answers.

1 If I weren't so poor *yesterday / at the moment*, I would have given some money to the street musician *now / yesterday*.

2 If Warren Buffet had given me half of his fortune *last week / at present*, I would be very rich *last week / now*.

b Match the statements in Exercise 4a (1–2) with the explanations (a–b).

a If something had happened in the past, the present would be different.
b If the present were different, something would have happened in the past.

5 Choose the correct answers.

1 If I *earned / earn* more money in my present job, I *wouldn't have gone / wouldn't go* for a job interview last week.
2 Sheila *would be able to / will be able to* go out now if she *hadn't spent / didn't spend* so much on clothes yesterday.
3 If the company *had invested / invested* more when they started, their profits *would be / will have been* bigger now.
4 If we *weren't / haven't been* such good friends, I *would have been / would be* furious when you crashed my car.
5 If I *were / had been* the president, I *would reduce / would have reduced* taxes as soon as I was elected.
6 She *would be / would have been* at home now if she *didn't miss / hadn't missed* her train.
7 Paul *couldn't have bought / couldn't buy* that new car last week if he *weren't / hadn't been* so well-off.

Conjunctions in conditional sentences

6 Choose the correct answers.

1 The company will be a success *even if / provided that* we all work hard.
2 *If / Unless* we get more customers, we will have to close.
3 *As long as / Even if* we get more customers, we may have to close.
4 We can move to bigger offices *as long as / unless* they're not too expensive.

7 Complete the sentences with *if*, *unless*, *even if*, *provided that* or *as long as* and the correct form of the verbs in brackets.

1 _____ you _____ (hurry up), we _____ (miss) the bargains in the sale!
2 We buy our office equipment from PenCo, which _____ (give) us a discount _____ we _____ (spend) more than £100.
3 I'm really grateful. _____ you _____ (not lend) me the money, I _____ (have) big problems now.
4 I _____ (come) with you _____ you _____ (pay). What time does the film start?
5 _____ we _____ (not run) a business, we _____ (have) more free time but we enjoy what we do.
6 _____ Peter _____ (ask) me to invest in his company, I _____ (not be) able to. I didn't have enough money at that time.
7 _____ you _____ (not work) so many hours, you _____ (not feel) so tired all the time. You really should try it.
8 _____ this _____ (be) my company, I _____ (not spend) so much on new computers last year.

Writing (Paper 2 Part 2: Article)

Lead in

1a How would your life change if you won a large sum of money? What problems might there be?

b What would you do with the money if you won? Discuss and make notes under these headings.

Spending	*Saving*	*Giving away*
_____	_____	_____
_____	_____	_____
_____	_____	_____

Understand the task

2 Read the task and answer the questions.
1 What are the two key parts to the question?
2 What does a reader expect from a good article?
3 How can you make your article interesting?

You see this announcement in an international magazine.

Articles wanted
Lucky winners!

What would you do if you won a large sum of money? How would your life change? Write an article answering these questions. Give reasons.

We will publish the best articles next month.

*Write your **article** in **140–190** words in an appropriate style.*

Plan your article

3a Choose three or four points from your notes in Exercise 1b for your article.

b Make a paragraph plan and add the points from your notes.

c Check your paragraph plan. Does it include:
1 a variety of answers? (not just a list of things you would buy)
2 a reason for each answer?

d In the exam, you can use the title in the question or invent one of your own. Think of possible titles for your article and choose the best one.

Language and content

4a In which part of the article might you find these extracts?

A Because you are rich, you are not necessarily happy. People ask you for money and if you spend everything carelessly, you are miserable again.

B I'll decide later what to do with the rest of the money but I won't buy luxury cars.

C It would be difficult to know what life would be like if I were rich suddenly but it would be very different.

b Now look at these extracts, which express the same ideas as those in Exercise 4a but are more engaging for the reader. First, match them with extracts A–C in Exercise 4a. Then complete the sentences using your own ideas.

1 Have you ever dreamt what life … ? What a … ! Everything would be …

2 Of course, money can't … . Suddenly, you discover … and if you spend the whole … you'll end up …

3 If you want to know … , I'm not sure. I'll decide … but you can rest assured that I …

c It is very important that you show a range of structures in your article. Read these sentences from a student's article and complete them with the correct form of the verbs in brackets.

1 The first thing I ___ (do) is ___ (start) by ___ (put) some money away and ___ (save) it.

2 Then I ___ (buy) my parents a new home. They ___ (deserve) it because they ___ (provide) me with everything I ___ (want) in my life even if it ___ (mean) they ___ (have to) go without.

3 It ___ (not be) right ___ (just/spend) the money on myself, so I ___ (give) some money to people who ___ (struggle) in the world.

d Adjectives can give an article 'colour'. Make these sentences more interesting by adding adjectives.

1 I'd give some money to my ___ parents.

2 I'd buy them a(n) ___ new home.

3 I'd give money to ___ people who are struggling.

4 I'd travel in ___ comfort.

5 I'd no longer want to stay in ___ hostels.

e Look at the phrases in the table. Then choose some and use them to write complete sentences for your article.

Giving opinions	To my mind, … The way I see it is that … I've always thought I'd …
Sequencing	The first thing … Then/After that/Next, I … Apart from that, I … And finally, I …
Giving explanations and reasons	After all, I … The (main) reason/One reason (I say that) is … Because of this I …

Write your article
➤ EXPERT STRATEGIES pages 177–178

5 Now write your article using the ideas and some of the language above.

Check your article
➤ EXPERT WRITING page 201

6 Edit your work using the checklist on page 198.

EXPERT LANGUAGE: Intensifying adverbs

Choose the correct answers.

1 After the win, his life changed *seriously / dramatically*.

2 At first we were *ridiculously / highly* happy.

3 A few weeks later, though, we were *bitterly / fully* disappointed.

4 I *clearly / thoroughly* remember you once saying you would give up work.

5 She has a lot of *seriously / deeply* held beliefs about the role of money in the world.

6 They were *greatly / totally* affected when they saw how happy I was.

7 I would *hugely / fully* understand if you spent the rest of your life travelling!

8 My life hasn't changed *highly / hugely*.

Speaking (Paper 4 Parts 3 and 4)

Vocabulary: Shopping

1a Look at the spidergram. In which of these places are you more likely to:
1 have to pay a fortune?
2 pick up a bargain in the sales?
3 find a 'one-off'?
4 go to the checkout?
5 get personal service?
6 be spoilt for choice?
7 get good value?

b Look at the places in the spidergram in Exercise 1a. Underline the stressed syllable(s).

c In which of the places in Exercise 1a would you expect to find the things in the box? More than one answer may be possible.

aisle   changing rooms   escalators   organic food   trolley

d What is a shop called where you can buy these things?
1 meat
2 medicine
3 flowers
4 newspapers
5 stationery
6 shoes

2 Complete the sentences with the correct form of *cost* or *price*.
1 'Where's the ___ tag on this dress?' 'Here. Oh dear! It ___ a fortune!'
2 I think this sofa is a very fair ___ . Very reasonable.
3 What's the total ___ of the computer? It seems very ___ !
4 We install the satellite dish at no extra ___ to the customer.
5 Look, these shoes are half ___ ! Great!

3 Complete the sentences with the words in the box. Who do you think is saying these things? What is the situation?

hang on	just	keep	offer	out of	pay	put	return

1 I'm sorry. We're _____ stock.
2 Do I have to _____ at the till?
3 Is this TV on special _____ ?
4 Could you _____ me through to your sales department?
5 Just _____ a moment. I'll go and have a look.
6 No, thanks. I'm _____ looking.
7 Sorry to _____ you waiting.
8 If it's faulty, you can _____ it and we'll exchange it for you.

Collaborative task

➤ EXPERT SPEAKING pages 179–180

4 Work in groups of three. Follow the instructions below.

Student 1:   You are the interlocutor. Turn to page 211 and give the instructions for the task.

Students 2 and 3:   You are Candidates A and B. Look at the spidergram in Exercise 1a and follow the interlocutor's instructions.

Task analysis

5 Read the Expert strategies on pages 179–180. Did you follow each piece of advice?

Three-way discussion

➤ EXPERT SPEAKING pages 179–180

6a Look at the Part 4 questions 1–6 below. Which question asks you to:

a make a prediction?
b describe something?
c make a comparison?
d check an opinion?
e give a reason?
f talk about the past?

1 Is it better to buy organic food than non-organic food?
2 Ten years ago, did people use to spend less time shopping?
3 Do you think you have to spend a lot of money to get nice clothes?
4 So you think some people like to go shopping as a hobby?
5 Do you think that people will do most of their shopping online in future?
6 How do most people do their shopping in your country?

b 🎧 31 Listen to two candidates answering one of the questions in Exercise 6a. Which question do you think they were asked? Do you agree with what they said?

c 🎧 31 Listen again and tick the expressions the candidates use. Why do they use each expression: to add to their own opinion, agree or disagree with the other candidate?

1 Apart from that ...
2 And there's another thing ...
3 Not only that ...
4 Actually ...

7 Work in groups of three. Take it in turns to be the interlocutor and Candidates A and B, and ask two questions each from Exercise 6a.

Task analysis

8 Discuss the questions about the task.

1 Did you give your partner an opportunity to respond to what you said?
2 Did you develop your answers fully?

Listening (Paper 3 Part 1)

Before you listen

1 Look at the task in Exercise 2 and decide what you have to listen for in each question. Mark the key words first.

Multiple choice

2 🎧 32 Do the task.

> EXPERT STRATEGIES page 178

You will hear people talking in eight different situations. For questions 1–8, choose the best answer (A, B or C).

1 You hear an advertisement on the radio. What is being advertised?
   A a television game show
   B a computer game
   C a board game

2 You overhear a man talking to a shop assistant. What is the man doing?
   A returning faulty goods
   B asking for his money back
   C trying to get some goods delivered

3 You hear a radio phone-in programme on the subject of cars. What is the caller doing?
   A blaming someone for something
   B asking for advice about something
   C making a suggestion about something

4 You hear part of a radio play. Where is this scene taking place?
   A in a bus station
   B in a shop
   C in a library

5 You overhear a woman talking in a travel agency. What is she complaining about?
   A the attitude of the staff towards her
   B the accuracy of the information she was given
   C the fact that her holiday arrangements were changed

6 You overhear a man talking on his mobile phone. Who is he talking to?
   A a hotel receptionist
   B a conference organiser
   C his secretary

7 You hear a radio announcement about a new service that's being offered in London. In which sector has the service been most successful so far?
   A travel
   B health
   C entertainment

8 You hear the beginning of a radio programme on shopping. What is the programme going to be about?
   A the disadvantages of e-commerce
   B a new idea that will help e-commerce
   C research into the success of e-commerce

Discussion

3 Answer the questions.
   1 Have you ever taken faulty goods back to a shop? If so, what was the problem? Did you get a cash refund or a credit note for goods?
   2 Have you ever felt you were being ripped off by a shop or a service provider?
   3 In what sorts of situation should travel agents or airlines pay compensation to travellers?

Use of English 1 (Paper 1 Part 2)

Lead-in

1 Discuss the questions.
1 Do you prefer to buy your food and other necessities in a street market or a supermarket?
2 What are the advantages and disadvantages of shopping at the same places every time?

Open cloze

➤ EXPERT STRATEGIES page 175

2a What advice would you give someone doing the task below? Check your answer with the Expert strategies on page 175.

b Read the title and the first sentence of the text. How much do you know about customer tracking?

c Do the task. Use the Help notes for support with certain items.

*For questions **1–8**, read the text below and think of the word which best fits each gap. Use only **one** word in each gap. There is an example at the beginning (**0**).*

Customer tracking

When you're stacking up grocery items at the checkout, you're probably not worried that your supermarket might (**0**) _be_ building a profile of the kind of shopper you are. After all, does it matter whether you buy (**1**) ___ brand of biscuits rather than another? Surely, nobody (**2**) ___ particularly interested! Well, supermarkets care. So much so that they issue 'loyalty' cards to offer what seem to be great bargains. They then use these cards to keep track (**3**) ___ how often you shop and (**4**) ___ your buying preferences are. Often, this information (**5**) ___ then 'shared' with other companies.

According (**6**) ___ one survey, 85 percent of UK consumers have a loyalty card. However, a number of shoppers (**7**) ___ becoming increasingly worried that these will be used to compile detailed profiles of their lifestyles. It is unclear where this practice will lead. Already, in some countries, customer profiling is used to track criminals. Will (**8**) ___ also be increases in insurance premiums for unhealthy eaters? Who knows what the future will hold.

➤ **HELP**

2, 5, 7 Do you need a singular or plural verb?
8 Do you need *they* or *there*?

Discussion

3 Discuss the questions.
1 Do you mind that shops may hold information about you?
2 Do you mind receiving unsolicited emails advertising products and offering deals?

Language development 2

Subject–verb agreement

> Verbs and their subjects should always 'agree'.
> *She hates shopping.* (singular subject, singular verb)
> *They think she's rich.* (plural subject, plural verb; singular subject, singular verb)
> But it's not always easy to know whether to use a singular or a plural verb form!
> A Use a singular verb after:
> *The news is boring.* (athletics, politics, the United States)
> *Ninety dollars is a lot of money.* (two weeks, thirty miles)
> *Neither of these shops sells what I want.* (each of, none of)
> *Hardly anyone goes to the market now.* (almost nobody)
> *Everyone uses the supermarket.* (everybody, every + noun)
> *More than one small shop has closed.* (one of, every one of, a total of)
> B Use a plural verb after:
> *People do their shopping online.* (the police, the military)
> *Glasses are becoming cheaper.* (scissors, trousers, jeans)
> *A number of chain stores have opened.* (both of, all of, the majority of, a couple of, a group of)
> C Some nouns can be followed by a singular or plural verb:
> the bank, the government, the family, the team, the school, the public
> *The staff is getting bigger.* (the staff as a single body)
> *The staff are not very happy with their pay.* (the staff as a collection of individuals)

1 Read the information above and read these sentences. Tick the correct ones and correct the mistakes in the wrong ones.

1 Everyone think it's a good idea.
2 The majority of us agrees.
3 The police are coming.
4 Neither of them know what to buy.
5 These jeans doesn't fit.
6 The news about the market wasn't good.
7 Ten euros aren't very much.
8 The company has a great future.
9 These scissors doesn't cut very well.
10 The United States have a new president.

2 Complete the article with the correct present simple form of the verbs in brackets.

> Home Previous Next Search
>
> ## *Variety – the spice of life?*
> Every supermarket (1) ___ (sell) up to 40,000 products but, according to recent research, many people (2) ___ (feel) that greater choice (3) ___ (cause) unnecessary stress. Hardly anyone (4) ___ (want) 600 kinds of coffee! Both men and women (5) ___ (seem) to want less choice when shopping.
> And none of us (6) ___ (be) happy to have more choice in other aspects of our lives; a significant number of people (7) ___ (say) they find it hard to decide what to eat. But whereas only ten percent of men (8) ___ (admit) that deciding what to wear is difficult, nearly all of the women (9) ___ (confess) that this is a major problem for them.
> However, none of those interviewed really (10) ___ (want) to change things. Too much choice is better than no choice at all!

it/ there

> A *there + be* = something exists
> *There are many more important jobs than hers.*
> B *It* replaces a noun.
> *'What's her job like?' 'It's quite interesting.'*
> C *It* is also used as an 'empty' subject to talk about time, weather and distance:
> *It's nine o'clock.   It's warm today.*
> *It's 24 kilometres to LA.*

3 Complete the sentences with *it* or *there* and the correct form of *be*.

> **Money-saving tips**
> (1) ___ lots of easy ways to save money. Here are just a few.
> • When you go food shopping, (2) ___ important to write a list and only buy what you need.
> • When choosing a restaurant, see if (3) ___ a 'set meal'. (4) ___ usually a lot cheaper.
> • These days (5) ___ many phone companies which offer cheap calls, so (6) ___ a good idea to compare different companies.

4 Answer the questions with *it* or *there*.
1 What's the date today?
2 How far is it from your house to where you work or study?
3 What shopping tips can you think of for your town?
There's a great market ...

Use of English 2 (Paper 1 Part 3)

Lead-in   **1**   Discuss the questions.
1 What features and facilities do you appreciate most in a shop?
2 What things frustrate you when shopping?

Word formation   **2**   Do the task. Use the Help notes for support with certain items.

➤ EXPERT STRATEGIES pages 175–176

For questions 1–8, read the text below. Use the word given in capitals at the end of some of the lines to form a word that fits in the gap in the same line. There is an example at the beginning (0).

Keeping customers happy

The **(0)** *decision* of many stores to cut costs by reducing the number of employees has	DECIDE
not been a success. Many stores now realise that if their staff suffer from **(1)** _____ ,	EXHAUST
they are far more likely to become **(2)** _____ with their customers, which is not a	PATIENCE
good idea in terms of sales figures.	
The U.S. department store Nordstrom knows that customers find poor **(3)** _____	SERVE
annoying. The company believes that the **(4)** _____ of its staff contributes in a big way	FRIEND
to customer **(5)** _____ and a desire to return to shop there. Therefore, it goes to a great	SATISFY
deal of trouble to **(6)** _____ a positive shopping experience for its customers.	SURE
For example, one of Nordstrom's customers was about to take a **(7)** _____ recently	FLY
and left her ticket on the counter by mistake when she was paying. When she saw	
what had happened, the assistant took a taxi to the airport and delivered the ticket	
(8) _____ to the surprised customer!	PERSON

➤ **HELP**

2 Do you need a prefix, a suffix or both?
4 Be careful with your spelling!

Discussion   **3**   Do you think service in stores is getting better or worse these days?

Word formation   **4**   Do the task. Use the Help notes for support with certain items.

➤ EXPERT STRATEGIES pages 175–176

For questions 1–8, read the text below. Use the word given in capitals at the end of some of the lines to form a word that fits in the gap in the same line. There is an example at the beginning (0).

Save or spend?

According to a recent survey, the British are poor savers in **(0)** *comparison* with other	COMPARE
nations in Europe. They may start out with good **(1)** _____ but many people end up	INTEND
putting aside only 5.5 percent of their income for 'a rainy day'. It is believed that only	
13 percent of people currently in **(2)** _____ in the UK are saving towards their	EMPLOY
(3) _____ .	RETIRE
One of the reasons for this is that the British spend around 16 percent of everything	
they earn on luxuries such as holidays and other forms of **(4)** _____ . As a result,	ENTERTAIN
(5) _____ problems and personal debt have increased sharply.	FINANCE
Owning a home is seen as a good **(6)** _____ by many British people. However, house	INVEST
prices are now so high that they are simply **(7)** _____ for many young people starting	AFFORD
out unless they receive some kind of **(8)** _____ from their parents. At the other end of	ASSIST
the scale, over 800,000 households now own a second home abroad.	

➤ **HELP**

6 Do you need a prefix, a suffix or both?
7 Is this an adjective or an adverb?

Discussion   **5**   Discuss the questions.
1 Are you a saver or a spender?
2 Do you think people should save more?
3 What are the consequences of living on credit?

Language development 3

Money and banks

1 Work in pairs and complete the quiz. You can use a dictionary to help you.

Money vocabulary quiz

1 Put a ✓ (= have money) or a ✗ (= not have money) next to the expressions in *italics*.
   a I'm a bit *short of cash* today.
   b The Jacksons *live from hand to mouth*. They simply *can't make ends meet*.
   c Lucinda's very *well-off*.
   d Peter *can't afford* to pay the rent this month. He's very *hard up*.
   e We're quite *comfortable*.
   f Are you *in debt*?
   g Mr and Mrs Johnson are very *wealthy*.

2 Choose the correct answers.
   a Asha borrowed a camera *to / from* Alex.
   b Will you lend the car *to / from* us for the weekend?
   c The company owes its success *to / from* its excellent training programme.
   d You're spending too much money *to / on* food.
   e Mike's wasting most of his money *on / into* clothes.
   f Ella paid some money *on / into* her bank account.
   g Carl changed his money *in / into* euros.
   h We've made a lot of money *from / by* computer games.
   i I've got no money *by / on* me.
   j When Sue died, she left her money *at / to* her brother.

3 Three of the nouns/noun phrases in each group cannot be used with the verb in bold. Cross them out.
   a **pay:** by cheque   the tickets   a deposit   you back   in cash   by credit card   a fine   a big profit   a bill   a discount
   b **earn:** a fortune   a living   a refund   your keep   a receipt   a good salary   interest   a loan

4 Replace the incorrect word in *italics* with a word or phrase from Question 3.
   a You get a huge *account* if you book in advance, so you'll save a lot of money.
   b Investors made a big *salary* of ten percent when their shares went up in value.
   c Don't worry! You'll get a full *withdrawal* if you cancel the holiday.
   d I see from my bank statement that rates of *investment* are very low at the moment.
   e We've just had a huge electricity *receipt*; I don't know how we're going to pay it.
   f Tara may earn a good *profit* every month but she's always in the red.
   g Mike got a £150 *cost* when the police caught him speeding.
   h How soon do you have to pay back that *lend* that you got from the bank?

2 How do you record topic vocabulary? For example, you could record money expressions in your vocabulary notebook under different 'money' headings, such as:

Banks   Shopping   Money problems

3 Discuss whether these statements are true for you.
   1 I like shopping for bargains.
   2 I think credit cards are dangerous.
   3 I'm happy to lend people money.
   4 I believe in living – and spending – for today.
   5 I think online banking is convenient but not secure.

Forming verbs

No change	
clean (adj)	clean (v)
record (n)	record (v)
Internal change	
hot (adj)	heat (v)
Prefix	
large (adj)	enlarge (v)
Suffix	
modern (adj)	modernise (v)

4a Read the information above about ways of forming verbs. Then look at the words in the box and decide what changes you need to make in order to form verbs. Write the verbs in the correct place in the table.

blood (n)   calm (adj)   choice (n)   critic (n)
danger (n)   dry (adj)   fat (adj)   import (n)   length (n)
name (n)   strength (n)   wide (adj)

b Match the definitions (1–4) with verbs from the table.
   1 talk about someone's faults
   2 bring goods into a country
   3 make someone unsafe
   4 decide on something

c Which of the verbs in the table would you use to talk about:
   1 making a road bigger?
   2 renovating an old house?
   3 making a class quieter?
   4 making a bridge stronger?

10A
> **Reading and Use of English:** Multiple choice (Part 5)
> **Language development:** The passive
> **Writing:** Semi-formal email (Part 2)

10B
> **Speaking:** Vocabulary: Transport; Long turn (Part 2)
> **Listening:** Multiple matching (Part 3)
> **Language development:** Hypothetical situations; *it's time, I'd rather, as if, as though*; Verb + preposition collocations; Verbs with similar meanings
> **Reading and Use of English:** Key word transformations (Part 4); Open cloze (Part 2)

Lead-in   **1**   **Discuss the questions.**

1 How far do you have to travel to your place of work/study or to take part in leisure activities? What method of transport do you use to get there?

2 How often do you travel abroad? How do you travel?

3 Read the quote by the contemporary travel writer Paul Theroux. How far do you agree or disagree?

> *'Travel is only glamorous in retrospect.'* (Paul Theroux)

133

Reading (Paper 1 Part 5)

Before you read

1 Read the title and introduction to the article. Do you think the writer's experiences of the USA will be good or bad?

Skimming

2 Read the article quickly and look at the map. Which places does the writer go to?

Multiple choice

➤ EXPERT STRATEGIES pages 175–176

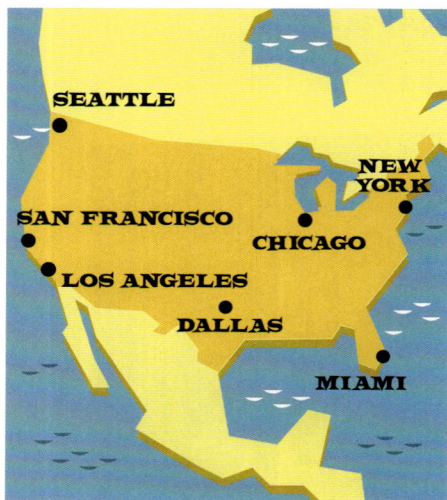

You are going to read an article in which a British journalist writes about his experiences in the USA. For questions 1–6, choose the answer (A, B, C or D) which you think fits best according to the text.

1 What was the writer's main impression when he first arrived in New York as a teenager?
   A a sensation of loneliness
   B the intense activity all around
   C how beautiful the weather was
   D that he would be very happy there

2 What does the writer remember about his early visits to the USA?
   A He found New York frightening.
   B It didn't live up to his expectations.
   C He didn't get to know the country very well.
   D He regrets wasting so much time in the cities.

3 The writer found Miami
   A unique.
   B elegant.
   C depressing.
   D disappointing.

4 What does the writer say about his first trip to LA?
   A He disliked its artificiality.
   B He ended up finding work there.
   C He felt as if he had been there before.
   D He didn't have a positive experience.

5 What does the writer mean by the expression *pushed the boat out* in line 22?
   A took strong action
   B left him to find his own way around
   C made a lot of progress
   D spent a lot of money

6 *This* in line 28 refers to
   A insulting Americans.
   B not having a passport.
   C travelling in the USA.
   D the population of the USA.

Vocabulary: Adjectives and nouns

4 Match the adjectives (1–5) with the nouns they are used with in the article (a–e).

1	sweet	a	smiles
2	sharp	b	neon lights
3	tasteless	c	tooth
4	clear	d	sky
5	broad	e	suits

Home   Previous   Next   Search

WELCOME TO THE USA

British television comedian and writer Dom Joly explains why he's happiest in the USA.

It was the summer of 1987 and I'd taken a train from Toronto to New York. I'd just left school and this was my first big solo adventure. I was almost dizzy with excitement as the train slowly pulled into Grand Central station, very early on a clear-skied New York morning. I can still remember hesitantly pulling my little black suitcase through the breathtaking central hall of the station; it was like stepping onto the set of a thousand familiar movies. There was something unique about the place – an energy that you could almost touch. All around me, New Yorkers rushed from destination to destination as though their lives depended on it. I remember feeling out of place, as if I wasn't really there, that I was floating high above the city.

I drifted out of the station into the metropolis that is New York. It was a world of huge shadows – the sun blanked out by the sheer enormousness of the Manhattan skyline. I rode the Staten Island ferry boat, conquered the Empire State building, roller-skated in Central Park. It was like meeting one of your childhood heroes and finding out that not only did they not disappoint but they were far, far cooler than you'd ever dared hoped. From that moment on, I've been obsessed but to begin with I, like most visitors, only really flirted with the USA – just visiting the cosmopolitan cities around her edges.

I first went to Miami by chance. I had to film there and I wasn't really looking forward to it. To me, Florida was all about tasteless neon lights and hideous theme parks. In a way, I was right. That's part of its appeal. This is, after all, the only city in the world where a yellow Ferrari makes sense. The gorgeous combination of fabulous climate, art-deco architecture and Cuban–Hispanic influence instantly made it one of my favourite cities in the world. Nothing quite beats sitting on the terrace of the Tides hotel, watching the beautiful people glide by. One breakfast, I was joined by the rapper Ja Rule and his pet lion: only in Miami, only in the USA.

People warned me about Los Angeles. 'Nobody walks anywhere, it's not a real city, it's all so fake.' Once again, they were right. It is those things, and you need to embrace them wholeheartedly to enjoy the place. My first time in LA, I was there for meetings with a film company and they really pushed the boat out. A stretch limousine whisked me in air-conditioned splendour to a famous hotel where Johnny Depp was having a drink in the garden. It really was a fairytale. Hollywood, Beverly Hills, Malibu – such familiar places to me through a thousand and one films and TV shows. Every sharp-suited executive at every meeting promised me the earth was mine. It was a merry-go-round of broad smiles and green lights. Of course, nothing came of any of this but I was living the cliché – the American dream. *line 22*

One of the most common insults thrown at Americans of late is that they are insular, disconnected from the world, with apparently only 20 percent of the population in possession of a passport. To us this seems unthinkable. When you travel in the States, it all makes sense. There's not that European need to travel 'abroad' when it'll take you a lifetime to discover your own country. To me, the USA is like a candy store and I'm the sweet-toothed kid waiting at the door, eager to sample new treats. I want to go to Hawaii and learn to surf, go to Texas and become a cowboy and then there's … . I've been there more times than to any other country and I've only scratched the surface. Every time I look out of a window, outside is the USA. *line 28*

Discussion   **5** Discuss the questions.

1 Which of the places in the article would you most and least like to go to?
2 Which country in the world have you most loved visiting?
3 If you could visit anywhere in the world, where would you go?

135

Language development 1

The passive

1a What type of holiday accommodation do you prefer (e.g. a hotel, a self-catering apartment or a campsite)? Why?

b Read the text and answer the questions.

1 What are the advantages of these self-catering apartments?
2 What possible disadvantages are there?

> These high-quality self-catering apartments are grouped around a central garden. They were built in the traditional Ottoman style by a team of highly skilled workers and have been designed to stay cool in summer. The rooms have all been decorated to a very high standard. A buffet breakfast is served around the pool for a small charge and a patio barbecue area is now being constructed. This will soon be completed and available for use by guests. Shops can be found within ten minutes' walk. We are sure you will have a wonderful holiday.

➤ EXPERT GRAMMAR, pages 195–196

c Find examples of the passive in the text in Exercise 1b. Why is the passive used here?

d Complete the table with examples from the text in Exercise 1b.

Passive form	Examples
Present simple	(1) _____
	(2) _____
Present continuous	(3) _____
Present perfect	(4) _____
	(5) _____
Past simple	(6) _____
will	(7) _____
Modal	(8) _____

2a Correct the mistakes in the text.

> Our apartments **(1)** *be situated* on the Bosphorus and have excellent views. Last winter they **(2)** *was redecorated*. Wifi facilities **(3)** *can been accessed* in all rooms and fire safety equipment **(4)** *have be installed* by the time you arrive.
>
> Smaller apartments **(5)** *are been built* at the moment and will be available next year. Also, permission **(6)** *has be given* to build two all-weather tennis courts.
>
> Availability **(7)** *must checked* with our booking service before making a reservation and guests **(8)** *will asked* to pay a deposit.

b Rewrite the sentences to make them more formal. Begin with the words in *italics*.

1 We are always improving *our facilities*.
2 We have modernised *all our flats* in the last two years.
3 We have equipped *our kitchens* to the highest standards.
4 Maids will make *the beds* daily.
5 You can find *the holiday village* two kilometres outside the town.
6 The village offers *a full programme of sports activities*.
7 We received *very few complaints* last year.
8 Guests may accommodate *extra people* on the sofa beds.
9 Our brochure indicates *the maximum number of people allowed in each caravan*.
10 You must return *keys* to reception on departure.

3 Read the information and answer the questions.

> A We sometimes use **the passive** when we want to continue the same theme. The new information is put at the end, for emphasis. Choose the correct answer in the example:
> *The telescope is very useful. It was invented* **by** / **from** *Galileo.*
>
> B **Some verbs** (e.g. *give, lend, send, show, promise*) **can have two objects** – a person and a thing. Which passive structure in the examples below do you think is more common, 1 or 2?
> **Active:** *The rest of the class* **gave Tania a present**.
> **Passive:** 1 *Tania was given a present* by the rest of the class.
> 2 *A present was given to Tania* by the rest of the class.
>
> C In news reports, **passive structures** are often used with *say, believe, consider, think*, etc. Complete the examples.
> 1 *We think Filton is planning ten new hotels.* (active)
> *Filton* **is** _____ **to be planning** *ten new hotels.* (passive + infinitive)
> 2 *Analysts say that SkyFly's profits are up.* (active)
> *It* **is** _____ **that** *SkyFly's profits are up.* (passive + *that* clause)
>
> D **Some verbs are followed by an infinitive without** *to* **in the active, but an infinitive with** *to* **in the passive.** Choose the correct answers in the examples.
> **Active:** *They heard the crowd cheer a long way away.*
> **Passive:** *The crowd was heard* **cheer** / **to cheer** *a long way away.*
> **Active:** *They made me empty all my bags at customs.*
> **Passive:** *I was made* **empty** / **to empty** *all my bags at customs.*

4 Complete the conversations with the correct passive form of the verbs in brackets.

1 A: Did Mozart compose the *Unfinished Symphony*?
B: No, I think _____ (compose/Schubert).

2 A: Why was there so much confusion?
B: Some people _____ (give) two tickets by mistake.

3 A: Why has that man been arrested?
B: I think he _____ (see) stealing some things.

4 A: When's the next election?
B: It _____ (believe) the prime minister will call one soon.

5 A: What's Megan doing next year?
B: She _____ (promise) a place at university.

6 A: Didn't Marie Curie discover penicillin?
B: No, I'm pretty sure _____ (discover/Fleming).

7 A: Do the police know how the burglar got in?
B: Yes, he _____ (think/hide) in the museum during the day.

8 A: What a lovely antique shop. Oh no! I've broken a vase!
B: Oh dear, I think you _____ (make/pay) for that!

5a Rewrite the text to make it more formal. Use the passive where appropriate.

> The town has changed a lot in the last 30 years. They have pulled down all the old factories and replaced them with hi-tech science parks. Many of the residents feel it's unfortunate that they have also demolished one of the older schools, as they will have to send their children by bus to the next town. Some people say that they will build a brand new school in the town in the next few years when the government provides extra funding. The newer residents in particular will appreciate that.

b What changes have happened in your town? What changes are planned for the future?

Golders Green, London, 2007

Golders Green, London, 1929

Writing (Paper 2 Part 2: Semi-formal email)

Lead-in

1 Discuss the questions.

1 In what situations might you write a letter/email:
   a to make a complaint?
   b to apologise?
2 Which of the situations would be:
   a very formal?
   b semi-formal?
   c informal?

Understand the task

2a Read the task. What will be the purpose of your reply? How formal will it be? Why?

b Underline the points in the question that you must answer.

You recently helped organise a college ski trip and you have received this email from a parent of one of the students who went.

> I understand you were one of the organisers of our son's ski trip. I have to say my husband and I were extremely dissatisfied with the arrangements. My son has informed us that the ski slopes were poor, the lessons were fewer than promised and the accommodation was inadequate.
>
> Can you please give us a satisfactory explanation?
>
> Yours sincerely,
>
> Nora White

*Write your **email** in **140–190** words in an appropriate style.*

Plan your email

3a Think of some possible explanations for the problems (e.g. why was the accommodation inadequate?). Then brainstorm some ideas under these headings for your email.

	Ski slopes	Lessons	Accommodation
Explanation:	_____	_____	_____
	_____	_____	_____

b Choose points from your notes in Exercise 3a and add them in paragraphs 2–4 in the paragraph plan.
Paragraph 1: Apology
Paragraph 2: Explanation 1: _____
Paragraph 3: Explanation 2: _____
Paragraph 4: Explanation 3: _____
Paragraph 5: Final comments (e.g. promise/offer, reassure, express hope): _____

c What might you say in paragraph 5? Make notes in the paragraph plan in Exercise 3b.

Language and content

4a Replace the phrases in *italics* in the sentences to make them less formal. Use the phrases in the box and make any other changes necessary.

---

a pity   couldn't get   get in touch   if we put you out in any way
not good enough   point out   told beforehand   unhappy about
weren't enough

---

1 There *were insufficient* intermediate slopes.
2 The accommodation was *unsatisfactory* – the rooms were too small.
3 We were *informed in advance* that there would be individual tuition.
4 They were *dissatisfied with* the standard of tuition.
5 I would like to *draw your attention to* what was said in your letter.
6 I tried to *make contact* with the group leader.
7 We *were unable to obtain* a satisfactory answer from the company.
8 I'd like to apologise *for any inconvenience caused*.
9 It was *unfortunate* that the instructors spoke poor English.

b How could you make these sentence openings less formal?
1 We were extremely concerned to hear that …
2 Having made enquiries to the company, …
3 To my astonishment, this proved not to be the case and …
4 I regret that single rooms were not included in the price …
5 I trust your son will continue to …

c Now rewrite these sentences to make them more formal using words and phrases from Exercises 4a and 4b.
1 Thanks for getting in touch.
2 It's a shame the beginners' slopes weren't very good.
3 If he'd wanted more lessons, he would have had to pay over and above.
4 Sorry about that but why didn't he tell us about it before we left?
5 There wasn't enough snow and that worried us a lot.

d Which of these are not normally used in more formal letters/emails?
1 *Dear …,*
2 contractions (*I'm, don't,* etc.)
3 question tags
4 *Yours sincerely,*
5 colloquial expressions

e Use the phrases in the table to write complete sentences for your email.

Agreeing	It is true that …
	It appears that what you say is correct and …
Apologising	I would like to express my regret that …
	I hope you will accept my apologies and …
Referring to a point	As for the question of …
	Regarding/Concerning (the point about) …
Concluding	We would like to assure you that …
	If you (should) need any …

Write your email

➤ EXPERT STRATEGIES pages 177–178

Check your email

➤ EXPERT WRITING page 203

5 Now write your email, using the ideas and some of the language above.

6 Edit your work using the checklist on page 198.

Speaking (Paper 4 Part 2)

Vocabulary: Transport

1a Which of the forms of transport in the photos have you used?

b Decide which word in each group is the odd one out and why.
  1 canoe, yacht, the tube, rowing boat
  2 moped, scooter, motorbike, delivery van
  3 tram, helicopter, glider, spaceship
  4 clutch, handlebars, accelerator, steering wheel
  5 deck, oars, carriage, mast
  6 hatchback, saloon, sidecar, estate

c Mark the stress on the words and phrases with more than one syllable in Exercise 1b.

2a Match the expressions in the box with different forms of transport. More than one answer may be possible.

> be forced to land   confirm your flight   disembark   fasten your seatbelt
> get clamped   get low on petrol   get points on your licence
> go on a cruise   it's two stops on the Northern Line   stop in a lay-by
> take a driving test   take on as hand luggage

b Correct the mistakes in the sentences.
  1 I'm tired. Let's get onto a taxi.
  2 I think we get out of the bus at the next stop.
  3 Oh, no! We've lost the last train! How are we going to get home?
  4 'Have you ever driven a horse?' 'Yes, I did when I was young.'
  5 Our ship parks in Cairo for a day. Let's go sightseeing there.
  6 What's the fare of the ticket? I haven't got enough money.
  7 It's a long travel there and back. We can't do it in a day.
  8 Wonderful! The train's exactly in time!

3 What are the best/worst things about modern transport?

Long turn

> EXPERT STRATEGIES pages 179–180

4a Look at the statements about Part 2 and decide if they are *True* (T) or *False* (F).
  1 You each have a minute to talk about the photos.
  2 You should describe each photo separately.
  3 You shouldn't include personal anecdotes.
  4 You can interrupt while the other candidate is speaking.
  5 There is only one part to the task.
  6 You each answer a personal question after the other candidate's turn.

b Look at the list of things (1–7) you might have to do in the exam. Match them with the phrases (a–g).
  1 talk about similarities
  2 talk about differences
  3 speculate about a picture
  4 give opinions on something
  5 ask for clarification/check information
  6 paraphrase
  7 correct what you say

  a I get the impression that …
  b So, do you want me to … ?
  c The obvious difference is that …
  d It's a kind of …
  e What I meant was …
  f As far as I'm concerned, …
  g In both of these situations …

c Add any other expressions you can think of.

How might the people be feeling in these situations?

➤ EXPERT SPEAKING page 211

5a **Work in groups of three. Follow the instructions below.**

Task 1

Student 1:   You are the interlocutor. Turn to page 211 and follow the instructions for Task 1.

Students 2 and 3:   You are Candidates A and B. Look at the photos above and follow the interlocutor's instructions.

➤ EXPERT SPEAKING pages 211–212

b **Work in the same groups. Follow the instructions below.**

Task 2

Student 2:   You are the interlocutor. Turn to page 211 and follow the instructions for Task 2.

Students 1 and 3:   You are Candidates A and B. Look at the photos on page 212 and follow the interlocutor's instructions.

Task analysis

6 **Compare and discuss your answers. Did you:**
1 follow the instructions?
2 speak clearly and accurately?
3 use appropriate vocabulary?
4 communicate what you wanted to say?
5 use the full minute?
6 give your personal view?

Listening (Paper 3 Part 3)

Before you listen **1** How do you prefer to get from place to place? Which of these factors are the most and least important for you?
• expense   • reliability   • convenience   • comfort
• environmental issues   • fun   • style

Multiple matching **2** 🎧 33 Do the task.

> **EXPERT STRATEGIES** pages 178–179

You will hear five short extracts in which people are giving reasons why they use bikes to get to work. For questions 1–5 choose from the list (A–H) the reason each speaker gives. Use the letters only once. There are three extra letters which you do not need to use.

A It's a safe way to travel.	Speaker 1 ☐ 1
B I found driving my car too stressful.	Speaker 2 ☐ 2
C I wanted to avoid being in large crowds.	Speaker 3 ☐ 3
D It's a reliable form of transport.	Speaker 4 ☐ 4
E I like surprising the people I work with.	Speaker 5 ☐ 5
F It helps me to get more work done.	
G I'm helping to keep the environment clean.	
H I bought it to save money.	

Task analysis **3** Compare and give reasons for your answers.

Discussion **4** Discuss the questions.
1 Do you agree that some people 'look down on' certain forms of transport?
2 How important are cars in your country as a status symbol? Which are the most prestigious cars to own?
3 Do you think it is the responsibility of the government to make public transport so cheap that it will persuade people to stop using their cars in urban areas?

Vocabulary: Transport **5** Answer the questions about yourself or your country. They include expressions from the recording.
1 Do any forms of transport regularly go on strike?
2 When is rush hour?
3 Do you prefer to drive second-hand or 'flash' cars?
4 Which public transport system is the most reliable?
5 Are motorists generally considerate to cyclists?
6 Which form of transport do you think is the most convenient?

Language development 2

Hypothetical situations

➤ **EXPERT GRAMMAR** page 196

1 Read the comments and answer the questions.
1 Which comments refer to a situation in:
   a the present?
   b the past?
   c the future?
2 What verb form is used in each case?
3 What's the difference between *wish* and *if only*?

> I wish public transport was better in this town.

> I wish I hadn't sold my motorbike. If only I'd kept it.

> If only I could afford a car.

> John is always complaining. I wish he would stop being so negative.

> If only the town council would set up a park-and-ride scheme.

wish, if only

A We often use *wish/if only* + **past simple** when we want our own situation to be different.
If only I **had** *a fast car.* (~~If only I would have a fast car.~~)

B We use *wish/if only* + **would** when we want another person or thing to be different.
I wish you would **change** *your mind about moving.* (~~I wish you changed your mind about moving.~~)

C We use *wish/if only* + **past perfect** to express regret for the past. *I wish I'd gone to the party last night.* (~~I wish I went to the party last night.~~)

2 What would you say in these situations? Use *wish* or *if only*.
1 Your friend has invited you to go out tonight but you have too much work to do.
   I wish I could go out tonight. If only I didn't have so much work to do.
2 You regret dyeing your hair bright red. Blonde suits you better.
3 Your brother is always borrowing your car without asking. You want him to stop.
4 It's late but you can't afford to get a taxi home, so you'll have to take the bus.
5 You're watching a film at the cinema but you don't like it at all.
6 Your flatmate has been in the bathroom for a long time and you want to use it yourself.

3 Complete the sentences so they are true for you.
1 I wish *I were taller* but I'm not.
2 I wish _____ but I'm not.
3 I wish _____ but I haven't.
4 If only _____ but I can't.
5 I wish _____ but I didn't.
6 If only _____ but he/she won't.
7 I wish I could _____ but I can't.

it's time, I'd rather, as if, as though

Here are some other phrases we often use to talk about hypothetical situations:

A *it's (about/high) time* + subject + **past simple**
It's (about) time we **went** *home.* (we should go now)
Don't you think it's time you **got** *a job?* (implies criticism)

B *would rather* + subject + **past simple/past perfect**
I'd rather you **didn't smoke** *in the house.* (I don't want you to)
I'd rather you **hadn't gone out** *last night.* (but you did – implies criticism)

C *as if/as though* + **past simple/present perfect/ past perfect**
You're looking at me as if/as though I **was/were** *crazy.* (but I'm not)
You look as if you've **seen** *a ghost!* (but you haven't)

4 Choose the option (A or B) that best describes the meaning of the sentence.
1 It's time you learnt how to drive.
   A You haven't learnt yet.
   B You don't have time to learn.
2 I'd rather you hadn't invited him to the party.
   A You didn't invite him.
   B You invited him and I'm annoyed.
3 You talk as if you had done all the work yourself.
   A You did all the work.
   B You didn't do all the work.

5 Complete the sentences with an appropriate verb in the correct form.
1 It's about time you _____ how to use that computer properly. You've had it long enough!
2 My brother treats me as if I _____ a child even though I'm only two years younger than him!
3 No, I don't want to phone her. I'd rather you _____ her.
4 He talks as though he _____ her but he hasn't. He's only seen her on TV.
5 Why did you buy me such an expensive gift? I'd rather you _____ something cheaper.

6 Complete the sentences using your own ideas.
1 The film was awful, wasn't it? I wish …
2 My room's in a complete mess. It's about time …
3 My best friend sometimes acts as if …
4 I don't have any money left! If only …
5 My brother has gone to work abroad. I'd rather …

Use of English 1 (Paper 1 Part 4)

Lead-in

1 What advice would you give to these two candidates?

> 1 I can't answer this question straightaway.

> 2 It's nearly time to stop and I haven't answered all these questions.

Key word transformations

> EXPERT STRATEGIES pages 175–176

2 Do the task. Remember that you usually have to make more than one change to the original sentence.

*For questions 1–6, complete the second sentence so that it has a similar meaning to the first sentence, using the word given. **Do not change the word given.** You must use between **two** and **five** words, including the word given.*

1 I'm sorry I didn't go to the party last night.
WISH
I _____ to the party last night.

2 I would prefer you to phone Jane.
RATHER
I _____ Jane.

3 The theatre was practically empty.
HARDLY
There was _____ the theatre.

4 People say that dancing is good for your health.
SUPPOSED
Dancing _____ good for your health.

5 You should stop going to late-night concerts.
TIME
It's _____ to late-night concerts.

6 I'd rather you didn't use my car.
MIND
Would _____ my car?

Task analysis

3 Discuss the questions about the task.
1 Which questions test language from page 143?
2 How does Question 6 require you to make more than one change?

Use of English 2 (Paper 1 Part 2)

Lead-in 1 Discuss the questions.
1 What is your most memorable car journey?
2 Was it a happy experience or a frightening one?

Open cloze 2a Choose the correct answers to complete the advice.
> EXPERT STRATEGIES page 175
1 Fill in the spaces *before / after* you have read the whole text.
2 Spend a *short / long* time on each gap.
3 Put a *word / short phrase* in each space.

b Read the title and text and answer the questions.
1 What seems to have happened to the man?
2 Why was he arrested?

c Do the task.

*For questions **1–8**, read the text below and think of the word which best fits each gap. Use only **one** word in each gap. There is an example at the beginning (0).*

The runaway car

In what seemed like a freak accident, John Adams, 27, a taxi driver, was trapped in his car, driving (0) _at_ 210 kph for 100 kilometres in rush-hour traffic.

'I took my foot (1) ___ the accelerator but it had jammed, so the car didn't slow (2) ___ . At first, with my foot on the brake, I was doing a steady 110 kpm. I managed to get (3) ___ to the police on my phone to ask for help but then I (4) ___ see smoke coming from the brakes. At that point, my speed went right up again and I had to concentrate (5) ___ trying not to crash. I remember thinking I was going to die.'

Adams was followed (6) ___ several police cars and a helicopter as he tried to avoid other traffic. His journey only ended when he crashed into a barrier. Amazingly, he managed to escape unhurt. However, after extensive tests on the car, (7) ___ mechanical defects were found and Adams was arrested on suspicion (8) ___ dangerous driving.

Task analysis 3 Which questions test:
1 verb + preposition collocations?
2 phrasal verbs?

Discussion 4 Discuss the questions.
1 Do you think Adams was telling the truth?
2 What would you do if the accelerator on a car you were driving got jammed?

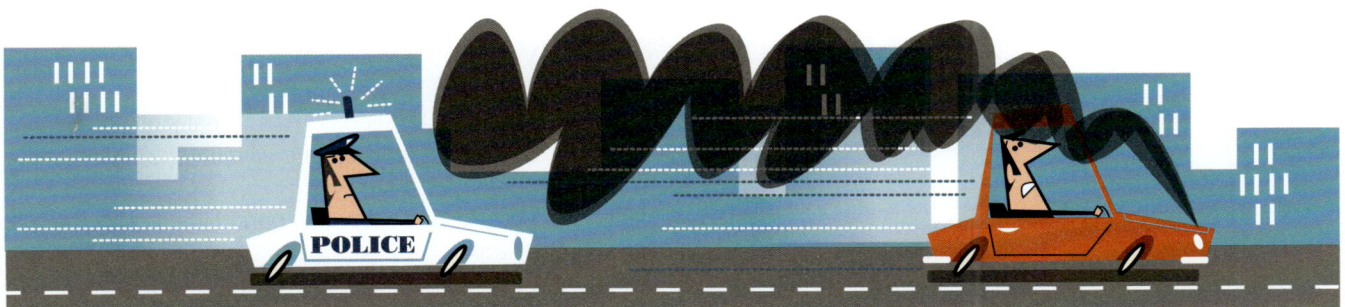

Language development 3

Verb + preposition collocations

1a Look at the examples from the text on page 145 and underline the verb + preposition collocations.

> *Adams was trapped in his car, driving at 210 kph.*
> *I had to concentrate on trying not to crash.*
> *Adams was followed by several police cars.*

b Choose the correct answers. Use a dictionary if necessary.

> Have you heard **(1)** *for / about / at* our Neighbourhood Watch scheme? It aims to prevent local people **(2)** *from / at / to* becoming victims of crime. It's no good simply complaining to the police **(3)** *of / by / about* the criminals who damage our cars in the street or who steal things that don't belong **(4)** *at / to / on* them.
> They can't cope **(5)** *by / at / with* the problem on their own. Since we set up the scheme, people have reported suspicious behaviour to the police and we have succeeded **(6)** *on / for / in* making our area a much safer place to live.

2 Choose the correct preposition for each gap and complete the sentences.

1 *for / on*
We had to wait half an hour ___ a table but it was nice to eat out and be waited ___ .
2 *about / of*
We're thinking seriously ___ starting a band. I suppose we'll have to think ___ a name for it!
3 *from / to*
The manager seems resigned ___ the fact that the leisure centre is losing money; I expect he'll resign ___ the job quite soon.
4 *as / for*
He's always been known ___ a singer more than an actor. He's best known ___ his love songs.
5 *of / from*
I turned down Andy's invitation to the cinema last week because I hadn't heard ___ the film. I haven't heard ___ him since then.
6 *for / to*
It was a great party but I'll have to apologise ___ the neighbours ___ making so much noise.

3 Complete the text with prepositions.

SPACE TOURISM: DREAM OR REALITY?

When I want a change **(1)** ___ my usual routine, instead of dreaming **(2)** ___ a perfect cruise on the open seas, I sometimes wonder **(3)** ___ putting my name down for a trip aboard a spacecraft. Of course, for the next few years recruitment for the very few places available is only aimed **(4)** ___ the mega-rich, since you have to pay huge sums **(5)** ___ the privilege – from $20 million to $100 million, depending **(6)** ___ how long you go for. However, compared **(7)** ___ a few years ago, when space tourism was just a fantasy, a number of companies are now seriously considering building hotels located **(8)** ___ space and before long, space travel will be something we can all look forward **(9)** ___ . They believe that low-cost options taking us 100–160 km into the earth's atmosphere will be available, maybe for as little as $20,000 a trip. Not surprisingly, though, some scientists object **(10)** ___ the idea that space will become crowded **(11)** ___ tourists. Nevertheless, when you're stuck in a traffic jam staring **(12)** ___ the stationary cars in front of you, it's not hard to see the attractions of travelling weightlessly through space at over 25,000 km an hour!

Verbs with similar meanings

> Some verbs of perception have similar meanings but are easily confused.
> *It is not just about **listening to** music.*
> *She **heard** a noise outside.*

4 Read the information above. Then choose the correct verb for each gap and complete the sentences. Put the verbs in the correct form.

1 *look / see / watch*
a I've ___ everywhere for my sunglasses. Have you ___ them?
b Do you want to dance? No, I'd rather just sit and ___ .
2 *gaze / peer / stare*
a You shouldn't ___ at people. It's rude.
b I ___ at the stage but I was too far away to see much.
c We stood and ___ at the wonderful view.
3 *hear / listen*
a I ___ hard but I couldn't ___ what she was saying.
b I could ___ to his songs all day – he's got a beautiful voice.
c Have you ___ that new band I was telling you about?
4 *feel / touch*
a I could ___ something ___ my shoulder.
b ___ how soft the material is.
c My brother doesn't let anyone ___ his CDs.

11 Well-being

Lead-in

1 Discuss the questions.
   1 How do you think the photos illustrate the theme of well-being?
   2 What is most important to *your* well-being?

Reading (Paper 1 Part 6)

Before you read

1a Look at the photo. Would you say this glass is half empty or half full? Do you think your answer reflects your character? How?

b Look at the title of the article and discuss the questions.

1 What do you think are 'the secrets of true happiness'?
2 Is it possible to learn how to be happy?

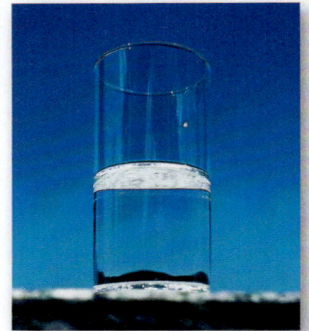

Gapped text

> EXPERT STRATEGIES pages 175–177

2 Do the task.

*You are going to read an article about the secrets of true happiness. Six sentences have been removed from the article. Choose from the sentences **A–G** the one which fits each gap (1–6). There is one extra sentence which you do not need to use.*

A That's why being part of a social group, such as a family, a community or a club adds to their overall sense of well-being.

B Other scientists, however, maintain that happiness is not so difficult to achieve.

C Such people, for example, seem to find satisfaction in activities which are meaningful and give a feeling of personal achievement.

D The latter develops in response to the experiences a person has during his or her life.

E There will always be someone else with more than you, so trying to compete can often lead to frustration and anxiety.

F To avoid this, it is important to pick a sport or activity you enjoy and which you do when you want to, rather than when you think you should.

G In other words, no matter how happy or unhappy an individual event may make us, this is just a temporary state.

Vocabulary: Word formation

3a Change the nouns into adjectives using the suffixes in the box. Check the spelling in a dictionary if necessary.

-able   -(i)ed   -(i)ous

1 contentment
2 satisfaction
3 frustration
4 anxiety

5 depression
6 stress
7 misery

b Have you experienced any of the feelings in Exercise 3a? When?

Discussion

4 Discuss the questions.

1 What did you find most interesting about the article? From your own experience, is there anything you strongly agree or disagree with?
2 What advice in the article do you think you would like to try?

Home | Previous | Next | Search

The secrets of true happiness

Lollie Barr reviews some recent research.

Everybody knows someone with a happy nature: the cheerful type of person with a positive attitude, who will always say a glass is half full rather than half empty. It's the person who is not easily put off when things go wrong and who appears to lead a happier life as a result. Such people may be healthier too, since there seems to be a link between happiness and good health. But what is the secret of happiness? And how can we achieve it?

Psychologists define this feeling of well-being as 'when thoughts and feelings about one's life are mainly positive'. The key seems to be contentment with what you already have, emotionally, materially and professionally. The more people try to keep up with others, for example, the more likely they are to be dissatisfied with life. **1**

David Lykken, Professor of Psychology at the University of Minnesota, is a leading specialist in happiness. As a result of studying 300 sets of twins, he now believes that happiness is more than 50 percent genetically determined. He also believes that we each have our own fixed 'happiness point', a level we always return to, whatever happens to us in life. **2**

But it is not necessarily the case that we are stuck with the level of happiness we were born with. This is because although a person's temperament is not easily changed, their character can be. The former determines what kinds of thing will make someone happy but not how much pleasure that person obtains from them. **3**

This is why Dr Isaac believes we need to study happy people and learn how to be like them. **4** They also tend to be interested in things other than themselves. This could be through their day-to-day work, for example, or by caring for others less fortunate, or by having some kind of spiritual focus to their life.

Happy individuals also tend to relate to other people and are able to give and receive affection. **5** They are, therefore, more likely to belong to things like sports teams, choirs and political parties. Researchers at Harvard University have found that people involved in such activities were happier than those who were not, and that this had nothing to do with how well-off people were financially.

Another factor in happiness appears to be physical activity. Exercise improves a person's mood and gets rid of tension. But there must be a balance between activity and rest because stress results in unhappiness. **6**

But mental activity can be just as important. Psychologists believe it's possible to train yourself to recognise happiness and, therefore, feel the benefits of it more often. The key is not taking your feelings for granted but rather learning to celebrate them and noticing times when you are happy. It is claimed that the more you recognise when there's a decision to be made about how you feel, the better you'll become at choosing happiness over misery.

Language development 1

Clauses of reason

➤ **EXPERT GRAMMAR** page 197

1 What do you do to relax?

2a Read extracts from an article about the Duchess of Cambridge and answer the questions.

   1 What can make us healthier?
   2 Why is Kate so positive?

A Some scientists claim that happy people are healthier *owing to* the influence of happy emotions on our immune system.

B Kate's positive, cheerful outlook is said to be *due to* her close family upbringing.

C *Because of* her interest in sports – tennis, netball, hockey, running, skiing, athletics – she keeps very fit.

D She is popular with the nation *as* she is attractive and charming, with a warm personality.

E *Since* she comes from Reading, she supports the city's football team.

F People are interested in the way she dresses *because* she wears clothes from high street stores as well as designer labels.

b The words and phrases in *italics* in Exercise 2a introduce an answer to the question *Why*? Which words/phrases can go in each sentence below?

   1 Mark left his job ___ it was stressful. (+ subject + verb)
   2 Mark left his job ___ the stress. (+ noun)
   3 Mark left his job ___ the fact that it was stressful. (+ *the fact that* + subject + verb)

c Complete the sentences with words and phrases from Exercise 2a.

1 Joe put on some music ___ he wanted to relax.
2 He had lost his job ___ his age.
3 The club had reduced its staff ___ the fact it was losing money.
4 But ___ he was a talented trainer, he knew he'd get another job.
5 ___ his many interests, he was never bored.
6 A lot of unhappiness is ___ boredom.

d Complete each sentence in three different ways, using the correct form of the word in brackets.

1 Dave was late for the meeting ... (snow)
  a because it _____ .
  b because of _____ .
  c due to _____ .
2 Marta decided to drive to work ... (rain)
  a as it _____ .
  b because of _____ .
  c since _____ .

Clauses of purpose

The expressions in **bold** express purpose. They introduce an answer to the question *what for*?

The office closes early	in order that	we can have a longer weekend.
	so that	
I like to go away	in order to	relax.
	so as to	
	to	
I take my phone	in case	anyone needs to contact me.

3a Read the information above. Then decide which words and phrases from the table can be used in each sentence.

1 I have a sauna once a week _____ relax. (+ verb)
2 The fitness centre stays open late _____ people can go after work. (+ subject + verb)
3 I usually call before I go _____ they're closed for any reason. (+ subject + verb: precaution)

b Choose the correct answers.

1 Get regular exercise *to / so that* keep yourself fit.
2 Take food and drink to work *in order that / in case* you can't stop for lunch.
3 Breathe deeply *in case / so that* your whole body relaxes.
4 Read an amusing book *in order to / in order that* reduce tension.
5 *In order to / In order that* you can see a problem clearly, change your routine.
6 Allow plenty of time for journeys, *in case / so that* there are delays.
7 Leave work on time *so as to / so that* spend time with your friends and family.
8 Only drink one cup of coffee a day *so as not to / not to* overstimulate your body.

Clauses of contrast

The expressions in **bold** connect contrasting ideas.

I ran all the way	despite	being exhausted. (+ -ing)
	in spite of	my exhaustion. (+ noun)
		the fact that I was exhausted. (+ the fact that)
	even though	it was very cold. (+ subject + verb)
	although	
	though	
Tom loves judo,	whereas	Mary prefers swimming. (+ subject + verb: contrasting but not contradicting ideas)

4 Read the information above and match the sentence halves.

1 My mother goes out to work whereas
2 He's still out of work despite
3 Jo is very active although
4 David isn't getting better even though
5 They always seem happy despite
6 He's unhappy in spite of the fact that
7 Sam gets a huge salary while
8 I'm feeling really tired in spite of

a his appetite has returned.
b he makes a lot of money.
c going for three interviews a week.
d having slept well last night.
e my father stays at home.
f his assistant hardly earns anything.
g their poverty.
h she hasn't been feeling well lately.

5 Complete the sentences using your own ideas.

1 Unfortunately, I can't join a gym even though ...
2 She couldn't sleep last night because of ...
3 I must call Mike so that ...
4 Despite ... , she was wearing a heavy coat.
5 Sheila phoned the restaurant to ...
6 He left his phone behind in spite of ...

Writing (Paper 2 Part 1: Essay)

Lead-in   **1**   Discuss the questions.

1 How can these things affect a person's happiness?
   a money   **b** other people   **c** exercise
2 Do you agree or disagree that happiness is something we are born with?

Understand the task   **2**   Read the task and decide if the statements are *True* (T) or *False* (F).

1 I am being asked to give a balanced view of both sides of an argument.
2 I am being asked for my opinion.
3 Examples are not important.
4 I should ignore all arguments except my own.
5 I must make three main points.

In your English class you have been talking about happiness. Now your English teacher has asked you to write an essay.

Write an essay using all the notes and give reasons for your point of view.

Whether you are happy or not depends on the personality you are born with. Do you agree?

Notes

Write about:

1 money

2 health

3 _____ (your own idea)

*Write your **essay** in **140–190** words in an appropriate style.*

Plan your essay   **3a**   Which of these would be good topics for Note 3?

1 caring for others	7 holidays
2 a positive attitude	8 possessions
3 keeping mentally active	9 one's job
4 family upbringing	10 religion
5 friends	11 hobbies
6 fame	12 home

b   Make a paragraph plan for an essay in which you:

1 state your opinion.
2 explain the reasons which support your opinion (or include one for contrast).
3 give your conclusion.

c Where in your essay will you indicate another point of view for balance?

d Write a topic sentence for each of the paragraphs in your plan. You can use these phrases or your own ideas.
1 It is true that …
2 Take …, for example.
3 Then consider …
4 The third thing I think is important is …
5 All of these …

e Make notes which support each topic sentence. (Note: A supporting sentence may not be necessary in a conclusion.)

Language and content

EXPERT LANGUAGE: Spelling

a Are there any words in English that you commonly misspell?
b Correct the spelling mistakes in the words.
1 imediately
2 seperate
3 unneccesary
4 truely
5 religous
6 therefor
7 niether
8 responsable
9 untill
10 definately
11 generaly
12 recieve
13 apparantly

c Correct the spelling mistakes in the sentences. The number in brackets tells you how many mistakes there are in each sentence.
1 It's extremely likley that there is a connection between health and hapiness. (2)
2 Now that you are over fourty, let me give you a peice of advise. (3)
3 For once, the goverment has definately no knowlege of what hapened. (4)
4 Unfortunatly, on that occassion the medecine had no affect whatsoever. (4)
5 The principal reason is that politcans are not sufficiently independant. (2)

Write your essay

> EXPERT STRATEGIES pages 177–178

Check your essay

> EXPERT WRITING pages 199–200

4a Write the linking words and phrases in the box in the correct place in the table.

| but | however | in addition | in fact | just as | on the other hand | similarly | whereas | yet |

Adding a point of view	Making a contrast

b Join the ideas using the linking words and phrases in Exercise 4a.
1 Money doesn't automatically make us happy. It makes some people very unhappy.
2 It is very stressful to lose money. If we are careful with it, it gives us security.
3 We should relax and laugh whenever possible. Being with friends can give pleasure. Spending time alone is important.
4 Getting too little sleep can cause unhappiness. Eating badly can affect our moods for the worse. Going for long walks can have a beneficial effect.

c Complete the sentences with a pronoun or *this, that, these*.
1 How we lead our lives – ___ is the main reason that ___ are happy or unhappy.
2 Money makes some people very unhappy because ___ always want more of ___ . I think ___ people are making a big mistake.
3 Then let's look at health. ___ is one of the major causes of unhappiness.
4 Such individuals are often interested in people other than ___ . ___ is why they tend to be happier than the rest of ___ .

d Decide which phrase is the odd one out and why. Then choose a phrase for your essay.
1 There is a common belief that …
2 According to …
3 They argue that …
4 My own opinion is that …
5 A growing number of people hold the view that …
6 However, there is also an argument that …

5 Now write your essay using the ideas and some of the language above.

6 Edit your work using the checklist on page 198.

Listening (Paper 3 Part 2)

Vocabulary: Health and fitness

1 Do you try and keep fit? Do you take regular exercise?

2a Work in pairs and complete the quiz.

Health quiz

1 In your view, what's the best way of improving:
   a strength?   b stamina?   c flexibility?   d coordination?
   (examples: weightlifting, swimming, running)
2 What advice would you give someone who wants to:
   a burn calories?
   b lose weight?
   c decrease cholesterol? (to help prevent a heart attack)
   d strengthen their immune system? (to protect against infection
      and disease)
   e lower their blood pressure? (to help prevent a stroke)
   f avoid obesity?
   g improve their circulation?
   h get more fibre in their diet?
   i look after their skin?
3 a What are the symptoms of:
   a flu?   b food poisoning?
   b Which part(s) of your body is/are affected by:
   a arthritis?   b migraine?   c bronchitis?   d tonsillitis?
4 Are these statements *True* (T) or *False* (F)?
   a Bread and potatoes are good sources of carbohydrates.
   b There are no calories in lettuce.
   c A lot of processed food lacks the vitamins and minerals found in
      fresh vegetables.
   d Eggs and nuts are low in protein.
   e Pasta is a good source of iron.

b Compare your answers in the quiz with other students and keep a
   record of any words you want to remember.

3 Complete the sentences with prepositions. Then check you
   understand the meaning of the words in *italics*. Use a dictionary if
   necessary.
   1 *Unsaturated fats* are much better ___ you than saturated fats.
   2 Tania is *allergic* ___ house dust. It makes her sneeze and her eyes itch.
   3 Jack went ___ water for several hours in the heat and he got very
      dehydrated.
   4 It took me ages to recover ___ a terrible *virus* that was going round.
      Antibiotics made no difference at all.

4 In your view, which is more important: exercise or a balanced diet?

Before you listen

5 a How much do you know about health around the world? Discuss the questions.
1 Which nationalities do you think have particularly healthy or unhealthy lifestyles? What are the reasons for this?
2 What are the most common diseases in the world today? Are some more common in specific countries?

b Look at the task in Exercise 6. Can you guess whether the missing word(s) will be nouns, verbs or adjectives and what the missing information might be? Remember you can use between one and three words.

Sentence completion

➤ EXPERT STRATEGIES pages 178–179

6 🎧 34 Do the task.

> You will hear a woman called Penny Flack, who is a nutritionist, talking about the effects of health and diet in some countries around the world. For questions **1–10**, complete the sentences with a word or short phrase.

> Eating for health
>
> Penny explains why financial support for **(1)** _____ is a current concern in many European countries.
>
> Penny would like certain **(2)** _____ aimed at children to be made illegal.
>
> Until recently, more money has been spent on food for **(3)** _____ than for schoolchildren in the UK.
>
> Penny mentions the recommendation to reduce **(4)** _____ intake by 50 percent.
>
> Penny points out that eating unhealthy **(5)** _____ is less common in France than in some other nations.
>
> Penny suggests that a re-think of the timing of their **(6)** _____ may benefit people.
>
> In a traditional Japanese diet, **(7)** _____ make up most of the daily calorie intake.
>
> The risk of **(8)** _____ in both Greenland and Japan is quite low.
>
> A link between omega-3 oils and better **(9)** _____ has just been found.
>
> Penny says that eating curry could improve the **(10)** _____ in old age.

Discussion

7 Discuss the questions.
1 Were you surprised by anything you heard in Penny's talk?
2 How does your country compare to the ones you heard about?

Vocabulary: Food

8 Think of as many examples as you can of food which comes under the following headings. Which is unhealthy and which is good for you, or acceptable in moderation?

Carbohydrates	Fat	Protein
pasta	olive oil	eggs

Speaking (Paper 4 Parts 3 and 4)

Lead-in

1a Read the statements about Parts 3 and 4 and decide whether they are *True* (T) or *False* (F).

1 Part 3
  a Candidates speak for three minutes on their own.
  b The task has two parts.
  c You are not allowed to disagree with your partner.
2 Part 4
  d You may be asked more than one question.
  e You should give short answers.
  f You should listen carefully to the other candidate.

b Look at the list of things (1–6) you might have to do in the exam. Match them with the phrases (a–f).

1 begin a discussion
2 involve the other candidate
3 disagree politely
4 ask for clarification
5 come to a conclusion
6 develop ideas

a I'm not quite sure what we have to do first.
b Why don't we start by … ?
c Do you think we should … ?
d Yes, but …
e I hadn't thought of that! We could also …
f So are we agreed that … ?

c Add any other phrases you can think of to Exercise 1b.

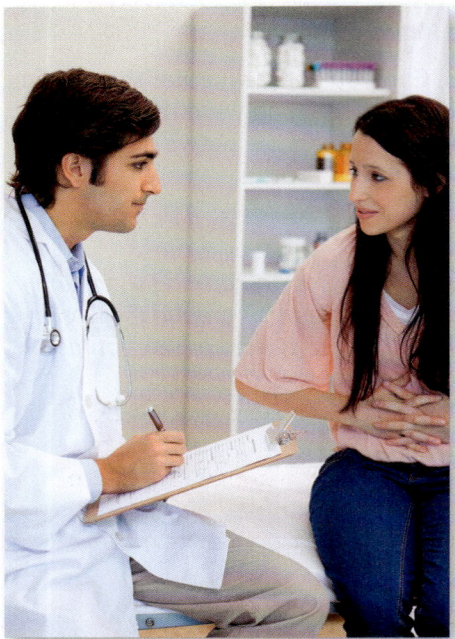

Collaborative task

➤ EXPERT STRATEGIES pages 179–180

2 Work in groups of three. Follow the instructions below.

➤ EXPERT SPEAKING page 212

Student 1: You are the interlocutor. Turn to page 212 and give the instructions for the task.

Students 2 and 3: You are Candidates A and B. Look at the spidergram on page 212 and follow the interlocutor's instructions.

Three-way discussion

➤ EXPERT STRATEGIES pages 179–180

3a Work in groups of three. Take it in turns to be the interlocutor and candidates and follow the instructions below.

Interlocutor: Ask the candidates some of the questions below. Ask *Why/Why not?* where necessary.

Candidates: Answer the interlocutor's questions.

1 Do you think we worry too much about our health?
2 Some people say that 'convenience food' is making us lazy. Do you agree?
3 Do you think smoking should be made illegal?
4 What do you think could be done to prevent obesity in children?
5 What are the advantages and disadvantages of vitamin supplements?
6 What do people do to stay healthy in your country?

Task analysis

b Discuss and compare your answers. Did you:

1 put your ideas across clearly?
2 keep closely to the task?
3 work well with your partner to complete the task?
4 use a range of vocabulary?
5 use correct grammar and pronunciation?

Language development 2

so/such; too/enough/very

1a Look at the examples and complete the rules.

> **so/such**
>
> Why is it **so difficult** to lose weight?
> You shouldn't eat **so many** sweets – they're bad for you!
> He walks **so fast** (that) I can hardly keep up with him.
> **Such bad behaviour** is not acceptable.
> He's **such a nice person** – everyone likes him.
> There was **such a lot** of salt in the food (that) I couldn't eat it.

1 We use _____ before adjectives, adverbs and quantifiers.
2 We use _____ before a noun phrase with an uncountable noun.
3 We use _____ + _____ before singular countable nouns.

b Look at the examples and answer the questions.

> **enough/too/very**
>
> Five hours a night isn't **enough sleep**.
> There aren't **enough facilities** for young people.
> It is**n't warm enough** (for us) to go swimming.
> He did**n't** run **fast enough** to win the race.
> **Too much** red meat isn't good for you.
> That health club is so expensive! It's much **too expensive** (for me) to join.
> I'm **very tired** – but not **too tired** to go out!

1 *enough* goes in front of a/an _____ and after a/an _____ or a/an _____ .
2 Match the words (1–3) with the definitions (a–c).
  1 *too* (+ adjective/quantifier)   **a** a lot
  2 *very* (+ adjective)   **b** as much as we want/need
  3 *enough* (+ noun/adjective)   **c** more than is good, reasonable or acceptable

2 Correct the mistakes in the sentences.
1 Jim's a so good doctor that everybody likes him.
2 My yoga class is great – I'm always too relaxed afterwards.
3 Paul has bought such an expensive fitness equipment!
4 The food is too much spicy for me to eat.
5 I think my diet's enough healthy overall.
6 I'm very tired to go jogging now.
7 John is so unfit so he can't even run for a bus.
8 There aren't rooms in this hotel enough for everyone.
9 You should be pleased with yourself for losing so weight.
10 I'm not enough old for to join that club.

as/like

> **A** Comparison: *like* + noun, *as if/though* + clause
> He's just **like** his father.
> I wish I could sing **like** Pavarotti (did).
> This looks/seems **like** a nice place.
> It seems **as if/like** (informal) he's going to be late. (likely situation)
> They treat me **like** their daughter/**as though I was** their daughter. (imaginary situation)
> The following verbs are often followed by *like* + noun or *as if* + clause: *feel, look, seem, smell, sound, taste*.
> It **looks like** rain/**as if** it is going to rain.
> He looks **as if** he had seen a ghost. (See Module 10B, page 143.)
>
> **B** Role, function: *as* + noun; manner: *as* + clause
> He's found a job **as** a barman.
> Please think of me **as** a friend.
> He arrived late, **as** he had warned us.
> Please do **as** I tell you.
> Other verbs followed by *as* are: *describe, be known, recognise, regard, treat*.
>
> **C** Examples: *like/such as* + noun
> Foods **like/such as** beans are a rich source of protein.

3 Read the information above and complete the sentences with *as, like, such as* or *as if/as though*.
1 I love sweet things _____ chocolates.
2 My friend Anna is looking for a job _____ an au pair.
3 Taking up yoga sounds _____ a good idea.
4 Foods _____ oranges are full of vitamin C.
5 He looks _____ he hasn't slept for a week.
6 _____ you can see, I've lost ten kilos!

4 Complete the extract from an email with *as, like* or *such as*.

> I'm working **(1)** __ a nurse in a clinic in the Himalayas and, since I live next to the clinic, people expect me to behave **(2)** __ a nurse all the time. **(3)** __ with any nursing job, my main task is to look after patients but here I also do other things, **(4)** __ help prepare the food and take it to the homes of sick people. The views from my bedroom are spectacular – it looks **(5)** __ paradise! And **(6)** __ you predicted, sometimes I feel I never want to go back home!

Use of English 1 (Paper 1 Part 4)

Lead-in

1a What advice would you give someone doing a key word transformation task? Check your answer with the strategy on page 176.

b Look at the completed key word transformation questions and correct the candidate's mistakes.

1 I remember the first time I met my wife.
MEETING
I remember *meeting my wife for* first time.

2 The tickets may be expensive, so take plenty of money.
CASE
Take plenty of money *in case of the tickets are* expensive.

3 By eight o'clock Tom was very tired, so he went to bed.
THAT
By eight o'clock, Tom *was too tired that he* went to bed.

4 We'll get into the stadium if we arrive by eight.
LONG
We'll get into the stadium *as long as we will arrive* by eight.

Key word transformations

➤ EXPERT STRATEGIES pages 175–176

2 Do the task.

> For questions **1–6**, complete the second sentence so that it has a similar meaning to the first sentence, using the word given. **Do not change the word given.** You must use between **two** and **five** words, including the word given.

1 You could stay with us next time you're in town.
PUT
We could _____ next time you're in town.

2 Jane had never eaten a meal that was as delicious as that one.
SUCH
Jane had never eaten _____ meal before.

3 'Do you want to buy my car or not?' Alan asked Judy.
WHETHER
Alan asked _____ to buy his car.

4 This car is too small for any more luggage.
ENOUGH
There _____ in this car for any more luggage.

5 Tom is not usually so bad-tempered.
LIKE
It is _____ so bad-tempered.

6 Jazz is less popular now than it was 50 years ago.
NOT
Jazz _____ it was 50 years ago.

Lead-in

3 Compare and discuss your answers.

Use of English 2 (Paper 1 Part 1)

Lead-in

1 Discuss the questions.

    1 How do you improve your mood when you're feeling low?
    2 How does shopping affect your mood?

Multiple-choice cloze

➤ **EXPERT STRATEGIES** page 175

2a Read the title and text quickly and answer the questions.

    1 What is retail therapy?
    2 In what ways can it be good and bad for you?

b Do the task.

*For questions **1–8**, read the text below and decide which answer*
*(**A**, **B**, **C** or **D**) best fits each gap.*

Retail therapy

Some people like to go shopping when they're feeling a bit under the (0) _C_ , as they claim that it (1) ___ them up. Unfortunately, while buying yourself treats may give a temporary 'buzz', in the long (2) ___ it is not to be recommended, as it can be the first (3) ___ towards shopping addiction and a debt problem.

However, some recent research proves that shopping also has its advantages. Walking is (4) ___ as being a good way of reducing the risk of coronary heart disease and on average, British women cover 214 km a year by going to the shops. This (5) ___ at about 4.45 km and 193 calories burnt for every two-hour trip. Going with a friend was found to be even better than shopping on your own because people (6) ___ to stay out longer and cover more distance.

So while retail therapy may not be the (7) ___ of all happiness, it can offer some health benefits, (8) ___ , of course, that we don't do it online!

0	A clouds	B mood	C weather	D moon
1	A comforts	B cheers	C takes	D raises
2	A time	B period	C moment	D run
3	A step	B position	C point	D direction
4	A believed	B said	C declared	D regarded
5	A gets round	B gives over	C works out	D makes up
6	A tend	B turn	C take	D hold
7	A branch	B heart	C plant	D root
8	A however	B provided	C nevertheless	D although

Discussion

3 Discuss the questions.
    1 Do you think shopping is good for your health?
    2 Which domestic activities:
      a help keep people fit?
      b are bad for you?

Language development 3

Health: Idiomatic expressions

1 a Look at the sentence from the text on page 159 and choose the correct meaning for the expression in bold.

Some people like to go shopping when they're feeling a bit **under the weather**.
a unhappy
b unwell

b Read the text and choose the correct answers in the sentences below.

George was (1) *feeling his age*. He hadn't (2) *been himself* for a while and he had been (3) *off his food*, which was unusual for him. He went to see his doctor, who said he was (4) *run-down* and needed a rest. The doctor told George to take a holiday and (5) *recharge his batteries*. He also said George needed to change his lifestyle, stop smoking and take more exercise. So George went to the south of France for three months and when he got back, he was (6) *in good shape*. His doctor gave him (7) *a clean bill of health*. That was 20 years ago. George is (8) *still going strong* today.

1 George *felt older and less energetic / wanted advice about staying young* when he went to the doctor's.
2 He went to the doctor's because he felt *different / unwell*.
3 Also, he *had no more food / didn't want to eat*.
4 The doctor said he *was very tired / had run too much*.
5 The doctor told George to *get back his energy / get a new battery*.
6 When George got back from holiday, he *had a good figure / was physically fit*.
7 His doctor said he was *clean / healthy*.
8 Today George is *fit and healthy / strong*.

c Check your answers to Exercise 1b in a dictionary. When you look up an idiomatic expression, look for the first noun, verb, adjective, adverb or preposition.

> **feel** /fiːl/ *v past tense and past participle* **felt** /felt/
> **feel your age** to realize that you are not as young or active as you used to be: *Looking at his grandson made him really feel his age.*

Health: Phrasal verbs

2 a Complete the sentences with the correct form of the phrasal verbs in the box.

come down with   cut down on   cut out   get over
give up   pick up   put on   take up

1 I think you need to _____ some weight after so long without food.
2 Why don't you _____ smoking altogether? You know it's bad for your health.
3 You've probably _____ a bug – there's something going round.
4 You ought to _____ sweet things and _____ chocolate completely.
5 You must be _____ a cold. You'll soon _____ it though.
6 You should _____ yoga to strengthen your muscles.

b Complete the conversations with the sentences in Exercise 2a.
a A: I've got backache.
  B: _____
b A: How many cigarettes do you smoke a day?
  B: About 20.
  A: _____
c A: I can't stop sneezing.
  B: _____
d A: I want to lose weight.
  B: Well, then, _____
e A: I feel very weak and thin after my illness.
  B: _____
f A: I've got a terrible stomachache.
  B: _____

3 Work in pairs. Take it in turns to ask your partner the questions.
1 Have you taken up a sport recently?
2 When did you last come down with something? Did you get over it quickly?
3 What do you think you should cut down on or cut out?

Lead-in

1 Discuss the questions.
   1 Which methods of communicating information and ideas are shown in the photos?
   2 What is the main purpose of each medium?
   3 What positive and negative effects have they had on our lives?

12A Bookworm

Reading (Paper 1 Part 5)

Before you read

1 a What do you read most/least often (e.g. newspapers, magazines, fiction books, non-fiction books, technical manuals)? Why?

b You are going to read an extract from a novel by Patricia Highsmith, which was made into a film. Look at the book cover and the title. What kind of novel do you think it is? (romance, historical, etc.)

Multiple choice

2 Do the task.

EXPERT STRATEGIES pages 175–176

*You are going to read an extract from the novel 'The Talented Mr Ripley'. For questions **1–6**, choose the answer (**A**, **B**, **C** or **D**) which you think fits best according to the text.*

1 What do we learn about Tom in the first paragraph?
   A He has already tried to steal Dickie's ring.
   B He is familiar with the details of Dickie's life.
   C He has just had an argument with Dickie.
   D He is unsure whether Dickie is asleep or not.

2 Why does Tom decide that he wants to kill Dickie?
   A He feels unfairly treated by Dickie.
   B He wants to get away from Dickie.
   C He thinks that Dickie has failed him.
   D He feels ashamed of Dickie's behaviour.

3 In the third paragraph, Tom plans how he will
   A cause Dickie to have an accident.
   B go and live in Dickie's apartment.
   C leave Dickie and return to Rome.
   D receive money intended for Dickie.

4 How does Tom feel at the thought of actually killing Dickie?
   A terrified of the consequences
   B unsure of what to do with the body
   C thrilled by the risks involved
   D confident of his ability to do it

5 The phrase *Tom knew why* in line 42 refers to the reason why
   A Tom was smiling.
   B Dickie was paying him attention.
   C Dickie was irritated.
   D Tom had a strange expression.

6 Why did Tom pretend to faint?
   A to annoy Dickie and start an argument
   B to distract attention from how he looked
   C to make a boring journey more interesting
   D to make Dickie more sympathetic towards him

Task analysis

3 Compare and justify your answers.

Vocabulary: Feelings: idiomatic expressions

4 a Find nouns and adjectives in the text that express feelings, emotions and reactions.
   nouns: hate, affection
   adjectives: enthusiastic

b Look at the expressions in bold in the text. Can you explain what they mean?

Discussion

5 a Discuss the story.
   1 What do you think happens next?
   2 Which character do you sympathise with most? Which one would you like to meet?
   3 Having read this extract, would you like to read the novel or see the film? Why/Why not?

b What are the advantages and disadvantages of making a film based on a novel? Give examples of films you have seen.

The Talented Mr Ripley

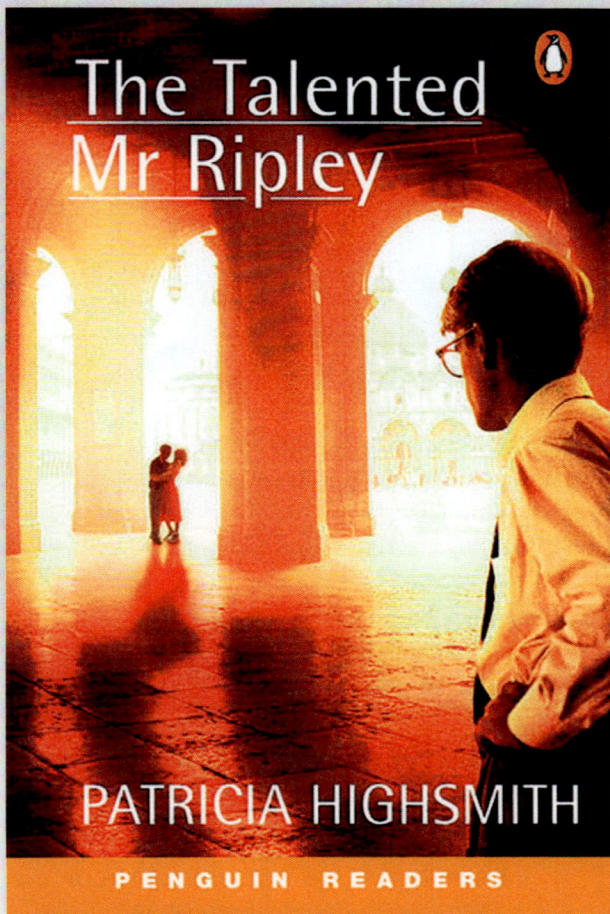

Dickie said absolutely nothing on the train. Under a pretence of being sleepy, he folded his arms and closed his eyes. Tom sat opposite him, staring at his bony, arrogant, handsome face, at his hands with the green ring and the gold signet ring. **It crossed Tom's mind** to steal the green ring when he left. It would be easy: Dickie took it off when he swam. Sometimes he took it off even when he showered at the house. He would do it the very last day, Tom thought. Tom stared at Dickie's closed eyelids. A crazy emotion of hate, of affection, of impatience and frustration was swelling in him, hampering his breathing.

He wanted to kill Dickie. It was not the first time he had thought of it. Before, once, twice or three times, it had been an impulse caused by anger or disappointment, an impulse that vanished immediately and left him with a feeling of shame. Now he thought about it for an entire minute, two minutes, because he was leaving Dickie anyway and what was there to be ashamed of any more? He had failed Dickie in every way. He hated Dickie because however he looked at what had happened, his failing had not been his own fault, not due to anything he had done, but due to Dickie's rudeness! He had offered Dickie friendship, companionship and respect, everything he had to offer, and Dickie had replied with ingratitude and now hostility. Dickie was just **shoving him out in the cold**.

If he killed him on this trip, Tom thought, he could simply say that some accident had happened. He could – he had just thought of something brilliant: he could become Dickie Greenleaf himself. He could do everything that Dickie did. He could go back to Mongibello first and collect Dickie's things, tell Marge any story, then set up an apartment in Rome or Paris, receive Dickie's cheque every month and forge Dickie's signature on it. He **could step right into Dickie's shoes**. He could have Mr Greenleaf Senior **eating out of his hand**.

The danger of it, even the inevitable temporariness of it, which he vaguely realised, only made him more enthusiastic. He began to think of how. The water. But Dickie was such a good swimmer. The cliffs. It would be easy to push Dickie off some cliff when they took a walk but he imagined Dickie grabbing at him and pulling him off with him and he tensed in his seat until his thighs ached and his nails cut red into his thumbs. He would have to get the other ring off too. He would have to tint his hair a little lighter. But he wouldn't live in a place, of course, where anybody who knew Dickie lived. He had only to look enough like Dickie to be able to use his passport. Well, he did, if he –

Dickie opened his eyes, looking right at him, and Tom relaxed, slumped into the corner with his head back and his eyes shut, as quickly as if he had passed out. 'Tom, are you OK?' Dickie asked, shaking Tom's knee. 'OK,' Tom said, smiling a little. He saw Dickie sit back, with an air of irritation, and Tom knew why; *line 42* because Dickie had hated giving him even that much attention. Tom smiled to himself, amused at his own quick reflex in pretending to collapse, because that had been the only way to keep Dickie from seeing what must have been a very strange expression on his face.

Language development 1

Connecting ideas

> EXPERT GRAMMAR page 197

1a Read the student's sentences, which describe a book he/she has read, and answer the questions.

1 Why did the student read the book?
2 What made it more difficult to understand?
3 Why do the characters sometimes sleep in the car?

a I read this book in order to find out more about the American way of life.
b As it was written by an American, it gives an accurate picture of life there.
c I had to read a lot of it before fully understanding the humour.
d If I'd known more about the USA before I started, I would have understood the book better.
e It's about two people who decide to drive across the USA.
f While they are driving along, they meet all kinds of people.
g Each night they arrive in a different town and feel exhausted.
h Because they don't know anyone, they have to find somewhere to stay.
i When they have found a hotel, they usually go out to eat.
j Sometimes they are so tired that they sleep in the car.
k However, they don't realise that they are being followed.

b Look again at the sentences in Exercise 1a and underline the words that are used to connect ideas. Then use the words to complete the table.

Type	Example	Example(s) from Exercise 1a
Relative pronoun	which, that	_____
Conjunction + clause	when	_____
Conjunction + -ing	after	_____
Clause of result	such a ... that	_____
Conditional	unless	_____
Linking conjunction	but, nevertheless	_____
Clause of purpose	to	_____
Clause of reason	since	_____

2 Correct the mistakes in the sentences.

1 The part what I liked best was the ending.
2 The main character is an old man who he has never left his home town.
3 It was a such good book that I couldn't stop reading it.
4 During the police look for the main suspect, Holmes makes other enquiries.
5 It is set in a town where there are a lot of factories in.
6 It can be helpful to see the film before to read the book in English.
7 If you will like science fiction, you'll probably like this book.
8 It is a good story despite the main character is not very realistic.
9 The police are called in for investigate the theft of a painting.
10 I didn't like the ending because of I thought it was disappointing.

Participle clauses

Participle clauses can be used in writing to make sentences shorter.

Look at the examples of shortened sentences from Exercise 1a:

A **present and perfect participles** (actions/situations at the same time or in sequence)

While they are driving along, they meet all kinds of people. →
Driving *along, they meet all kinds of people.*

Because they don't know anyone, they have to find somewhere to stay. →
Not knowing *anyone, they have to find somewhere to stay.*

When they have found a hotel, they usually go out to eat. →
Having found *a hotel, they usually go out to eat.*

B **past participles** (for passives)

As it was written by an American, it gives an accurate picture of life there. →
Written *by an American, it gives an accurate picture of life there.*

C **past participles used as adjectives**

Each night they arrive in a different town and feel exhausted. →
Each night they arrive in a different town, ***exhausted****.*

3 Look at the information in the box and complete the second sentence so that it has a similar meaning to the first sentence. Use participle clauses.

1 Since Jackson is an immigrant himself, he decided to write about immigrants.
____ an immigrant, Jackson decided to write about immigrants.
2 As he writes in the first person, he brings the story to life.
____ in the first person, he brings the story to life.
3 Because he has experienced problems himself, he writes very realistically.
____ problems himself, he writes very realistically.
4 Although the book was criticised at first, it was a huge success.
Although ____ at first, his book was a huge success.
5 Despite the fact that she has had many problems, the protagonist never gives up.
Despite ____ many problems, the protagonist never gives up.
6 Now that I've read this one, I can't wait for his next novel!
____ this one, I can't wait for his next novel!
7 I got to the end of the book and felt completely satisfied.
I got to the end of the book, ____ .

4 The sentences below explain what the book *Heat and Dust* is about. Look at the clues in brackets and connect the ideas in the sentences using language from Exercises 1–3. In each case, combine the sentences to make one long sentence.

1 The book was written by a woman. She lived in India for many years. It tells us a lot about life there. (participle; relative)
Written by a woman who lived in India for many years, the book tells us a lot about life there.
2 It is about a young English woman. She goes to India with her child. She wants to find out the true story of her grandmother. (relative; reason)
3 Her English grandparents lived in India together. Her grandmother fell in love with an Indian man. (contrast)
4 She arrives there. Then she starts to follow the same life path as her grandmother. She falls in love with an Indian. (perfect participle; conjunction + clause)
5 It is set in two periods and tells two women's similar stories. It shows that lifestyles and attitudes change a lot over two generations. Love and relationships never change. (participle; contrast)

Writing (Paper 2 Part 2: Review)

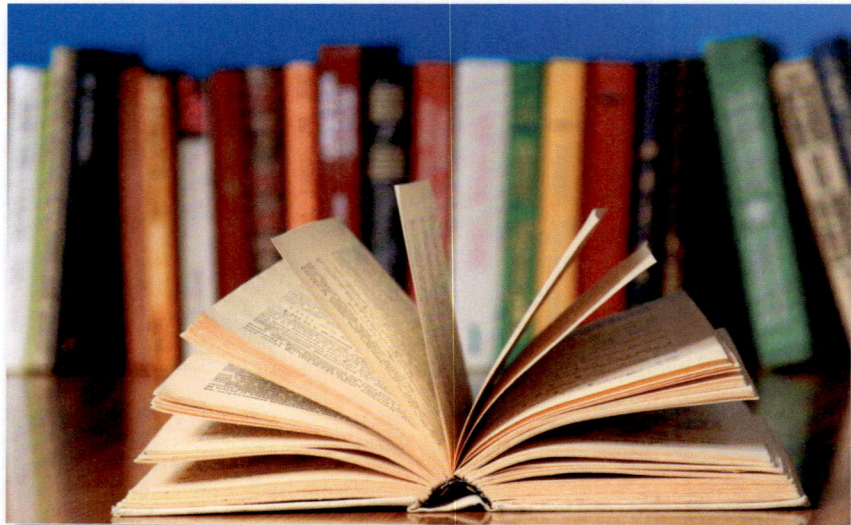

Lead-in

1 Discuss the questions.

1 What books have you read recently?
2 Think of a novel with an unusual storyline. What was it about? What did you like most/least about it?

Understand the task

2 Read and analyse the task. Think about the purpose of a review, your style and what you must include in your answer.

You have seen this announcement in an international magazine.

BOOK REVIEWS WANTED

Have you read a book recently with a story that has held your attention? Write a review of the book, explaining what the story is about and whether the characters are convincing. Tell us whether or not you would recommend it both to younger and older readers.

The best reviews will be published in the magazine.

*Write your **review** in **140–190** words in an appropriate style.*

Plan your review

3a Answer the questions about the book you are going to review.

1 What kind of story is it (e.g. mystery, crime)?
2 Which aspects of the book are you going to focus on? (Read the question again.)

b Make notes under these headings.

Characters	Events	Setting

c Number the events in your notes in the order they occur.

d Choose the most important points for your review.

e Number the paragraphs in the best order for your review.

Paragraph ___: the characters (with examples)
Paragraph ___: general conclusion + recommendation (with reasons)
Paragraph ___: brief statement (opinion)/setting + summary of storyline
Paragraph ___: meaning of story (optional)
Paragraph ___: brief opinion + further details of storyline

Language and content

4a Put the adjectives in the box under one of the headings in your notes in Exercise 3b. More than one answer may be possible.

lifelike weak unexpected passionate moving predictable imaginative brave disappointing lovely original successful entertaining unconvincing appealing clever attractive boring sensitive awful impressive

b In context, would the adjectives in Exercise 4a be *Positive* (P) or *Negative* (N)?

c Can you think of any other adjectives you could use? Add them to your list from Exercise 4a.

d Read the sentences. Which words could you use instead of the phrases in *italics* to avoid repetition?

1 They're very well-drawn characters, especially the evil *well-drawn characters*.
2 I think this is one of his later novels. If *it is one of his later novels*, it is an extraordinary achievement.
3 Some people who write novels *write novels* because they have something to say.
4 Do you know this book? If *you don't know this book*, I strongly recommend it.

e How would you complete these sentence openings for your review?

1 This is a story about …/This novel tells the story of …
2 It is set (in/on) …/It takes place (in/on) …
3 The character(s) I like most/least …
4 The reason I feel that … is …
5 I think it is (written quite cleverly/extremely well written) because …
6 It's full of …
7 The best part of the book is when …
8 I like/don't like the beginning/ending because …
9 I found the story …
10 I think … would enjoy … most.

EXPERT LANGUAGE: Attitude phrases

Choose the correct answers.

1 *To be honest / As far as I know*, I don't think it's a very original story.
2 *Roughly speaking / Generally speaking / Strictly speaking*, she writes romantic novels rather than spy thrillers.
3 *According to me / As far as I'm concerned*, this is his best book to date.
4 *It goes without saying / In person* he was the most interesting character.
5 *No doubt / Presumably / Without doubt*, it was a wonderful read. Give it to a friend for their birthday!
6 *Not surprisingly / Quite honestly / Truly*, the story was not as well developed as I'd hoped.

Write your review

➤ EXPERT STRATEGIES pages 177–178

Check your review

➤ EXPERT WRITING page 205

5 Now write your review using the ideas and some of the language above.

6 Edit your work using this checklist. Have you:

1 answered both parts of the question sufficiently? (storyline + characters)
2 expressed yourself clearly and avoided repetition?
3 given reasons for your opinions?
4 included enough detail? (but not too much)
5 used a range of words, expressions and structures?

Speaking (Paper 4 Parts 1–4)

Vocabulary: Press and advertising

1a Look at the photo. Find an example of:
1 a local paper.
2 an news website.
3 a red-top newspaper.
4 a broadsheet.

b Look at the photo again and find an example of:
1 a headline.
2 a column.
3 a 'breaking news' item.
4 a sports section.
5 a colour supplement.

c What do these people do on a newspaper?
1 a foreign correspondent
2 a crime reporter
3 a columnist

d Choose the correct answers.
1 News of the couple's separation *beat / hit* the headlines the next day.
2 The star decided to issue a *press / newspaper* release.
3 The journalist rushed to *find / meet* his deadline before the newspaper went to *publication / press*.
4 Most newspapers have regular *qualities / features* such as TV guides, classified ads and weather *forecasts / predictions*.
5 There are so many *shiny / glossy* fashion magazines nowadays and they are full of advertisements for all the well-known brand *companies / names*. Whether they want to *promote / support* an older design or *take off / launch* a new one, they all have to try and *seize / grab* the attention of the reader.

2a Choose the correct word for each gap. Then write it in the correct form to complete the sentences. Use a dictionary if necessary.
1 *day, circulate, reader*
   The Sun is a best-selling ____ tabloid newspaper published in the UK. It has the highest ____ of any newspaper in the UK, with a current ____ estimated at almost 7 million.
2 *journal, editor*
   Some people say that standards in ____ are declining and that the ____ content of all newspapers has gone downmarket, with too many items revolving around celebrities.
3 *commerce, advertise*
   In most public service broadcasting, there are no ____ . The only form of ____ that is allowed is of its own programmes.

b Make a note of any words you want to remember and mark the main stress. Here is an example.

PERSON	ACTIVITY
(who collects and writes news stories)	
Journalist	Journalism

3 Discuss the statements.
1 There are so many sources of news nowadays that newspapers are no longer important.
2 All adverts are dishonest. They do not give us a true picture of a product.
3 Adverts have very little influence on what we buy.

Part 1: Conversation

➤ EXPERT STRATEGIES pages 179–180

4 Work in groups of three. Take turns to be the interlocutor and candidates. Follow the instructions below.

➤ EXPERT SPEAKING page 213

Student 1: You are the interlocutor. Turn to page 213 for a list of questions to choose from. Ask Candidates A and B some of the questions. Stop after two minutes.

Students 2 and 3: You are the candidates. Answer the questions. Look at the strategies on pages 179–180 for points to remember.

Part 2: Long turn

➤ EXPERT STRATEGIES pages 179–180

Why do people choose to get their news in these ways?

5a Work in pairs. Read the interlocutor's instructions below and do Task 1.

Task 1

Student A: Here are your photos. They show people finding out about the news. I'd like you to compare the photos and say why people choose to get their news in these ways. (*one minute*)

Student B: Do you believe everything you read in the newspapers? (Why/Why not?) (*30 seconds*)

b Work in the same pairs. Read the interlocutor's instructions below and do Task 2.

Task 2

Student B: Look at the photographs on page 213. They show two different kinds of radio interview. I'd like you to compare the photos and say which you think makes the most interesting interview. (*one minute*)

Student A: Do you like to spend a lot of time finding out what is happening in the world? (Why/Why not?)

Part 3: Collaborative task

➤ EXPERT STRATEGIES pages 179–180

6 Work in pairs. Read the interlocutor's instructions below and do the task.

Look at the spidergram on page 213. I'd like you to imagine that a college wants to offer classes to retired people in the community. These are some ideas they are thinking about and a question for you to discuss. Talk to each other and decide the advantages of these subjects. (*two minutes*)

Now you have about a minute to decide which subject would be the best for retired people. (*one minute*)

Part 4: Three-way discussion

➤ EXPERT STRATEGIES pages 179–180

7 Work in pairs. Take turns to ask each other these questions. You have four minutes for this.

1 Do you think it's better to have a personal tutor or be in a class?
2 Some people say that education is wasted on young people. Do you agree?
3 Do you think that the internet is a good learning tool? (Why/Why not?)
4 Why do you think some people find it difficult to learn a foreign language?
5 What can we learn from travel?
6 How do people like to spend their retirement in your country? (Why?)

Listening (Paper 3 Part 4)

Before you listen

1a Which newspaper do you usually read? What do you like about it? How does it compare with other papers?

b Look at the task in Exercise 2 and read the questions. Don't look at the options yet. Then discuss these questions.
1 What personal qualities do you think are necessary to be a journalist?
2 Discuss possible answers which you might hear.

Multiple choice

➤ **EXPERT STRATEGIES** pages 178–179

2 🎧 35 Do the task.

> *You will hear a radio interview with a man called Mike, who is a journalist. For questions 1–7, choose the best answer (A, B or C).*

1 What convinced Mike to follow a career in journalism?
   A a course he took
   B his lack of success in business
   C the advice of a family member

2 What type of training did Mike have once he started work?
   A He studied for formal qualifications.
   B He worked closely with a more experienced colleague.
   C He received feedback on his work from newspaper readers.

3 When Mike first started working with the police, they
   A were unsure whether to trust him.
   B had little time to spend with him.
   C refused to accept drinks from him.

4 Why didn't Mike use the information he gained about Prince Charles?
   A It was against the law to do so.
   B He had promised that he wouldn't.
   C It was felt to be unfair to do so.

5 According to Mike, what is a journalist's most important quality?
   A being committed to the job
   B having good writing skills
   C feeling sure of your abilities

6 What does Mike say about modern journalism?
   A It's not as exciting as it used to be.
   B It's no longer as sociable as it was.
   C It's less demanding than in the past.

7 What disadvantage of journalism does Mike warn young people about?
   A the financial insecurity
   B the disruption to domestic life
   C the competitive atmosphere

Discussion

3 Discuss the questions.
1 Do you think you have the right qualities to be a journalist?
2 What aspects of the job would you like/dislike?

Use of English 1 (Paper 1 Part 1)

Lead-in

1a Decide if the statements are *True* (T) or *False* (F).
In Paper 1 Part 1:
1 you need to know the meaning of the missing word.
2 what the whole text is about is not important.
3 you need to know whether the missing word would go with other words in the context.

b What advice would you give a candidate about this part of the paper?

Multiple-choice cloze

➤ **EXPERT STRATEGIES** page 175

2 Read the text quickly and answer the questions.
1 What image do advertisers of men's fragrances usually try to create?
2 What is unusual about the advertisement which is described?

3 Do the task.

*For questions **1–8**, read the text below and decide which answer (**A**, **B**, **C** or **D**) best fits each gap. There is an example at the beginning (**0**).*

| Home 🏠 | Previous ‹ | Next › | | Search 🔍 |

What are they trying to tell us?

The aim of advertisers is to get their product (0) *C*, and in the competitive world of men's fragrances, image and (1) ___ name are all-important. To advertise their fragrances, most lifestyle magazines try to (2) ___ an emotional impact by featuring an image of a glamorous male model in his early 20s. This is usually accompanied by a picture of the product, the name and sometimes a (3) ___ phrase, all of which (4) ___ an important part in the publicity campaign.

In one advert, the bottle of fragrance is in the (5) ___ of a book. Unusually, the male model looks intellectual and unmasculine and is wearing thick-framed glasses. The image of his head is merged with words from a story, typed on a large (6) ___ typewriter. (7) ___ the man is meant to look stylish so that the fragrance will (8) ___ to more serious, less sporty types, or perhaps to women who would like their men to be like that.

0	**A** sensed	**B** remarked	**C** noticed	**D** witnessed
1	**A** label	**B** brand	**C** mark	**D** logo
2	**A** take	**B** feel	**C** make	**D** occur
3	**A** quick	**B** brief	**C** small	**D** intense
4	**A** play	**B** take	**C** do	**D** make
5	**A** size	**B** picture	**C** character	**D** shape
6	**A** old-fashioned		**B** old-time	
	C behind the times		**D** out of date	
7	**A** Nevertheless		**B** For instance	
	C Presumably		**D** Eventually	
8	**A** attract		**B** charm	
	C appeal		**D** call	

Discussion

4 Discuss the questions.
1 Do you think adverts are dishonest?
2 What things do you think should not be allowed in TV adverts? Why?

Language development 2

need + -ing/ to be done; have/ get something done

A *need + -ing/to be done*

Active: *Someone* **needs to** *check the adverts to make sure they're legal.*

Passive: *The adverts* **need checking** | *to make sure*
The adverts **need to be checked** | *they're legal.*

B *have/get something done*

- We can use *have/get something done* when we arrange for someone to do something for us. *We think of the ideas ourselves but we* **have/get the adverts** *made for us.*
- We can also use *have/get something done* when someone else does something to us that we don't want.
We **had** *our office* **broken into** *last night.*
(had = not my fault)
I **got** *my nose* **broken** *in a fight. (got = my fault)*

1a Read the information above and correct the mistakes in the sentences. Rewrite each sentence in two different ways.
1 The advert's too long. It needs shorten.
2 Those posters are out of date. They need to replace.

b What needs doing? Respond to the sentences using *need* + *-ing* and the verbs in the box

---

clean   cut   rebuild   repaint   tidy up   water

---

1 This garden's a mess.
2 The grass is long.
3 The plants all round the house are very dry.
4 That wall's fallen down.
5 Those windows over there are filthy.
6 The paint on the doors is coming off.

c Read the notes and explain how to make a TV advert using *needs to be.*

How to make a TV advert
1 first raise money
2 then write advert
3 prepare script and bring to life
4 find good production company
5 hire experienced director
6 recruit well-known actors
7 shoot advert in studio you can afford

2a Complete the conversations using *have/get something done.*
1 A: Let's scan these images. Have you got a scanner?
   B: No, *I'll get them scanned* at the office.
2 A: Where's your DVD player?
   B: I _____ (steal).
3 A: Let's repair your computer ourselves.
   B: No, _____ .
4 A: Have you checked the tyres on the jeep?
   B: No, _____ .
5 A: Shall we install the washing machine ourselves?
   B: No, _____ .
6 A: These knives are very blunt.
   B: Yes, _____ . (sharpen)

b Why do we go to these places? Answer using *have/get something done.*
1 a dentist's
2 an optician's
3 a dry cleaner's
4 a hairdresser's
5 a manicurist's
6 a photographer
7 a picture framer's
8 a tailor's

c Which of these things do you do yourself? Which do you have done for you?
1 paint your room when it needs decorating
2 mend your TV when it's broken
3 tidy the house/apartment where you live
4 clean your car
5 service your car
6 clean your coat when it's very dirty
7 do the gardening

3 Discuss the questions.
1 If you could have some of your clothes made especially for you, which ones would they be and what would you have done?
2 If you could have a house built for you, where would you have it built and how would you have it designed?

Use of English 2 (Paper 1 Part 3)

Lead-in

1 Discuss the questions about Paper 1 Part 3.
  1 Is it better to read the text line by line or sentence by sentence?
  2 Should you answer the questions in order or leave any you can't do and come back to them?

Word formation

> EXPERT STRATEGIES pages 175–176

2 Read the text in Exercise 3 quickly and answer the questions.
  1 Why are the paparazzi so keen to get their photographs?
  2 How do they defend what they do?

3 Do the task.

For questions 1–8, read the text below. Use the word given in capitals at the end of some of the lines to form a word that fits in the gap in the same line. There is an example at the beginning (0).

The paparazzi

The private lives of celebrities continue to generate (0) *endless* public interest, which is reflected in massive newspaper and magazine (1) _____ when certain photos are published. The paparazzi, the photojournalists who get these pictures, are able to sell them to the press for (2) _____ amounts of money.

END
SELL

BELIEF

The paparazzi show great (3) _____ when they decide to take photos which they know will make them rich. Some will go as far as searching through rubbish bins at a celebrity's home. There is general (4) _____ of this practice among the general public and many want to ban it. There have been a number of high-profile (5) _____ over the years.

DETERMINED

APPROVE

COMPLAIN

However, the paparazzi argue that celebrities have no right to any (6) _____ because their jobs involve being in the public eye. The argument is still going on but it has proved difficult to take (7) _____ against them. And as long as people continue to buy newspapers and magazines which print these photos, it is (8) _____ whether the paparazzi will ever be stopped.

PRIVATE

ACT

DOUBT

4 Read the text in Exercise 5 and answer the questions.
  1 Who do special advisers work for?
  2 In which two ways do they influence voters' opinions?

5 Do the task.

For questions 1–8, read the text below. Use the word given in capitals at the end of some of the lines to form a word that fits in the gap in the same line. There is an example at the beginning (0).

Special advisers

Every (0) *government* likes to show itself in the best possible light. In the UK, this has recently been reflected in the (1) _____ increase in the number of special advisers who have become very (2) _____ in the world of politics.

GOVERN
DRAMA
POWER

These people are given (3) _____ for making sure that all news is good news. In order to do this, it is necessary to build up a good relationship with the newspaper (4) _____ who they want to support them. In this way, the advisers hope to influence the way in which a story will be reported – a practice which many people worry is beginning to reduce the (5) _____ of the press.

RESPONSIBLE

EDIT

FREE

Advisers also have the task of writing (6) _____ 'soundbytes' for speeches. Now that there is such a wide (7) _____ of ways to communicate a message, it is even more important to speak and write (8) _____ if you want to get the voters' attention.

MEMORY
VARY
IMAGINE

Language development 3

Word formation: Review

1a Complete the table. Use a dictionary if necessary.

Adjective	Adverb	Noun	Verb
responsible			✗
		belief	
	worryingly		
embarrassing			
			recognise
variable			
		decision	
			imagine
legal			
	satisfactorily		
			approve
		amazement	

b Form the opposites of these words using prefixes.

1 legal (adj) ____
2 responsible (adj) ____
3 romantic (adj) ____
4 appear (v) ____
5 accurately (adv) ____
6 moral (adj) ____
7 probable (adj) ____
8 logical (adj) ____
9 regular (adj) ____
10 perfectly (adv) ____

c Complete each sentence with a word from Exercises 1a and 1b that has a similar meaning to the words in brackets. More than one answer may be possible.

1 The newspaper was ____ to reveal secret information about the Queen. (not thinking about the effects of their actions)
2 It was an ____ to the company that so many people complained about their adverts. (something uncomfortable)
3 Greenco says it is an environmentally friendly company, so it seems ____ that its leaflets are not made of recycled paper. (not based on careful thought)
4 It is ____ to make a false claim in an advert. (against the law)
5 To everyone's ____ , our low-cost advertising campaign was a big success. (great surprise)
6 News editors mustn't hesitate. They have to be ____ . (able to make up their mind quickly)
7 Many of the figures quoted in the newspaper were ____ . (not correct)

2 Complete the second sentence so that it is similar in meaning to the first sentence. Use the words in brackets and the correct form of one of the words in the box.

fashion   relation   survive   use

1 The police and the media are getting on well these days. (better)
The police and the media have a ____ these days.
2 This bag is no good at all – it's got a hole in it. (absolutely)
This bag is ____ – it's got a hole in it.
3 I used to buy that music magazine long before everyone else bought it. (became)
I used to buy that music magazine long before it ____ .
4 The doctors said he would probably live. (chance)
The doctors said he had a good ____ .

3a Complete these statements about magazines with the correct form of the words in brackets.

1 I read a couple of great computer magazines each month. They're very _____ (profession) produced.

2 Some men's magazines are quite _____ (entertain) but I find others completely _____ (read).

3 If I had to _____ (general), I suppose I prefer magazines with _____ (stimulate) articles about things that are happening in the world.

4 I have great _____ (admire) for magazines about cooking. They are so _____ (create) and I don't really like to _____ (critic) them. However, sometimes I find their recipes a bit _____ (rely).

5 I hate magazines that insult my _____ (intelligent). So many of them are just about the _____ (relation) of famous people. Not only are such articles extremely _____ (bore), I find them rather _____ (offend).

b Discuss the questions.

1 What kinds of magazine do you read. Why?
2 What kinds of magazine do you dislike? Why?____

Exam reference

Paper 1: Reading and Use of English (1 hour 15 minutes)

There are 7 parts to this paper, with a total of 52 questions. Each part of the paper contains a text. In Parts 1–4, there are accompanying grammar and vocabulary tasks. In Parts 5–7, there are a range of texts and accompanying reading comprehension tasks, each testing specific aspects of reading (e.g. understanding gist or finding specific information).

- Part 1: multiple-choice cloze: one short text with eight gaps and a set of four options for each
- Part 2: open cloze: one short text with eight gaps
- Part 3: word formation: one short text with eight gaps
- Part 4: key word transformations: six separate items
- Part 5: four-option multiple-choice questions: one long text with six questions
- Part 6: gapped text: one long text with six sentences removed and jumbled
- Part 7: multiple matching: several short texts or sections of a continuous text, with ten options

Questions in Parts 1, 2 and 3 carry one mark each. Questions in Part 4 receive up to two marks each.

EXPERT TASK STRATEGY (ALL TASKS)

- For all text-based tasks, read the titles and skim the text quickly before you begin, to get a general sense of what it's about and how it's organised.
- Read the instructions carefully and check how long you have to do the task. Make sure you answer all the questions.
- Notes can be made on the question paper but your answers must be transferred to the answer sheet before the end of the test.
- Do not leave gaps. Make a guess if necessary but answer all the questions.

Questions in Parts 5 and 6 receive 2 marks each and in Part 7 one mark each.

Part 1: Multiple-choice cloze

➤ See page 19 for an example.

There is a text with eight gaps and four options (A–D). You have to decide which answer is correct.

You are tested on your awareness of vocabulary: what the words or expressions mean and how they fit into the context. Examples are nouns, adjectives and verbs followed by prepositions (e.g. *love of*, *succeed in*), fixed phrases (e.g. *above average*, *do without*), phrasal verbs (e.g. *take after* (*someone*)), linking words (e.g. *although*, *in case*), adverbs (e.g. *particularly*, *nearly*) and sets of words with similar meanings (e.g. *travel*, *voyage*, *journey*, *excursion*).

EXPERT TASK STRATEGY

- Read the text carefully before and after each gap and try to guess what kind of word or phrase fits the gap and meaning best.
- Look at the four options and decide which one goes with the words that come before and after each gap.
- If you are not sure, cross out the options which you know are incorrect and then decide on the most likely answer.
- When you have finished, read through the whole text to make sure that it makes sense and that the options fit grammatically in the context.

Part 2: Open cloze

➤ See page 31 for an example.

There is a text with eight gaps. You have to complete each gap with one word only so that the sentence makes sense. There are no options.

The main focus is on grammar but you may also be tested on nouns/verbs/adjectives, etc. with prepositions (e.g. *interested in*, *a way of*), fixed phrases (e.g. *on his way home*, *at least*) and phrasal verbs (e.g. *get on with someone*).

Grammar areas include verb forms (e.g. auxiliaries, passives), pronouns (e.g. relative pronouns – *who*, *which*, etc.), comparative forms (e.g. *more*, *less*, *than*, *as … as*), articles (e.g. *a/an*, *the*), determiners (e.g. *this*, *these*); possessives (e.g. *of* used for possession), conditionals, quantifiers (e.g. *one of*), time conjunctions (e.g. *before*, *while*), linking expressions (e.g. *because/but*; *neither/nor*, *it/there*, *make/do*, *whether … or not*, *let/allow*, *as/like*, etc.).

EXPERT TASK STRATEGY

- Think about what kind of word is needed in each gap (a preposition, an article, an auxiliary verb?).
- Write only one word in each gap. Do not use contractions.
- When you have finished, read the text again and make sure that it makes sense and that your spelling is correct.

Part 3: Word formation

➤ See page 33 for an example.

You are given a text with eight gaps. There is a word in capital letters at the end of some of the lines and you have to change the form of the word so that it fits a gap in the same line. The main focus is on vocabulary and the word could be a noun, adjective, adverb or verb.

For the word to make sense in context, you may have to add a prefix (e.g. *un-*) or a suffix (e.g. *-able*), or both, to change it into a noun, adjective, verb or adverb. You may need to make some words negative or plural according to the context, change some verbs into participles (e.g. *write – written*) and some adjectives into superlatives (e.g. *big – biggest*). You might have to make internal changes (e.g. *strong – strength*) or compounds (e.g. *rain – raindrop*). You won't need to make more than two changes to the original word.

EXPERT TASK STRATEGY

- Read the line with the gap in it in the context of the paragraph and the whole text.
- Work out the part of speech of the missing word and whether it is positive or negative, singular or plural. There may be more than one change required (e.g. adding a prefix and a suffix).
- Write the correct form of the word in the gap.
- Read the text again to make sure that it makes sense and that your answers are spelt correctly.

Part 4: Key word transformations

➤ See page 18 for an example.

There are six 'lead-in' sentences. You are also given the beginning and end of a sentence and you have to complete it so that it has a similar meaning to the first sentence, using different structures.

There is a 'key' word, which you must use, and which you must not change in any way. Using the key word involves making more than one change to the original sentence. You have to use between two and five words, including the key word. Contracted forms (e.g. *haven't*) count as two words.

You are tested on grammar, vocabulary and collocation. Each question receives two marks; one mark may be given if there is a small error.

Grammar areas tested include: active and passive verb forms, comparatives and superlatives, direct and reported speech, clauses of purpose and result (e.g. *so … that*), verbs + *-ing/to*-infinitive, modals, *wish/if only/it's time* + past, conditionals, verbs with two objects, quantity (e.g. *hardly any*), adverbs, *it/there*, *make/let/allow*, *despite/in spite of*, *since/for*, *prefer/would rather/had better*, *remember/forget*, *lend/borrow*, *in case*, *too/enough*, *so/such*.

Vocabulary areas include: collocations with prepositions (e.g. *be good at*), phrasal verbs (e.g. *look forward to*), changing nouns to verbs and fixed expressions (e.g. *out of work*).

EXPERT TASK STRATEGY

- Read both sentences and the key word and work out what is missing from the second sentence.
- Identify what part of speech the key word is and how it will fit into the new sentence.
- Write down the missing words, making sure that you do not change the key word in any way.
- Read your completed sentence to check that it has the same meaning as the first one, that it makes sense and that it is spelt correctly.
- Make sure you have not written more than five words, including the key word. Contractions count as two words.
- Be careful you do not add any words that are not necessary.

Part 5: Multiple choice

➤ See pages 22–23 for an example.

This part has six multiple-choice questions with four possible answers (A, B, C and D). It tests detailed understanding of the text and may require understanding of opinions and attitudes, main ideas, purpose and an ability to work out the meaning of vocabulary and understand the relation between words and phrases (e.g. *What does 'it' refer to?*). The final question may test general understanding of the text (e.g. *Who was the text written for? Where does the text come from?*).

EXPERT TASK STRATEGY

- Read each stem (question or unfinished sentence) and highlight the key words.
- For each question, find the part of the text that it relates to and highlight that part. The questions are in the same order as the text.
- Read the relevant part of the text very carefully.
- Look at the question and four options again and decide on the answer. There may be similar views elsewhere. However, only one part will match the meaning exactly, although it will not be expressed in exactly the same way.
- If you are not sure exactly which option is correct, cross out the ones which you know are incorrect and then choose the one that is most likely.

Part 6: Gapped text

➤ See pages 36–37 for an example.

Six sentences have been removed from the text, jumbled and put in a box after the text. The task is to decide where in the text each sentence comes from. There is a distractor sentence which doesn't fit anywhere.

This task tests your understanding of text structure – how the text is organised, both logically and thematically. To do the task, you have to be aware of the logical sequence of the text by looking for key words and ideas, and understand how grammatical and lexical devices are used to link sentences and paragraphs (e.g. *Having done that, she left.*).

EXPERT TASK STRATEGY

- Read the base text carefully to get the general idea of how the text is structured.
- Read the sections before and after each gap in order to predict what kind of information is missing.
- Underline any clues which might help you (e.g. verb forms, reference words like pronouns, etc., time references and nouns or verbs which might be repeated later – possibly in a different way).
- Look at the seven sentences and underline any grammatical links (e.g. the same verb form), topic links, parallel phrases, near-synonyms, etc.
- Choose the best option for each gap. If you are not sure about a gap, go on to the next question and return to it later.
- Read through the completed text and make sure you have chosen a sentence to fit in each gap and that you have not used the same one twice.
- Make sure that the 'distractor sentence' doesn't fit anywhere.

Part 7: Multiple matching

➤ See pages 64–65 for an example.

The task is to match ten statements or questions to paragraphs (a group of different paragraphs related in theme, or a single text divided into paragraphs).

This part focuses on your ability to scan texts quickly in order to find specific information, opinions, etc. related to the questions. Although the text may seem long, you do not need to read it in detail and the information required can usually be located fairly quickly.

EXPERT TASK STRATEGY

- Read the questions and mark the key words before reading the text.
- Scan each section quickly to find the information related to the questions. The information in the text will not be written in the same way as it is in the options, although it will have the same meaning.
- Highlight possible answers.
- Read the section of the text you choose again more carefully. Be careful: there may be similar ideas or information in another section.
- Leave any question you are not sure about but remember to go back to it later and choose the most likely answer.

Paper 2: Writing (1 hour 20 minutes)

There are two parts to this paper and one task in each, of between 140 and 190 words. Both parts carry equal marks.

Part 1 is compulsory, with no choice of task. You write an essay based on a title and notes.

Part 2 has a choice between three tasks. You will be asked to write an email/letter, an article, a report or a review. The instructions specify the context, the type of text, the target reader and the purpose for writing. You should read the instructions carefully as all relevant information must be included.

Assessment is based on the following criteria:
- successful completion of the task
- how appropriate the writing style is
- how well-organised the text is
- the range of language

EXPERT TASK STRATEGY (BOTH TASKS)

- Answer the question, including all relevant points.
- Consider the target reader carefully so that you use the appropriate tone and level of formality.
- Plan your writing.
- Organise your answer in a way that is appropriate to the task type (e.g. headings in a report).
- Use a wide range of vocabulary and sentence structures, including complex sentences where appropriate.
- Use discourse markers (e.g. *however*, *as well as that*) effectively.
- Try to engage the reader's interest.
- Try to keep approximately within the recommended word limit. If you write too much, you run the risk of including irrelevant information and repetition of ideas. If you write too little, you may not include all the required points.
- Leave enough time to check your answers.

Part 1: Compulsory essay

➤ See Expert writing, pages 199–200 for examples.

For Question 1, you are required to write an essay of between 140–190 words. It must be based on the title and notes given, as well as an idea of your own. The subject will be a general one, requiring no specialised knowledge. You give an opinion and provide reasons for your opinion. The number of paragraphs will probably be between three and five and include a brief introduction and conclusion.

Part 2: Choice of task

➤ See Expert writing, pages 201–205 for examples.

In Part 2, you choose one of three tasks. There is a clear context, purpose and target reader given for each task, and you must write between 140 and 190 words.

Questions 2–4

Letter or email: A letter or email is written as a response to part of a letter or email in the task. The question will identify a target reader and a purpose for writing, and the level of formality should be appropriate to the reader. The letter or email may be informal – to a friend or a colleague – or more formal, for example to a magazine editor or possible employer.

Article: This is often written for a newsletter, website or magazine and the context – usually a topic of general interest – will be clear from the question. You should write in an appropriate style and try to engage the reader's interest. There is usually some opinion or comment.

Report: You are expected to provide the reader (e.g. your boss, your teacher, a group of colleagues) with factual information in a neutral style on a given situation, outlining the aim of the report and making suggestions or recommendations so that the reader can decide on a course of action. The report should be clearly organised and may include bullet points and headings.

Review: You will usually write a review for an English-language website, magazine or newspaper, expressing a personal opinion about something which you have experienced (e.g. a film, website or holiday). The purpose of a review is to give the reader a clear idea of what it is like, describing and explaining it in an interesting way so that the reader knows whether the writer is recommending the book, film, etc., and the reasons why.

Paper 3: Listening (approx. 40 minutes)

This paper has four parts and a total of 30 questions. Each part is accompanied by recorded texts and comprehension questions and each recording is heard twice. Recordings can include two speakers (e.g. interviews and conversations) or monologues (e.g. talks and announcements). There is a mixture of shorter extracts (around 30 seconds each) and longer extracts (of around three minutes) in a variety of accents.

Part 1: Multiple choice (short extracts)

➤ See page 86 for an example.

In this part, you will hear eight short unconnected recordings of one or two people speaking in different situations, and one question for each extract. There are three options to choose from (A–C). Each extract lasts approximately 30 seconds and you hear each extract twice before you go on to the next one. In this part, the questions are recorded, as well as being in your answer booklet, so that you have time to think about the recording coming up.

Each question requires you to 'tune in' and listen out for clues so that you can understand a main idea, an agreement between speakers, an opinion, etc. (e.g. *What are the people talking about? How does the teacher feel? Who is speaking? Where are the children?*).

Part 2: Sentence completion

➤ See page 44 for an example.

This is a longer extract (approximately 3–4 minutes) with one person speaking, which may be a lecture, radio talk, etc. You are required to complete ten sentences, with a maximum of three words. This part tests detail, stated opinion and specific information. The questions are in the same order as the information on the recording and all the words you have to write are on the recording and are usually concrete nouns or noun phrases. However, the words are not in the same order as on the recording – it is not a dictation.

EXPERT TASK STRATEGY
- Before you listen, read the sentences carefully and highlight key information.
- Try and guess the information which may be missing.
- As you listen, try to complete the sentences with words you hear on the recording. You need to write 1–3 words.
- The second time you listen, fill in any information which you did not complete the first time. Don't leave a blank.

Part 3: Multiple matching

See page 58 for an example.

You will hear five short related monologues of approximately 30 seconds each. You hear all the extracts together once, before you hear them all again a second time. The task is to match each of the five extracts to one of eight statements on a list. Three of the statements are not used.

As in Part 1, this part of the paper tests your ability to listen for the general meaning, main points and detail, and to pick up clues and get information about the context, ignoring irrelevant information.

EXPERT TASK STRATEGY
- Read the sentences and highlight the key words.
- Think of possible paraphrases that you might hear.
- The first time you listen, try to identify what the speaker is talking about and choose the option which matches most closely.
- During the second listening, check that the statements match exactly what the speakers say.

Part 4: Multiple choice

See page 30 for an example.

This is a longer extract (approximately 3–4 minutes) and is an interview or a discussion between two speakers. There are seven questions and the task requires you to choose answers from three options (A, B or C).

This part requires you to identify opinion, attitude, detail, gist, specific information and main idea.

EXPERT TASK STRATEGY
- Read the questions and options before you listen and highlight the key words.
- Predict what you need to listen for.
- Listen for the ideas in the options being expressed in a different way.

Paper 4: Speaking
(approx. 14 minutes in total)

This paper is divided into four parts, each of which focuses on a different type of conversation between speakers. You are assessed on how well you speak in the whole of the speaking test, based on the following criteria:
- how accurate and appropriate your vocabulary and grammar is
- the fluency and range of your language
- whether your pronunciation can be understood
- your ability to speak for a longer period without too much hesitation
- your ability to use linking words (e.g. *next, however*) to organise your ideas
- your ability to have a conversation with other people
- how well you work with your partner or interlocutor to carry out the task

There are always two examiners present. One of the examiners (the interlocutor) explains the tasks and asks the candidates questions, while the other (the assessor) assesses the candidates and gives marks.

In Parts 1 and 2, the candidates speak mainly to the interlocutor and in Parts 3 and 4 with each other (the other candidate). You may or may not know your partner. You should speak as clearly and naturally as possible.

EXPERT TASK STRATEGY (ALL PARTS)
- Listen to the interlocutor's instructions carefully so that you know what you have to do.
- Don't be afraid to ask him/her to repeat anything if necessary.
- Use a wide range of vocabulary and structures. This is your chance to show how well you speak English.
- Avoid repeating yourself.
- Speak clearly.
- Give yourself thinking time by using expressions such as *let me think* or *I haven't given that much thought but …* However, don't overuse them.
- Paraphrase if you can't think of a word.
- In Parts 1, 3 and 4, participate fully but don't dominate – encourage your partner to speak as well.

Part 1: Conversation (approx. 2 minutes)

See pages 112–113 for an example.

The interlocutor will ask you and the other candidate personal information (for approximately two minutes). You will have to use a range of social language and verb forms in order to talk about such things as where you live, your family, what you do in your spare time and your future plans.

Part 2: Long turn (4 minutes in total)

➤ See pages 84–85 for an example.

You are each given two photos on the same topic. You have to listen to the task, which is also printed on the page with the photos.

The task has two parts: you are given a minute to compare the photos and give your personal reaction to them. The focus is on organising your ideas and expressing yourself clearly.

You also have to answer a question after your partner has spoken, so you need to look at his/her photos and listen to what he/she says, so that you can be prepared to comment. You have 30 seconds to answer.

Part 3: Collaborative task (approx. 3 minutes)

➤ See pages 28–29 for an example.

You work with your partner for three minutes to complete a task, using a spidergram which the interlocutor gives you.

The first part of the task, which takes two minutes, involves discussing ideas and giving opinions based on the question and notes on the spidergram. There is then a one-minute decision-making task. There are no right or wrong answers and it is not necessary to agree with each other.

In this part, you are tested on your ability to work together on a task: you are expected to take turns at speaking, sometimes leading the conversation, trying to involve your partner and coming to an agreement. However, how you work together on the task is more important than any decision you may come to.

For this part, you need to be able to ask for, give and react to opinions and suggestions, speculate, interrupt and start and finish a discussion.

Part 4: Discussion (approx. 4 minutes)

➤ See pages 70–71 for an example.

In this part, you will be asked questions which develop ideas related to the topic in Part 3. The discussion will open up into more general areas.

This is an opportunity to show how much language you know. Although this part of the test is led by the interlocutor, you must try and share the discussion equally; give your own opinions but also listen to and involve your partner. The interlocutor will stop you after approximately four minutes.

Cambridge English: First: Top 20 questions

1 How many marks are needed to pass the exam?

To pass the exam with a grade C, you need around 60 percent of the total marks.

2 Do I have to pass each paper in order to pass the exam?

No. The papers don't have individual pass and fail marks. The final grade (A, B, C, D or E) is arrived at by adding the weighted marks from all the papers together.

3 Are marks deducted for wrong answers?

No. If you're not sure, make a guess – you may be right.

4 Am I allowed to use a dictionary?

No.

5 In Paper 1 (Reading and Use of English), if one part has more questions, does it mean it is more important?

No. The parts are equally weighted, so that a part with fewer questions has more marks.

6 In Paper 1 (Reading and Use of English), how long should I spend on each question?

This is up to you. You can do the tasks in any order. Knowing how to use your time well is a part of the test.

7 In Paper 1 (Reading and Use of English), Parts 2, 3 and 4, if I'm not sure, can I give two alternative answers?

If there are two answers and one of them is wrong, no marks are given. So, it's better to decide which of your answers is best!

8 What happens if I misspell a word in Paper 1 (Reading and Use of English), Parts 2, 3 and 4?

All spelling must be correct in these parts.

9 In Paper 1 (Reading and Use of English), Part 4, what happens if I make a small mistake in a key word transformation?

There are 2 marks for each answer, so you could still get 1 mark even if there was a small error.

10 In Paper 1 (Reading and Use of English), Part 4, do contractions count as one word or two?

Two (e.g. *don't* = two words: *do* + *not*).

11 In Paper 2 (Writing), what happens if I don't use all the given information?

You will lose marks. The examiners are looking for both the correct information and good language. So read the question, the input text and/or the notes very carefully.

12 In Paper 2 (Writing), how should I lay out the addresses?

Don't include addresses. If you do include them, the examiners will ignore them, as this is not part of the task.

13 In Paper 2 (Writing), what happens if I write too many or too few words?

The word count is given as a guide only. Don't waste time counting; the examiners don't, they are more interested in your English! It is unlikely that answers under 140 words will contain enough information/ideas to fulfil the task. Over-long answers are more likely to contain mistakes. Plan your time so that you write about the right amount and have time to check what you have written.

14 What happens if I misspell a word in Paper 3 (Listening)?

As long as the word is recognisable, you will get a mark. Spelling is not tested in Paper 3.

15 How many times will I hear each recording in Paper 3?

Each recording is played twice.

16 In Paper 3 (Listening), Part 2, do I have to use the words in the recording or other words?

The word(s) you need to write are heard in the recording and are heard in the same order as the questions.

17 In Paper 3 (Listening), Part 2, what happens if my answer is too long to fit on the answer sheet?

Most answers are single words, numbers or groups of 2–3 words. If you think the answer is longer, then it is probably the wrong answer. If you write information which is not the answer, in addition to the answer, you will not get the mark, as you have not shown that you know exactly what the answer is.

18 In Paper 4 (Speaking), do I have to go with another student? Can I choose my partner?

You cannot be examined alone as the ability to discuss with another student is being tested in this paper. In some centres you can choose your partner, in others not. You should ask the local organiser. Don't forget that in Parts 1, 2 and 4 of the Speaking test, you talk to the examiner, not to your partner.

19 Is it a good idea to prepare what you are going to say in Part 1?

It's a good idea to practise but don't forget that the examiners give marks for natural communication in English. If you give a prepared speech which doesn't answer the examiner's question, you will lose marks.

20 What if my partner makes lots of mistakes or doesn't talk in Part 3?

Don't worry. The examiners will help if necessary. Don't forget: you are not in competition with your partner. If you can help them, this will impress the examiners. Remember that Part 3 is about interaction, so you have to ask and answer questions as well as say what you think.

Expert grammar

Module 1

1 Present situations, habits and states
(pages 10–11)

A Present situations and habits

1 We use the present simple for:
- habits:
  I clean my teeth every night.
- permanent or long-term situations:
  I come from Australia.
  They live near the sea.
- facts:
  Ice melts in the heat.

Typical time words and expressions used with the present simple include: *usually, always, never, hardly ever, as often as I can, twice a day, whenever I can.*

2 For surprising or annoying habits (things that happen very often/too often), we use the present continuous (+ *always*) or *keep* (*on*) + *-ing*:
Kate's always giving me chocolates. I don't know why!
She's always saying silly things. (It's annoying.)
She keeps (on) saying silly things.

3 We can also use *tend to* for things that usually happen:
He tends to interfere in other people's business.
Men don't tend to live/tend not to live as long as women.

4 We use *will* for:
- the typical way a person behaves:
  My brother will sit for hours just reading a book. (with a time expression e.g. *for hours*)
- stating what we think/assume is true:
  That'll be your sister on the phone. Can you answer it?

B Present events and changing situations

We use the present continuous for:
- something happening now:
  I'm watching TV at the moment.
- temporary situations:
  She's studying economics.
- changing/developing situations:
  It's getting dark.

Typical time expressions used with the present continuous include: *at present, currently, at the moment, for the time being, today.*

2 State verbs (page 11)

We use the present simple with certain verbs that describe a state rather than an action:
I like college.
That cake looks good.
I believe you.

Some examples of state verbs are verbs of
- appearing (e.g. *appear, seem, look*)
- thinking (e.g. *doubt, feel, gather, know, mean, remember, think, understand, expect*)
- feeling (e.g. *dislike, hate, love, want, wish, prefer*)
- sensing (e.g. *hear, see, smell, taste, sound*)
- owning (e.g. *belong, need, owe, own*)

Other state verbs include: *promise, agree, deny, depend, fit, mean, involve, matter*

These verbs are not normally used in the continuous, except when they describe a mental or physical action or process:
I'm thinking of you all the time. (mental action)
He's appearing in a new film. (physical action)

3 Past habits and states (page 11)

1 We can use the past simple (with a time word/expression) for past habits.
Every day I got up at 7 a.m. and went to work by bus.

2 We use *used to* + infinitive for habits/states which are no longer true:
I used to go out every Friday. (habit)
We used to live in Bridgetown. (state)

3 We can use *would* for habits (but NOT states) which are no longer true:
When I was younger, I would help my mother in the kitchen.
(BUT NOT: ~~When I was younger, I would live in Barbados.~~)

4 Comparatives and superlatives (page 17)

A Types of comparison

1 We use the comparative form or *as ... as* to compare two or more people, things, places, etc.
Chloe is a better singer than Hannah. (to a higher degree)
Harry is as good a dancer as Ryan. (to the same degree)
Amy is less confident than Katie. (to a lower degree)
Amy is not as confident as Katie. (to a lower degree)

2 We use the superlative form when we want to pick out one person, thing, place, etc. from all the others:
Ben Nevis is the highest mountain in Scotland.

B Adjectives

1 Regular adjectives:

		Comparative	Superlative
one syllable	*old*	*older* (than)	(the) *oldest*
	large	*larger* (than)	(the) *largest*
one syllable with one vowel + one consonant at the end	*big*	*bigger* (than)	(the) *biggest*
one or two syllables with -y at the end	*happy*	*happier* (than)	(the) *happiest*
two or more syllables	*careful*	*more careful* (than)	(the) *most careful*

2 Exceptions:
- One-syllable adjectives:
  *I feel **more ill** today than I did yesterday.*
  *I feel **colder/more cold** today than I did yesterday.*
  *We got more and **more lost**.* (adjectives formed from past participles)
- Some common two-syllable adjectives (e.g. *clever, gentle, simple, shallow, narrow, pleasant, cruel, polite, quiet, stupid*):
  *clever – clever**er/more** clever – clever**est/the most** clever*
- Two-syllable adjectives ending with -y:
  *He looks much **happier/more happy** these days.*
- Ungradable adjectives (e.g. *superior, unique, fundamental*) do not have a comparative form.

C Adverbs

1 We don't use *more/the most* with adverbs which have the same form as adjectives (e.g. *hard, fast, early, long, quick*):
  *fast – fast**er** – fast**est***
  *early – earl**ier** – earl**iest***
2 With most other adverbs, we use *more/(the)most*:
  ***more** carefully – the **most** carefully*
  Note:
  In informal English, you will sometimes hear -er/-est adjectives instead of the more 'correct' more/most adverbs:
  *We walked much **slower** than usual.* (instead of much more slowly)

D Irregular adjectives/adverbs

	Comparative	Superlative
good/well	*better* (than)	(the) *best*
bad/badly	*worse* (than)	(the) *worst*
much	*more* (than)	(the) *most*
little	*less* (than)	(the) *least*
far	*farther/further* (than)	(the) *farthest/furthest*
old	*elder/older* (than)	(the) *oldest/eldest*

E Sentence patterns

1 comparative + *than*:
  *The festival is more popular **than it used to be**. (than + clause)*
  *He's better at cooking **than me**. (than + object pronoun)*
  *He's better at cooking **than I am**. (than + subject pronoun + verb)*
  Note
  The *than* clause is sometimes not stated:
  The city is getting more crowded these days. (i.e. than it was before)
2 *the + superlative + in/of*:
  *The celebration is the biggest **in** Latin America.*
  *It was the hottest night **of** the year.*
  Note:
  The is not always used with the superlative form:
  Try your hardest!
  Jack and Jessica were best in the class.
3 *the + superlative + clause*:
  *It's **the** prettiest costume (**that**) **I've ever seen**.*
4 *less/(the) least* (the opposite of *more/(the) most*):
  *He's **less intelligent than** his sister. He's **the least intelligent person** (that) I know.*
  Note
  more commonly used: *He's **not as** intelligent **as** his sister.*
5 comparing quantities:
- We use *more/less* and *the most/the least* to compare quantities:
  *She spends **more/less** than her brother does.* (i.e. more/less money)
  *She earns **the most/least**.* (i.e. the most/least money)
- In formal style, *fewer/fewest* is used before plural nouns:
  *There are **more/fewer** (**of** us) here each year.* (plural countable noun)
  *I spend **more/less** (**of** my) time practising the piano.* (uncountable noun)
6 patterns:
  *In the next few years the internet will get **quicker and quicker**.* (to show an increase)
  The earlier we leave, the earlier we get there. (The two changes go together.)
  ***The better the weather, the more crowded** the roads.*
  ***The less** you earn, **the less** you have to spend.*
  The sooner, the better.

Module 2

1 Past simple, present perfect simple, present perfect continuous (pages 24–25)

A Past simple

1 Form: Regular verbs add *-ed* (e.g. *stay – stayed*), but there are many verbs with irregular forms (e.g. *see – saw, go – went*). In questions and negatives, we use *did/didn't* + infinitive.

2 We usually use the past simple with a time word/ expression (e.g. *yesterday, last night, two years ago*) to talk about:
- completed actions at a particular time in the past:
  *I **went** to Rome last Thursday.*
- completed situations over a definite period of time in the past:
  *I **worked** at a summer camp when I was younger.*
- past habits, repeated actions/situations in the past:
  *We **went** to the beach every summer.* (past habit)
- past actions which happened quickly one after the other:
  *When I **arrived**, they **turned** off the television and **started** cooking.*

B Present perfect simple

1 Form: *have* + past participle

2 The present perfect simple connects the past and the present. We use it to talk about past actions and situations:
- in a time period that is unfinished.
- that are relevant to the present. When they happened is not important.
  *I've **taught** in China. It's an amazing country.* (important experience in my life, which is unfinished; it doesn't matter when I taught there)
  Compare this with the past simple: *I **taught** in China in 2012.* (definite time in the past)
  *The doctor's **arrived**.* (He's here now.)
  *I've **worked** as a gardener for ten years.* (the ten-year period until now)

3 The uses of the present perfect simple include:
- a talking about experiences:
  *Have you ever **met** a famous person?* (at any time in your life; it doesn't matter when)
  *I've never **lived** abroad.* (= at no time)
  *He's **travelled** widely for his job.*
- b talking about things completed in the past with a result now:
  *I've **hurt** my leg. I can't walk.* (past event – we are not thinking *when* it happened, but it's relevant now)
- c talking about things recently completed (often with *just* before the main verb):
  *Look! The conference has **just started**.* (= a short time ago)

d things that have (or have not) happened up to now, often with:
- *yet*, for something we expect to happen (*Yet* comes at the end of the sentence and is used only in questions and negative sentences.)
  *Have you **sent off** the application **yet**?*
  *I **haven't sent** it off **yet**.* (NOT ~~I have sent it off yet.~~)
- *still*, for something we expected to have happened by now:
  *They **still** haven't called me.* (NOT ~~They have still called me.~~)
- *already*, to refer to the time before now. (*Already* goes before the main verb or at the end of the sentence and is used in positive sentences and questions.)
  *Have you **already met** the boss?*
  *I've **already** met him.*
- other adverbials, such as *so far, up to now* and *recently*.
  *I've **read** the first three chapters **so far**.*
  *She's **been** very quiet **up to now**.*
  *I **haven't seen** Joe **recently**.*

e unfinished actions or states which started in the past and continue now:
  *I've **lived** in this town for five years.* (NOT ~~I live in this town for …~~)
  *She's **been** a teacher since she left university.*
  Note
  Gone and *been* are both used to make the present perfect of *go*, but with different meanings:
  *He's **gone** to London.* (He's in London now – it doesn't matter when he left.)
  *He's **been** to London once in his life.* (A past experience – he isn't in London now.)

C Present perfect continuous

1 Form: *have* + *been* + *-ing*.

2 We use the present perfect continuous to talk about activities in a period of time that is unfinished. It places focus on the activity in progress, not the finished action. We use it to refer to:
- a recent temporary activity:
  *I've **been getting** work experience.*
- a recent repeated/extended activity:
  *Your colleague has **been ringing**.*
  *She's **been answering** enquiries all morning.*

3 Present perfect continuous vs present perfect simple
- The present perfect continuous focuses on the activity, which is often temporary, not on whether the activity is finished or not. The present perfect simple can be used to focus on the completion of an activity:
  *'Why are you so dirty?' 'I've **been cleaning** my room.'* (Maybe the cleaning is finished, maybe not.)
  *I've **cleaned** my room. Do you want to see it?* (The cleaning is finished.)

- With state verbs such as *be*, *know*, etc. we usually use the present perfect simple, not the present perfect continuous. (See page 182 for state verbs.)
  She's been a teacher since 2012. (NOT *She's been being ...*)

D *for* and *since*

We use *for* and *since* to answer *How long ... ?* We use:
- *for* with a period of time (*for three weeks, for a month, for four hours, for days*):
  *I've been waiting for my exam results **for** three weeks.* (NOT *during three weeks*)
- *since* with a point of time (*since 2012, since last week, since we were students*):
  *We've been living in this flat **since** last year.*

2 Articles (page 32)

A Indefinite article

We use the indefinite article (*a/an*) with singular countable nouns:
1 when we introduce something new, unfamiliar or unexpected to another person:
  *I need **a** new school uniform.*
  *It's **a** good university to go to.*
  *There's **an** old woman in the street.*
2 In descriptions and classifications (to say what kind of thing):
  *It's **a** lovely day, isn't it?* (description)
  *It's **a** big hotel.* (description)
  *What **a** nice town!* (description)
  *The play was **a** comedy.* (classification)
3 with jobs:
  *My sister is **a** doctor.*
4 to mean 'all':
  ***An** orange has a lot of vitamin C.* (= all oranges)
  (We also say: *Oranges have a lot of vitamin C.*)
5 to mean 'every', in expressions of time/quantity/speed:
  *twice **a** week*
  *two euros **a** kilo*
  Note:
  We use *one* instead of *a/an* when we want to emphasise the number. With plural or uncountable nouns, we use *some*.

B Definite article

We use the definite article (*the*) with singular or plural countable nouns and with uncountable nouns:
1 when the other person knows who or what we are referring to:
  *Where's **the** car?* (you know which car I mean)
  *Do you know **the** people at that table?* (you can see them)
  *There's a man and a woman outside. **The** woman says she's your sister.* (I have already mentioned the woman.)
2 to refer to something unique:
  ***The** earth goes round **the** sun.* (it's the only one)
3 in certain expressions:
  *He joined **the** police/**the** army/**the** navy.*

*Let's go to **the** shops/**the** cinema/**the** theatre/**the** bank.*
*She plays **the** piano/**the** violin.*
*I went to **the** airport/**the** bus station.*
4 in some general statements:
  *Who invented **the** telephone?* (inventions)
  ***The** tiger is in danger of extinction.* (species; We also say: *Tigers are in danger of extinction.*)
5 with these proper nouns:
  - oceans and seas (***the** Pacific ocean*)
  - rivers (***the** Amazon*)
  - groups of islands (***the** Bahamas*)
  - mountain ranges (***the** Alps*; BUT: not with individual mountains: *Mount Fuji*)
  - deserts (***the** Sahara*)
  - countries with plural nouns and political terms (***the** USA, **the** Netherlands, **the** Czech Republic*)
  - groups of people (***the** Germans, **the** rich*)
  - hotels/cinemas/theatres (***the** Ritz, **the** Variety Theatre*)
  - newspapers (***the** Times*)
  - political bodies (***the** government, **the** Labour Party*)

C No article

We do not use an article:
1 when we refer to something general or abstract:
  ***Houses** are getting much more expensive.*
  *He's making good **progress**.*
  *He's got a lot of **courage**.*
  *He's studying French **history**.* (BUT: ***the** history of France*)
2 before institutions, when someone is part of the institution:
  *He's at **university/school/church**.*
  *She's in **prison/hospital**.*
  *He's at **college** at 8:30.* (He's a student there – part of the college.)
  *I got to **the** college at 8:30.* (I was visiting – refers to the building.)
3 before:
  - people's names: *My name's **Eric Davies**.*
  - most countries: *He lives in **Germany**.*
  - continents: *Have you been to **Asia**?*
  - counties: *They come from **Yorkshire**.*
  - villages/towns/cities: *She works in **London**.*
  - parks: *We went for a walk in **Hyde Park**.*
  - streets: *I did some shopping in **Oxford Street**.* (BUT: ***the** High Street*)
  - languages: *I speak **French**.*
  - sports: *He plays **golf**.*
  - illnesses: *Bob's had **appendicitis**.*
  - go + -ing: *We often go **skating**.*
  - meals: *at **breakfast***
  - most expressions of time/dates/seasons: *last week, at 5.30, in June, on time, in autumn*
4 in certain expressions:
  *at home I watch **television*** (BUT: *I listen to **the** radio*)
  *go to **work/bed**, go **home***
  *go by **bus/train/car***

3 Forming adjectives (page 34)

1 Most common adjectives have no special endings.
large   rich

2 Sometimes we add a suffix to a noun or verb to form an adjective:
comfort (n.) → *comfort**able*** (adj.)
live (v.) → *live**ly*** (adj.)
Some common adjective suffixes include:
- noun → adjective: *wood**en***, *sens**ible***, *child**ish***, *fam**ous***, *music**al***
- verb → adjective: *act**ive***, *care**ful***, *help**less***, *sleep**y***

3 A number of adjectives end in *-ly* and look like adverbs:
lively   friendly   lovely   lonely   deadly

4 Some adjectives have the form of the past or present participle: (See also: page 189.)
*The children were very **excited**.*
*The news was really **exciting**.*

5 In two-part adjectives, the second part is often a participle:
well-known, beautifully dressed, time-consuming

Module 3

1 Adjectives and adverbs (pages 38–39)

- We use adjectives to identify or describe something (a noun) in more detail. Adjectives in English do not change with the noun they modify.
*a **small** town   **small** towns*
- We use adverbs to add more information about a verb, an adjective, another adverb or a clause/whole sentence.
*Go **quickly**!*
*She's **really** nice!*
*He runs **incredibly** fast.*
***Naturally**, I was very tired.*

A Gradable and ungradable adjectives

1 An adjective which is gradable can be used in the comparative and superlative forms (e.g. *cold, colder, the coldest*). We can use an adverb of degree to make it stronger (e.g. **very** *cold*) or weaker (e.g. **fairly** *cold*).

2 Ungradable adjectives are extreme (e.g. *furious, awful*) or absolute (e.g. *dead, correct*). We can use an adverb which emphasises them, but not an adverb which makes them stronger or weaker:
absolutely *furious* (NOT **very** ~~furious~~)
completely *wrong* (NOT **fairly** ~~wrong~~)
totally *exhausted* (NOT **very** ~~exhausted~~)

B Order of adjectives

Normally, no more than three adjectives go before the noun. Adjectives go in a particular order according to what type of adjective they are.

The usual order of adjectives is:
opinion/judgement + size + age + shape + colour + pattern + nationality + material (+noun):

a	**small**	**red**	**silk**	scarf
	(size)	(colour)	(material)	
a	**lovely**	**old**	**Italian**	car
	(opinion)	(age)	(nationality)	
a	**big**	**round**	**wooden**	table
	(size)	(shape)	(material)	

C Forming adverbs

1 In most cases, we add *-ly* to an adjective to form the adverb: *careful* → *careful**ly***
If an adjective ends in *-ll*, we add *-y*: *full* → *full**y***
If an adjective ends in *-y*, the *-y* changes to *-i*: *happy* → *happ**ily***
In some cases, other changes are needed:
fantastic → *fantastic**ally***
remarkable → *remarka**bly***   *true* → *tru**ly***

2 *Good* is an exception and is irregular: *good* → *well*

3 Some adjectives have *-ly* endings (e.g. *friend**ly**, live**ly**, lone**ly**, sil**ly***). We cannot add *-ly* to make these into adverbs. Instead, we use *in a ... way/manner/fashion*:
*He smiled **in a friendly way**.*

4 Some adverbs have the same form as the adjectives: *fast, hard, straight, far, early*
*He works **hard**.* (adverb)
*He's a **hard** worker.* (adjective)

5 Some adverbs have two forms with different meanings:
*I worked **hard** all morning.*
*He has **hardly** changed at all.* (almost not)
*The bus came ten minutes **late**.*
*I've been feeling ill **lately**.* (recently)

D Position of adverbs

1 We can use different types of adverbs and adverbial phrases in different positions in a sentence, but not always in every position. The most 'neutral' position for adverbs is at the end of the sentence, but they can go in front/mid position for emphasis:
***Occasionally**, he misses the bus.*
*He **occasionally** misses the bus.*
*He misses the bus **occasionally**.*
BUT NOT: ~~He misses **occasionally** the bus.~~
(between verb and object)

2 Most frequency adverbs (*always, often, never*, etc.) go before the main verb, but after the verb *be*:
*He **always walks** to work.*
*He is **always** late.*

3 Adverbial phrases of frequency (*every week, twice a year*, etc.) can't go in mid position:
***Every summer** we go there.*
*We go there **every summer**.*
BUT NOT: ~~We **every summer** go there.~~
~~We go **every summer** there.~~

E Adverbs of degree

We use adverbs of degree to make adjectives and adverbs stronger or weaker.

1 The adverbs *very* and *extremely* collocate with most gradable adjectives:
very/extremely *impressive/lively/beautiful*

2 The adverb *absolutely* collocates with most ungradable adjectives:
absolutely *wonderful/gorgeous/exhausted*

3 Other adverbs often tend to collocate with certain adjectives, although these collocations are not exclusive:
utterly *useless/delightful/miserable*
highly *skilled/educated*
totally *crazy/exhausted*
completely *different/relaxed*

4 The adverbs *quite* and *rather* can have more than one meaning, depending on the adjective/adverb they are used with.
- *quite* + adjective (= moderately, fairly)
The book was **quite** good./It was **quite** a good book.
I like him. He's **quite** nice.
(This use of *quite* is not common in American English.)
- *quite* + ungradable adjective/adverb (= completely, absolutely)
The news was **quite** extraordinary.
He was **quite** right to make a complaint.
- *rather* + negative adjective (= moderately)
He's **rather** a lazy student./He's a **rather** lazy student.
- *rather* + positive adjective (= very)
She's **rather** good at maths.

2 Verbs followed by an *-ing* form or infinitive (page 46)

I have **missed being** in the jungle. (verb + *-ing*)
I **hope to go back** soon. (verb + *to*-infinitive)
I **saw** him **leave**. (verb + bare infinitive)

A Verbs followed by an *-ing* form

admit, adore, appreciate, avoid, can't face, can't help, can't resist, can't stand, carry on, consider, delay, deny, detest, dislike, don't mind, enjoy, fancy, feel like, finish, give up, imagine, involve, keep (= continue), mention, mind, miss, postpone, practise, put off, resent, risk, suggest, understand

B Verbs followed by a *to*-infinitive

afford, agree, aim, appear, arrange, ask, attempt, can't afford, can't wait, choose, claim, decide, demand, deserve, expect, fail, guarantee, happen, help, hope, learn, manage, offer, plan, prepare, pretend, promise, refuse, seem, swear, tend, threaten, turn out, want, wish

Note:

Many verbs followed by a *to*-infinitive express a concern for the future (e.g. *arrange, expect, hope, intend, plan*).

C Verbs followed by an *-ing* form or a *to*-infinitive

1 Verbs with a small or no change in meaning:
- *begin, bother, can't bear, can't stand, continue, hate, intend, like, love, prefer, propose, start*:
I **started recording/to record** the solar eclipse. (no difference in meaning)
Don't **bother putting on/to put on** the protective glasses just yet. (no difference in meaning)
-ing sometimes suggests a general statement (and acts like a noun) and the *to*-infinitive suggests a specific action in the future:
I **prefer camping** to staying in hotels. (general preference; NOT ~~I'd prefer to camp to stay in hotels~~.)
I'**d prefer to go** by bike but you can walk. (specific occasion)

2 Verbs with a change in meaning: *forget, go on, mean, need, regret, remember, stop, try*
- I'll never **forget seeing** you looking so miserable. (= forget that I did something in the past)
Don't **forget to send** the email! (= forget that you need to do something)
- I **remember locking** the door. (= remember that I did something in the past)
Please **remember to write** to me. (= remember that you need to do something)
- He **went on talking** and talking. (= continued)
He **went on to ask** me how old I was. (= changed the activity/subject)
- Being a good photographer **means having** a lot of patience. (= involves)
Did you **mean to leave** the house unlocked? (= intend)
- I **need to have** a bath. (= I must – it's important)
This room **needs painting**. (= somebody needs to do it – passive meaning)
- I **regret spending** so much on that trip. (= I did something I wish I hadn't.)
I **regret to tell** you that you owe me some money. (= I am sorry that I have to tell you this.)
- **Stop worrying!** (= no longer do something)
She **stopped to talk** to me. (= stop something and do something else)
- **Try changing** the bulb. (= see what happens – experiment)
I **tried to phone** you last night. (= make an effort)

3 Some verbs of the senses (e.g. *see, hear, feel*):
- I **heard** her **sing** a lovely song. (I heard the whole song.)
I **heard** her **singing** a lovely song. (I heard part of it.)
- He **saw** the book **fall off** the shelf. Then he picked it up.
He **saw** the book **falling off** the shelf and caught it.

D Verbs followed by a bare infinitive

1 modal verbs:
I **might go** to the meeting, but I **can't stay** long.
Note
ought **to**:
You **ought to tell** him the truth.

2 *let* and *make*:
My boss **let me go** home early because I wasn't feeling well.
The teacher **made us do** the exercise again.
Note
The passive form of *make* is:
We **were made to** do the exercise again. (*be made* + *to*-infinitive)

3 *would rather* and *had better*:
We**'d rather stay** at home tonight.
I**'d better go** now or I'll be late.

Module 4

1 Narrative forms (page 52)

Narrative forms are used to talk about the past, often in stories and anecdotes. They include the past simple (see page 184), past continuous, past perfect simple and past perfect continuous.

For time conjunctions often used with narrative forms, see page 53.

A Past continuous

1 Form: *was/were* + *-ing*
2 We use the past continuous:
  • to talk about an action or (temporary) situation that was in progress at a particular time in the past:
    On Friday night we **were listening** to a CD.
  • to talk about a past action/situation that was interrupted by a shorter action (we use the past simple for the shorter action):
    We **were listening** to a CD when the telephone **rang**.
  • to talk about two actions that were in progress at the same time:
    We **were listening** to a CD while my brother **was reading** a book.
  • for background descriptions (e.g. to set the scene in a story):
    (We went out into the street.) It **was raining** hard and people **were carrying** umbrellas.
  • for annoying or surprising typical behaviour/past habits, with *always*:
    She **was always smoking** in the house.
  • to talk about planned events that did not happen (future in the past):
    We **were meeting** Jane the next day but she didn't come.

Note:
  • We use the past continuous to focus on the activity or its effect on us. We are not saying whether or not the action is completed. With the past simple, the action is always completed.
  • With state verbs such as *have, seem, know*, etc. we usually use the past simple, not the past continuous. (See page 182 for state verbs.)
    I **knew** him well. (NOT ~~I was knowing him well.~~)

B Past perfect simple

1 Form: *had* + past participle
2 We use the past perfect simple to talk about actions or events before a past time:
    When we got to the airport, the plane **had already left**.
  It is particularly important when stressing that one event finished before another began. However, if the order of events is clear, we often prefer the past simple:
    The plane **left** before we got there.

C Past perfect continuous

1 Form: *had* + *been* + *-ing*
2 We use the past perfect continuous for an activity over a period of time up to a specific time/event in the past:
    Before I came to London, I**'d been working** in Paris.
    They**'d been waiting** for an hour when the bus finally arrived.

Note:
  • We use the past perfect continuous to focus on the activity or its effect on us, not the completed action.
  • With state verbs such as *have, seem, know*, etc. we usually use the past perfect simple, not the past perfect continuous. (See page 182 for state verbs.)
    It **had seemed** difficult to do. (NOT ~~It had been seeming …~~)

2 Quantity (page 59)

A Countable nouns

Countable nouns can be singular or plural. They refer to things we can count (e.g. *one car, two cars*). We can use *a/an* with singular countable nouns:
  I took **an** umbrella and **a** coat with me.

B Uncountable nouns

  • Uncountable nouns have no plural. They refer to things we cannot count, such as liquids (e.g. *water, milk*), materials (e.g. *wool, metal*) or abstract qualities (e.g. *progress, behaviour*). We use *some/any* with uncountable nouns, not *a/an*:
    some/any progress (NOT ~~a progress/two progresses~~)
  • Examples of some common uncountable nouns are: *accommodation, advice, behaviour, bread, butter, electricity, food, fun, furniture, health, information, knowledge, luggage, money, music, news, research, salt, scenery, spaghetti, traffic, travel, trouble, weather, work*

C Countable and uncountable nouns

1 Some nouns can be either countable or uncountable:

Countable	Uncountable
a chicken (the animal)	*some chicken* (the meat)
a chocolate (a sweet or a drink)	*chocolate* (the substance)
two coffees (two cups of coffee)	*some coffee* (the substance)
a glass (of milk)	*glass* (the substance)
a hair (a single hair)	*my hair* (the hair on my head)
I've seen the film many times. (occasions)	*I don't have much time.*
a good cheese (a variety of cheese)	*I like cheese.* (in general)
a paper (a newspaper)	*Have you got any paper?* (the material)
The house has eight rooms.	*There isn't much room.* (it's crowded)
a (parking) space	*There's no space for the armchair.*
He's got two businesses.	*do business* (buy and sell)

2 We can 'count' some uncountable nouns by using a countable expression:
a piece/bit of bread/news/information/advice
a drop of water/milk
a slice of bread/toast/cake
an item of news

3 Determiners (page 59)

For examples of determiners that go with countable and uncountable nouns, see page 59. Note that:
- Some determiners go with countable nouns (e.g. *many*), some with uncountable (e.g. *much*) and some can go with both (e.g. *a lot of*).
*There weren't **many people** at the party.*
*We haven't got **much time**.*
***A lot of people** brought presents.*
*He spends **a lot of time** in his studio.*
- there is a difference in meaning between *few/little* and *a few/a little*:
*There are **a few** people.* (= some)
*There are **few** people.* (= not many/hardly any)
*There's **a little** time.* (= some)
*There's **little** time.* (= not much/hardly any)

4 *-ing* and *-ed* adjectives (page 62)

1 *-ed* (past participle) adjectives describe our reaction to something/someone:
*I was very **bored** with/by the play.*
2 *-ing* (present participle) adjectives describe the thing/person/event/experience that causes the reaction:
*The play was very **boring**.*

3 Other common pairs of participle adjectives include: *amused/amusing, annoyed/annoying, depressed/depressing, disappointed/disappointing, excited/exciting, interested/interesting, terrified/terrifying, tired/tiring*

Module 5

The future (pages 66–67)

A Future forms

A variety of forms can be used to talk about the future:
- *be going to* + infinitive
- present continuous
- *will/shall* + infinitive
- present simple
- *be to* + infinitive
- *be due to/be about to* + infinitive
- *be on the point of* + *-ing*
- future continuous (*will/shall/going to + be + -ing*)
- future perfect (*will/going to + have +* past participle)
- future perfect continuous (*will + have + been + -ing*)

B Future meanings

1 Planned events
- We use *be going to* for intentions, things we've already decided:
I'm going to read the new book by Steve Jones. I bought a copy last week.
- We use the present continuous (+ a time word/expression) for arrangements:
I'm taking my driving test tomorrow. I applied a few weeks ago.
- We use the future continuous for a planned/routine action without personal intention:
***Will** you **be going to** the psychology lecture tomorrow? If so, could you lend me your notes?*
2 Fixed events
- We use the present simple (+ a time word/expression) for timetables and programmes:
*The bus **leaves** in half an hour.*
*My French classes **finish** next week.*
- We use *be to* + infinitive for formal official arrangements:
*The Queen **is to** visit Australia next year.*
3 Unplanned events
We use *will/shall* for events decided more or less at the moment of speaking (e.g. offers, promises, requests, refusals, decisions):
*I **won't lend** her any money. She never pays it back.* (decision)
*It's cold in here. **Will you** close the door?* (request)
*That looks heavy. **Shall I help** you?/I'll help you.* (offer)
*I **won't tell** anyone, don't worry.* (promise)

4 Predictions
- We use *be going to* when we notice something in the present which will make something happen:
  I feel ill. I think I'm going to be sick.
  It's very cloudy. I'm sure it's going to rain.
- We use *will* when we expect something to happen – it is our opinion based on experience/knowledge:
  Computers will be/won't be as intelligent as humans any time soon.
  The sun will rise at 6.30 a.m. tomorrow.
  To show how certain we are, we often use *will* with phrases like *I expect, I'm sure, I think, I don't think*, etc. We also often use these phrases with modal verbs to refer to the future.
  I'm sure he'll help you if you ask him.
  We may/might/could be there before midnight.

5 For events close to happening, we can use *be about to + infinitive* or *be on the point of + -ing*:
  The Russians are about to launch a new spacecraft.
  They're on the point of launching a new spacecraft.
  We can use *be due to + infinitive* for planned events:
  The bus is due to arrive at nine o'clock tomorrow.

6 We use the future continuous for actions in progress at a certain time in the future:
  We'll be flying around in cars when you grow up!

7 We use the future perfect for something completed before a specific time in the future:
  We'll have finished before you get back. (OR *We may have finished* … if we are less certain.)

8 We use the future perfect continuous for something that may not be completed/may be ongoing at a specific time in the future:
  I'll have been learning English for five years by the time I take the exam.

9 Future in the past
  Sometimes when we are talking about the past, we want to refer to something that was in the future at that point in the past. We use the same structures that we use for talking about the future, but change the verb forms:
  I was going to come but I changed my mind.
  We arrived at the building where the interview was to take place.

10 In time clauses with a future meaning, we use the present simple:
  When you see Tom, give him a big kiss for me. (time clause)

Module 6

1   Relative clauses (pages 80–81)

A   Relative pronouns

Relative clauses provide additional information about a noun, a clause or a sentence. They begin with a relative pronoun.

Relative pronoun(s)	Used to refer to …
who, whom	people
which	things, animals
that	people, things, animals
when	time
where (which + preposition)	place
whose	possession

B   Defining relative clauses

1 Defining relative clauses (without commas) provide essential information:
  The man who/that witnessed the accident is over there. (people)
  That's the car which/that won the race. (things)
  It was the moment when I knew for sure. (time)
  He's the man whose drum kit is for sale. (possession)
  That's the house where William Shakespeare lived. (place)

2 We usually place a preposition at the end of a relative clause:
  That's the house which I used to live in. (place)
  But we place a preposition before the relative pronoun in more formal English:
  The delivery date for your smartphone will depend on the postcode area in which you live.
  We also place a preposition before the relative pronoun when the relative clause is very long, or to be more formal:
  This is the email in which he said he was looking forward to coming home.
  The meeting to which you are invited starts at 9 a.m.

3 The relative pronoun can be left out if it is the object of the verb in the relative clause:
  The concert (which/that) we went to was three hours long.

4 Reduced relative clauses: participle clauses (see page 81) and infinitives can sometimes replace relative clauses, especially in informal contexts.
  People buying this CD will be disappointed. (= who buy)
  The car parked outside belongs to Tara. (= which is parked)
  The last person to leave the studio should switch the lights off. (= who leaves)

C Non-defining relative clauses

1 Non-defining relative clauses are more common in written English than spoken English. They provide extra information (between commas) not essential to the sentence. The sentence would make sense without the clause:
*My mother, **who lives in Scotland**, is 94.*
*She was ill, **which was very unusual for her**.* (Here, *which* refers to the whole main clause, not just the subject.)

2 Note the pattern after numbers and words like *some, many, most, neither*:
*There were a lot of people in the house, **some of whom** I'd met before.*
*I did German and Italian at university, **neither of which** I had learnt before.*

3 *That* is not used in non-defining clauses and object pronouns cannot be omitted:
*This book, **which** my father gave me, is over 50 years old.*
(NOT ~~This book, **that** my father gave me, ...~~)

2 Adjective/Noun + preposition (page 88)

Adjective + preposition

addicted to, afraid of, amazed at/by, annoyed with, aware of, bad at, capable of, crazy about, delighted with/about, dependent on, different from, familiar with, famous for, fed up with, full of, good at, guilty of, interested in, jealous of, keen on, kind to, late for, married to, proud of, ready for, related to, responsible for, satisfied with, similar to, surprised at/by, terrified of, tired of, worried about

Noun + preposition

advertisement for, advice on/about, answer to, apology for, appointment with, attitude to, cause of, change in, collection of, comment on, congratulations on, cure for, danger of, decrease in, delay in, demand for, dependence on, difference between, difficulty in/with, effect on, escape from, example of, excuse for, help with, hope for, increase in, influence on, interest in, introduction to, lack of, need for, objection to, opportunity for, payment for, preference for, preparation for, protection from, punishment for, reaction to, reason for, reference to, reply to, respect for, search for, success in/at, worry about

Module 7

Modals (pages 94–95)

Modals express our attitudes and emotions to an event or situation. The modal auxiliary verbs are: *can, could, may, might, must, will, would, shall, should, ought to* and *need to*. There are other non-modal verbs and expressions (e.g. *be able to, have to, allow*) which we can sometimes use instead of modal verbs.

A Form

Present time			
		modal +	infinitive
You		can	go.

Past time				
		modal +	have +	past participle
You		could	have	gone.

Note:
- *he/she/it can go* (There is no change in the third person.)
- Modal verbs have no infinitive form.

B Permission

1 We use *can, could* and *may* to talk about permission:
- *can*:
Can we sit by the window? Is that all right? (asking for permission)
You **can** use my computer – that's OK. (giving permission)
- *could*:
Could we move to the other table? (asking for permission; more polite than *can we … ?*)
She said that I **could** go to the party. (reporting permission)
- *may*:
May I leave class early today? I've got a job interview. (asking for permission – for more formal situations)

2 We can use other non-modal verbs and expressions to talk about permission:
- *let* + object + infinitive
My parents **let** me **eat** whatever I want.
Note:
let does not have a passive form. We use *be allowed to* instead.
- *allow to/be allowed to* + infinitive
The organisers **allow** you to go backstage afterwards. (allow + object + *to*-infinitive)
I **was allowed** to leave class early today. (passive + *to*-infinitive)
Note:
In a sentence like this, where the permission resulted in an action, we can't use *could*.
(NOT ~~I could leave class early today.~~)
- *permit/be permitted to* + infinitive
You **are permitted** to smoke only in the designated areas. (formal)
Smoking **is permitted** only in the designated areas. (rules made by someone else – more formal than *allow*)

C Prohibition

1 We use *can't, couldn't, mustn't* and *may not* to talk about prohibition:

- *can't*:
  He **can't** go to a nightclub. He's too young. (prohibition)
- *couldn't* (past form of *can*):
  He said I **couldn't** use it. (he refused permission)
- *mustn't*:
  You **mustn't** eat in the library. Please be quiet! (direct order)
  Note: the past form of this sentence is:
  We **weren't allowed to** eat in the library.
- *may not*:
  Candidates **may not** leave the room during the exam. (prohibition)

2 We can use other non-modal expressions to talk about prohibition and rules that are made by someone else:

- *be + not supposed to* + infinitive (informal)
  You're **not supposed to** park here.
- *allow to/be allowed to* + infinitive
  My manager **won't allow me to take** the day off.
  You're **not allowed to take** photographs here.
- *permit to/be permitted to* + infinitive
  You **are not permitted to smoke** in here.
  Smoking **is not permitted** here. (more formal than *allow*)
- *forbid/ban*
  Cars are **forbidden/banned** in the town centre. (prohibition – very strong)
  Note: *Forbid* is more likely to be used in formal notices than when speaking.

D Obligation and necessity

1 We use *must/mustn't* to express strong obligation or necessity:

- *must* (stronger than *should/had better*):
  I **must** get the tickets straightaway. (I, personally, feel it is necessary.)
  Note: For the future of *must*, we use *will/'ll have to*. For the past, we use *had to*:
  I'**ll have to** hurry or I'll miss the last train.
  She **had to** go home because she felt ill.
- *mustn't* (stronger than *shouldn't*):
  You **mustn't** forget your keys. (an obligation NOT to do something)

2 We can use other non-modal verbs and expressions to talk about strong obligation and necessity:

- We use *have (got) to* when the situation or someone else (not the speaker) makes something necessary:
  I **have to** work late tonight. My boss says so.
  We'll **have to** invite my mother next time. (The situation makes it necessary.)
  I **had to** go to the doctor's yesterday. (past time – it was necessary)

- We use *make* for a strong obligation imposed by someone else:
  Her parents **make** her wash the dishes. (*make +* object + infinitive)
  She **is made to** wash the dishes. (passive + *to*-infinitive)

3 We use *should/shouldn't* and *ought to/ought not to* to express a slightly less strong obligation or a duty/responsibility:
  You **should/ought to** phone and let them know you'll be late.
  They **shouldn't** leave without permission.

4 *Should have/ought to have* is used when something was the right thing to do, but you didn't do it:
  You **should have/ought to have** gone to bed early last night. You look tired. (You didn't go to bed early.)
  Note: *Shouldn't have* is commonly used, but *ought not to have* is rare.

5 *Be supposed to* is a non-modal expression we use to talk about our responsibilities and the correct way of doing things:
  What time **are we supposed to** be at the office?

E Lack of obligation/necessity

1 We use *don't have to/haven't got to, needn't/don't need to, needn't have* and *didn't need to* to express lack of obligation or necessity:

- *don't have to/haven't got to*
  You **don't have to** wash those shirts. They're clean. (It's not necessary.)
  Note: *Have got to* is more informal than *have to*.
  We use *didn't have to* as the past form of both *don't have to* and *haven't got to*:
  I **didn't have to** go to the doctor's yesterday. (It wasn't necessary.)
- *needn't/don't need to*
  You **needn't/don't need to** wash those shirts. They're clean. (It's not necessary.)
  Note: *need* can be a modal verb (negative = *needn't*) or an ordinary verb (negative = *don't need*).

2 We use both *needn't have* (modal verb) and *didn't need to* (ordinary verb) when we talk about past time, but they have different meanings:
  There were plenty of seats on the train. We **didn't need to stand**. (It wasn't necessary.)
  There were plenty of seats on the train. We **needn't have stood**. (It wasn't necessary, but we did stand.)

F Advice and recommendations

1 We use *should(n't)/should have, ought to/ought to have* to give advice and make recommendations. (*Ought to* is less common than *should*.)
  You **shouldn't/ought not to** go to work today – you really don't look well. (advice)
  You **should** see it – it's a great film. (recommendation)

Note: The past forms (*should have/shouldn't have*) suggest criticism:
*You **should have** told me you weren't coming. I waited for ages!*
*He **shouldn't have** shouted at her.*

2 The non-modal expression *had better (not)* is stronger than *should/shouldn't*:
*It's cold. You**'d better** wear a coat.* (It's the best thing to do.)
*Hurry up! We**'d better not** be late.*

For modals of speculation and deduction, see page 101.
For modals of ability, see page 116.

Module 8

Reported speech (pages 108–109)

'I want to give you something,' he said. (direct speech)
*He **said** (that) he **wanted** to give me something.* (reported speech)

A   Reported statements

1 To report something said in the past, we normally change forms one step back in time. This is sometimes called 'backshift':

Direct speech	Reported speech
Present	
*'I **don't like** you.'*	*She said she **didn't like** me.*
*'We**'re leaving**.'*	*They said they **were leaving**.*
*'I**'ve** never **been** to China.'*	*He said he **had** never **been** to China.*
*'I**'ve been working** out.'*	*He said he **had been working** out.*
Past	
*'I **saw** him.'*	*He said he **had seen** him.*
*'I **was having** lunch.'*	*He said he**'d been having** lunch.*
Future	
*'I**'ll help** you.'*	*She said she **would help** me.*
*'We**'re going** out.'*	*They said they **were going** out.*
Some modals	
*'I **can't** read it.'*	*He said he **couldn't** read it.*
*'We **must** go.'*	*They said they **had to** go.*
*'I **may** be late.'*	*She said she **might** be late.*
*'You **needn't** call him.'*	*He said I **needn't**/**didn't need to** call him.*

2 No backshift is needed with:
- the past perfect simple and continuous:
  *'I **had seen** him.'* → *He said he **had seen** him.*
  'They'd been working since noon.' → *He said they**'d been working** since noon.*
- the modals *would, should, might, could, ought to* and *mustn't*:
  *We **might** go out for meal.* → *They said they **might** go out for a meal.*

3 Sometimes backshift is needed with other forms, depending on the context. Compare:
*He **said** he **wanted** to give me something.* (reporting the past)
*He **said** he **wants** to give me something.* (We are emphasising it is still true.)
*He **said** he **had wanted** to give me something.* (to emphasise one thing happened before the other)
*He **had said** he **had wanted** to give me something but he changed his mind.* (*said/wanted* happened before *changed his mind*)

4 Some changes in common time and place words are:

Direct speech	Reported speech
today	*that day*
tomorrow	*the next day/the following day*
next (week)	*the following (week)*
yesterday	*the day before/the previous day*
last (year)	*the (year) before/the previous (year)*
a (month) ago	*a (month) before*
this	*that*
here	*there*
come	*go*
bring	*take*

B   Reported questions

- To report questions, we use a reporting verb (e.g. *ask, want to know, wonder*) and the same word order as in statements:
  'Do you like science fiction films?' → *He asked if **I liked** science fiction films.*
- For *yes/no* questions, we use *if* or *whether*:
  'Are you coming with us?' → *He asked **if** I was going with them.*
  'Do you want tea or coffee?' → *She asked me **whether** I wanted tea or coffee.*
- For *wh-* questions, we use the *wh-* question word:
  'When is she leaving?' → *He wanted to know **when** she was leaving.*
- In questions with modals, only *can* and *may* change:
  *'**Can** you tell me the way?'* → *She asked if I **could** tell her the way.*

*'**Could** you tell me the way?' → She asked if I **could** tell her the way.*
*'**May** I interrupt for a moment?' → I asked if I **might** interrupt for a moment.*

C Reported requests/commands

- To report requests and commands, we use the reporting verbs *ask/tell* + object + *to*-infinitive:
*'Come here, please!' → He **asked me to go** there.*
- For negative requests and commands, we use *ask/tell* + object + *not* + *to*-infinitive:
*'Please don't speak so quickly.' → He **told/asked me not to speak** so quickly.*

D Reporting verbs

1 Some reporting verbs simply report the speaker's words (e.g. *say, tell, state, answer, reply*). Other reporting verbs tell us something about the speaker's intention. The choice of verb sometimes depends on how we interpret what the person was saying:
*He **persuaded** me that he wanted to give me something.*
Some common reporting verbs include: *admit, advise, claim, convince, feel, insist, persuade, suggest, think, urge, warn.*

2 Different reporting verbs have different patterns:
- verb + *to*-infinitive (e.g. *agree, ask, offer, promise, refuse, threaten*):
*He **refused to see** her.*
- verb + object + *to*-infinitive (e.g. *tell, advise, ask, invite, order, persuade, remind*)
*I **told her** to come.* (NOT ~~I told to her to come.~~)
- verb + *-ing* (e.g. *admit, deny, report, suggest, recommend*)
*He **denied having been** there.*
*They **suggested trying** the new Chinese restaurant.*
- verb + object + *that* (e.g. *tell, advise, convince, persuade, promise, remind*):
*They **told me that** I should come back later.*
(NOT ~~They told to me that ...~~)
- verb + object + preposition + *-ing:* (e.g. *congratulate on, accuse of, blame for, discourage from*):
*They congratulated **him on passing** the exam.*
*He accused **her of cheating**.*
*They blamed **us for breaking** the window.*
*She discouraged **me from going** to the concert.*
Note:
- *apologise **to** + object + **for** + -ing: I **apologised to her for being** late.*
- *insist **on** + -ing:*
*We **insisted on seeing** the manager.*
- verb (+ preposition + object) + *that* (e.g. *say, admit, complain, explain, mention, suggest*). With these verbs the hearer is not the direct object:
*Ann **said** (to him) **that** she felt tired.* (NOT ~~Ann said him that ...~~)

Module 9

Conditionals (pages 122–123)

We can categorise conditionals into three main groups:
- likely or real events/situations:
If you're the last to leave the office, can you please turn out the light?
- unlikely (or imaginary) events/situations:
If I had four million euros, I'd give some of it to charity.
- unreal events/situations in the past:
If we'd saved more money, we would have bought a bigger house.
Note:
The main clause can come before the *if* clause in conditional sentences, but the punctuation is different:
If it rains, we won't have a picnic. (A comma comes after the *if* clause.)
We won't have a picnic if it rains. (There is no comma between the clauses.)

A Zero and first conditionals (likely or real)

1 We use the zero conditional for facts that are always true. We use it when both events happen. In zero conditional sentences, *if* means *when*:
- present simple + present simple:
*If/When you **press** this switch, the laptop **comes** on.* (always true; normal event/fact)
- past simple + past simple:
*If/When the weather **was** bad, we always **stayed** indoors.* (past habit)
2 We use the first conditional for events/situations that are likely to happen. We use:
- present simple + modal (with present/future meaning)
If there's an earlier train, I'll catch it. (possible/likely situation + result)

If you **need** a ticket,	I **can** book you one. (offer)
	I'**ll** get you one. (promise)
	I **might** be able to get you one. (possibility)

- present simple + *going to*
*If there's a good clothes sale on, I'm definitely **going to buy** a new coat.*
- present simple + imperative
*If the phone **rings**, please **answer** it.* (instruction – for a possible event)
We can use other conjunctions to introduce conditions (e.g. *as long as, provided that, even if, unless*):
*I'm going to leave **unless** you turn that music down!* (= if you don't)
*She won't go **even if** she's invited.* (= whether or not)
*I'll cook dinner **as long as** you do the washing-up.* (= only if)

Note:

If we are sure something will happen, we use *when*:

When I leave college, I'm going to become a teacher.
(NOT *If I leave ...*)

3 There are other possible patterns for situations/events which are likely or possible:

- modal + modal/imperative:
  If you**'ll** just **wait** a moment, **I'll see** what I can do. (request)
  If you **should get** lost, **go** into the Tourist Office. (less likely, but possible)
  If it**'ll help** you to sleep, **open** the window. (result)
- present continuous + modal/imperative:
  If you**'re expecting** someone, I **can** leave.
- present perfect + modal/imperative:
  If you**'ve finished** your work, we **can** go.

B Second conditional (unlikely or imaginary)

1 We use the second conditional for unlikely or imaginary events/situations in the present or future. We use past + *would/could/might* + infinitive:

If you **went** abroad, you **might learn** something about foreign cultures. (unlikely that you will go, but possible)
If you **were driving** to London, which way **would you go**? (imaginary – you're not driving)
If he **didn't have** a car, he**'d find** it difficult to get to work. (imaginary – he has a car)

2 Both *was* and *were* can be used with *If I/he/she/it ...* :

If I **were** rich, I wouldn't work.
If I **was** rich, I wouldn't work. (not normally used in formal English)

3 *Were* can start the sentence and replace *if* in formal English:

Were you really ill, I'd look after you, but you're perfectly OK.

4 We sometimes use *should* instead of *would* after *I* and *we* in more formal contexts (e.g. formal emails and letters):

I **should** be grateful if you would contact me ...

5 We can use the second conditional for offers, suggestions, advice and requests:

I **wouldn't do** it if I **were** you. (advice)
Would you **mind** if I **used** your phone? (request)

Note:

- An offer can be made more or less direct, depending on the type of conditional used:
  If you **need** the key, I **can** probably find it. (first conditional: direct)
  If you **needed** the key, I **could** probably find it. (second conditional: less direct; I'm less sure you need the key.)
  If you **were to need** the key, I **could** probably find it. (second conditional: even more tentative, polite)

- We can also make polite requests using *If you would ...* :
  If you would take your seats, ladies and gentlemen, **we'll start** the meeting.

C Third conditional (unreal or imaginary)

We use the third conditional for unreal or imaginary events/situations in the past, often to express regret or criticism. We use:

- past perfect + *would/could/might* + *have* + past participle:
  If I **had heard** the alarm, I **would have woken up** on time. (But I didn't hear it, so I overslept.)
  I **would have helped** her if she **had asked** me. (But she didn't, so I didn't help her.)
- *had* at the start of the sentence can replace *if* (formal):
  Had you been ill, I **would** have looked after you.

D Mixed conditionals

It is possible to mix the second and third conditionals, particularly when a past event has an effect in the present:

I **would be** married now if I**'d had** the courage to propose to her.

If you **were** more intelligent, you **would have thought** about that before.

Module 10

1 The passive (pages 136–137)

- In passive sentences, the action, event or process is more important/has more emphasis than who or what does the action:
  Breakfast **is served** in the garden.
- If we want to mention the person doing the action (the agent), we use *by*:
  I was robbed last night **by** a man in a dark jacket.

A Form

	subject +	be +	past participle
Present simple	It	is	made in Taiwan.
Present continuous		is being	
Past simple		was	
Past continuous		was being	
Present perfect		has been	
Past perfect		had been	
be going to		is going to be	
will		will be	
Future perfect		will have been	
Present/future modal		may be	
Past modal		must have been	

- Positive sentences: *It **was made** in Taiwan.*
- Negative sentences: *It **wasn't made** in Europe.*
- Questions: ***Was** it **made** in Taiwan?*

Note:

Verbs that do not take an object (e.g. *arrive*) do not have a passive form. (NOT *She was arrived*.)

B Sentence structure

1 In an active sentence, the subject is the person/thing that does the action. In a passive sentence, the subject is the person/thing to whom/which something happens:

Active	subject +	active verb +	object
	Alice Munro	*won*	*the prize.*
Passive	subject +	passive verb +	agent
	The prize	*was won*	*by Alice Munro.*

2 In a sentence with two objects, there are two possible sentence structures, but we usually make the person the subject of the passive sentence:

Active

subject	active verb	ind ob +	dir ob
He	*gave*	*Sue*	*a CD.*

Passive

Sue was given a CD. (more common)

A CD was given to Sue. (possible, but less likely)

3 We can use the passive with reporting verbs such as *say, expect, suppose, agree, know, think, understand, claim,* to talk about an opinion held by some people/a lot of people/experts, etc. The following patterns can be used:

- subject + passive + *to*-infinitive

Our team	*was expected*	*to do well.*
It	*is supposed*	*to be a fine day tomorrow.*

- *it* + passive + *that*

It	*has been agreed*	*that we have to make improvements.*

4 Some verbs (*see, hear, make, help, know*) are followed by an infinitive (without *to*) when they are active, but a *to*-infinitive when passive:

*They **heard** him **shout**. → He **was heard to shout.***

C Use

1 The passive is more often used in written language (e.g. newspapers, reports, scientific writing, notices and announcements). It can often sound formal and impersonal:

*Customers **are requested** not to leave their bags unattended.*

2 The passive can be used to take personal responsibility away from the speaker:

*Income tax **will be increased** next year.*

3 We sometimes use the passive to continue the theme of what is being talked about. In the following sentence, the new information – *Beethoven* – is put at the end for emphasis:

*This is a marvellous symphony. It **was written** by Beethoven.*

4 In informal English we can sometimes use *get* + past participle with a passive meaning, for things that happen by accident or unexpectedly:

*The postman **got bitten** by a dog.* (= was bitten)

*How **did** your car **get damaged**?* (= who/what was it damaged by?)

2 Hypothetical situations (page 143)

A Present situations

1 We use *wish/if only* + past simple (or past continuous) when we are unhappy with a present situation and want it to be different:

*I **wish** I **was** a bit slimmer.* (OR *I wish I **were** a bit slimmer.*)

*I **wish** we **weren't sitting** in a classroom right now.*

*If only I **could** swim.* (but I can't)

2 We use *wish/if only* + other person/thing + *would* when we are annoyed with something:

*I **wish** you **would stop** biting your nails!*

*I **wish** it **would** stop raining!*

B Future situations (imaginary or unreal)

We use *wish/if only* + *could* when we wish for a change in the future that will probably not happen:

*I **wish** I **could** see her.* (I want it to happen, but it probably won't.)

Note

We can use *hope* + present simple to refer to future situations:

*I **hope** I **pass** my driving test.* (This future event IS possible.)

C Past situations (regret)

We use *wish/if only* + past perfect when we are sorry about a past situation, but it is impossible to change it now:

*I **wish** I **had worked** harder at school.* (but I didn't)

*I **wish** we **had taken** a different route.* (but we didn't)

Note

If only is used to express a strong wish that things could be different – it is more emphatic than *wish*:

*If only we **knew** the truth.*

*If only I **could** sing.*

*If only you **would** keep your room tidy.*

*If only we **had managed** to get tickets for the show.*

Module 11

Clauses of reason, purpose and contrast
(pages 150–151)

A   Identifying clauses in sentences
1   A clause has a subject and a verb, and it: either
   - forms a sentence:
     I was walking home …
   - or part of a sentence:
     … when I met Pete.
2   There are many ways of joining clauses in sentences, e.g.
   - with words like *who, which*, etc. (See Relative clauses, page 190.)
     She was talking to a man who looked like Brad Pitt.
   - with *if* (See Conditionals, page 194.)
     I'll let you know if I hear from her.
   - with *than* (See Comparatives and superlatives, page 182.)
     I feel much better than I did yesterday.
   - with time conjunctions like *when, while,* etc.
     (See Time conjunctions, page 53.)
     She was on her way to work when I saw her.

B   Clauses of reason
*He couldn't see **because** he wasn't wearing his glasses.*

Other connecting words/expressions include:
   - *because of, for, owing to, due to* (+ noun)
     *She couldn't concentrate **because of** the noise.*
   - *as, since* (+ subject + verb)
     ***As** she was out, I left her a message.*
   - *seeing that, owing to the fact that, due to the fact that* (+ subject + verb)
     ***Owing to the fact that** their flight was late, they missed the meeting.*

C   Clauses of purpose
*I exercised regularly **to** keep fit.*

Other connecting words/expressions include:
   - *in order to, so as to* (+ infinitive)
     *We left early **in order to** catch the first train.*
   - *in order that, so that, for fear that, in case* (+ subject + verb)
     *We left early **so that** we could catch the first train.*

D   Clauses of contrast
*I went to work **despite/in spite of** the fact that I felt very tired.*

Other connecting words/expressions include:
   - *in spite of, despite* (+ noun/present participle/perfect participle):
     *She fell asleep, **in spite of** the cold.*
     *He stayed awake, **despite** being tired.*
   - *although, though, even though, even if, much as, whereas, while, however, no matter how (much/many/badly), in spite of the fact that* (+ subject + verb)

Although it was cold, she fell asleep.
*He was tired. **However**, he stayed awake.*
Note:
While and *whereas* contrast ideas that don't contradict each other:
*Nurses' salaries have risen **while/whereas** doctors' salaries have fallen.*

Module 12

Connecting ideas; Participle clauses
(pages 164–165)

In participle clauses, the subject of the participle must be the same as the subject of the main clause.
Being a French teacher (= me), I speak French very well.
1   Present participles:
   *I stayed awake all night, **thinking** about the book I'd read. (= and thought)*
   ***After phoning** you, I realised my mistake. (time: = After I phoned)*
   ***In/On trying** to open the door, I broke my key. (time: = While I was trying)*
   ***Being** a pilot, I knew how to fly the plane. (reason: = As I was a pilot)*
   ***Having** a pilot's licence, I knew how to fly the plane. (reason: = As I had)*
   *I wrote **telling** her the news. (purpose: = in order to tell her)*
   ***Despite not feeling** well, I went into work (contrast: = Despite the fact that I didn't feel well)*
   *The man **living** next door is an old friend of mine. (relative: = who lives)*
2   Perfect participles:
   ***Having done** most of the course, I want to finish it. (reason: = Since I've done – active)*
   ***Having been given** a pay rise, I decided to celebrate. (time: = After I had been given – passive)*
3   Past participles:
   Past participles are used for passives and are found more in writing than conversation:
   ***Seen** from this distance, it looks quite attractive. (= When it is seen)*
   ***Although built** fairly recently, it looks quite old. (= Although it was built)*
   *Cars **made** in Japan are very common in Europe. (= which are made)*

Expert writing

Contents

Introduction

The Expert writing section aims to help you with your writing in preparation for Paper 2 of the *Cambridge English: First* exam.

First, there is a checklist, for you to use every time you complete a piece of writing.

Then, for each type of writing that might come up in the exam, there is an example question (Task), a model answer to that question, with notes to help you, and another exam question (Further practice) for extra practice.

If you are working on your own, read the task and the model answer carefully. Refer back to the pages in the main modules for more information and help. Then do the task in 'Further practice', following the guidelines here and in the main modules.

If you are working with a teacher, he/she will tell you when and how to use the Expert writing section.

Writing checklist

Content and style

- Is your answer the right length? If you write less than 140 words, you probably haven't answered the whole question; if you write more than 190, the examiner may not read it and it will be a waste of valuable time.
- Have you answered all parts of the question? You will lose marks if you don't include all the required information.
- Have you explained your points clearly?
- Do you think your reader will be happy with your answer (e.g. If it's an article, is it interesting to read?)?
- Is your style appropriate (e.g. Does the context require you to be formal or informal? If it's an article, is it lively?)?

- Is your style consistent (e.g. no very informal words in a formal letter)?
- Will your writing have the effect you want on your reader?

Organisation

- Have you divided your answer into paragraphs?
- Does each paragraph have one main idea? (A related idea in the same paragraph is possible if the connection is close.)
- Are the paragraphs in a logical order?
- Is there a supporting sentence (possibly an example) for the opening sentence of the paragraphs? (This is not always necessary in an introduction or conclusion, or a section of a report.)
- Have you used linking expressions to connect ideas between paragraphs (e.g. *however, on the other hand*)?
- Would headings and sub-headings be appropriate (e.g. in a report)?

Language

- Have you included a range of grammatical structures (e.g. in an essay: present simple, modals, conditionals)?
- Is there a good range of vocabulary (e.g. in an article, adverbs: *life changed dramatically*; in a review, adjectives: *powerful performance*)?
- In a review, have you used the language of personal opinion (e.g. *I thought the best thing about it was … , …. was rather disappointing*)?
- Is your vocabulary specific, not general (e.g. *an enjoyable meal* not *a good meal*)?
- Have you used a range of appropriate linking expressions (e.g. *but, so, after, because* within a sentence, and *finally, what's more* to connect ideas in two sentences)?
- Have you used time expressions appropriately (e.g. *when, after, as soon as*)?
- Have you used appropriate opening and closing phrases in an email or letter (e.g. opening an informal email: *Good to see you again the other night*; closing a formal letter: *I look forward to hearing from you.*)
- Is your handwriting easy to read?
- Are your spelling and punctuation correct? You will not automatically lose marks for poor spelling, punctuation and handwriting, but it will affect the examiner's general impression.
- Have you checked for grammar mistakes, in particular the ones you know you often make?

Part 1: Essay (1)

Task

In your English class you have been talking about the role of women in the workplace. Now your English teacher has asked you to write an essay.

Write an essay using all the notes and give reasons for your point of view.

Not many women reach top positions in the workplace. Do you think this is fair?

Notes
Write about:
1 what is important for women
2 childcare
3 _____ (your own idea)

Write your **essay** in **140–190** words in an appropriate style.

Model answer

Start with a general statement in your own words.

State your own point of view clearly.

You can state the context using one of the notes.

Start the paragraph with a strong topic sentence.

Show awareness of another point of view.

Show awareness of another point of view.

Add a supporting sentence (e.g. making a suggestion).

Give reasons for your point of view.

To conclude, summarise your argument.

In many countries more than half the workforce are women and yet there are relatively few top female company directors and politicians. This is clearly not right.
At one time, men were expected to get a job and women to stay at home but times have changed. Women also like to work and most still want to have a family.
Some people argue that women are too busy to commit to full-time careers at the top. It is true that providing good childcare is not easy if working hours are unreasonably long, but it should be the responsibility of the company to accept flexible working arrangements.
Another argument is that women are less aggressive and competitive than men and find it harder to get the best jobs, but, again, this is unreasonable. Women are ambitious too, but if their nature is different in other ways, companies should take that into account. The workplace needs the female skills of being good communicators and not just in junior positions.
In my view, the current situation is unacceptable and companies should make it possible to have a male–female balance at the highest levels.

Further practice

In your English class you have been talking about environmental issues. Now your English teacher has asked you to write an essay.

Write an essay using all the notes and give reasons for your point of view.

We are damaging the environment for our children. What can be done about it?

Notes
Write about:
1 pollution
2 animals and plants
3 _____ (your own idea)

Write your **essay** in **140–190** words in an appropriate style.

Part 1: Essay (2)

Task

In your English class you have been talking about vegetarianism. Now your English teacher has asked you to write an essay.

Write an essay using all the notes and give reasons for your point of view.

Do you think humans should eat meat?

Notes
Write about:
1 traditional food
2 health
3 _____ (your own idea)

Write your **essay** in **140–190** words in an appropriate style.

Model answer

Introduce the topic in the first paragraph, giving the 'whole picture' and an introduction to both sides of the argument.

Have a separate paragraph for the other side of the argument.

Summarise your view in the conclusion, using different words from the introduction. You might want to add some further comment.

Most people think that since animals eat other animals, it is natural for humans to eat meat. However, some religions disagree, and a growing number of people are choosing to become vegetarians for non-religious reasons.

First, I'd like to put the arguments in favour of eating meat. Humans have always hunted and eaten animals. When people stop eating meat, they are avoiding the main food that gives them energy. Besides, we use the animals' fur and skin for clothes and shoes.

On the other hand, many vegetarians believe that eating meat is not only unnecessary, but it is also unhealthy. We can easily grow plants that give us all we need in our diet, and meat can cause serious diseases.

Another strong argument against eating meat is that the way we farm animals is cruel, as well as damaging to the environment, as we are destroying rainforests to provide land for animals.

In my view, there are strong health reasons for not eating meat. However, if we become vegetarians for moral reasons, I think we should also not wear fur or leather.

Add supporting information.

Use linking words to show the sequence of your ideas and when you are making an extra point.

Explain the topic, giving specific examples.

Have a separate paragraph for a different point.

Further practice

In your English class you have been talking about professional sport. Now your English teacher has asked you to write an essay.

Write an essay using all the notes and give reasons for your point of view.

Are sports stars paid too much money?

Notes
Write about:
1 special talent and fitness levels
2 other professions
3 _____ (your own idea)

Write your **essay** in **140–190** words in an appropriate style.

Part 2: Article

Task

You see this announcement in an international magazine.

Articles wanted
Life on a desert island

Imagine you were on a desert island. What important object, person or place in your life would you miss most? What would be the reasons?

Write us an article answering these questions. We will publish the best articles in the magazine.

Write your article in 140–190 words in an appropriate style.

Model answer

Add a short title to catch the reader's attention. Make sure it is relevant. You can use the one in the question or invent one of your own.

Give specific examples to bring your article to life.

Finish with a sentence which summarises what you have said.

Life on a desert island

How would you feel about living on a desert island? I can't imagine anything worse! I'd miss a lot of things but most of all, I would miss my home.

My home is a small house on the outskirts of a city. It was built about 50 years ago and has a small garden. In the summer, our country gets very hot but our house is always cool. You'd probably think our house is nothing special, but I have lived there all my life and all my friends live nearby. It's a happy place, where I feel completely safe. Whenever I go away, I look forward to coming back, lying on my bed, reading a book and listening to my brother and sister arguing downstairs!

I love travelling and meeting new people, but if I were on a desert island, I'd be away from the place I love most: my home; and I would hate that.

Introduce the topic. Although you don't know your readers personally, you can address them directly and ask them a question. It helps to involve them.

Your style will not be formal (e.g. you might use contractions). This article has a personal style. Others might have a more neutral style.

Further practice

You see this announcement on your college English-language website.

Articles wanted
My favourite hobby

What is your favourite hobby? How did you get started? Why do you enjoy it?

Write us an article answering these questions. We will publish the best articles on our website.

Write your article in 140–190 words in an appropriate style.

Expert writing

Part 2: Informal email/letter

Task

You have received this email from your English-speaking friend, Jean.

I hear you organised a surprise birthday party for your mother. I'd love to hear about it. What kind of party did you organise? Who did you invite? How did it go? Do tell me.

Love,

Jean

*Write your **email** in **140–190** words in an appropriate style.*

Model answer

Open with an informal greeting.

Start your reply by referring to the sender's email/letter.

Give the reason for replying.

Start a new paragraph as the topic has changed slightly. Use an informal linking word/phrase.

When you close, make an excuse to finish.

Hi Jean,

Good to hear from you again. I hope you're still enjoying your job.

I'm glad you asked me about the party I planned for my mother's birthday. Well, I have to say it was a fantastic success. I told mother we were taking her out for a quiet meal at a local restaurant with just the family, but in fact, I'd hired a large room in a hotel and invited all her old friends!

Anyway, I picked mother up and told her I'd changed my mind. We were going to have a meal in a hotel. You should have seen her face when she walked into the room and everyone cheered! She just couldn't believe it and burst into tears. Then the party got going and it didn't finish until four in the morning. We were absolutely exhausted, but mother had had a wonderful time.

Must dash now – I've got to go to college. Hope to hear from you soon.

Love,

Tania

Use contractions.

Use some exclamation marks (but not too many) to express emotion.

It's good to use a range of appropriate vocabulary and informal expressions.

Short sentences are acceptable.

Make sure you finish with an informal phrase.

Further practice

You have received this email from your English-speaking friend, Marco.

Thanks for offering to put me up in February while I'm on my language course. What will the weather be like at that time of the year? What should I bring with me? Will you be around in the evenings? Perhaps we could do something together.

All the best,

Marco

*Write your **email** in **140–190** words in an appropriate style.*

Part 2: Formal email/letter

Task

You see this announcement in an English-language college prospectus.

Scholarships

Every year, two scholarships are offered to candidates from overseas who can show how our one-year course in English and American studies would help their career.

Scholarships cover fees, accommodation and food, but not transport or personal spending money.

To apply, write a letter explaining why you think you deserve a scholarship.

*Write your **letter** in **140–190** words in an appropriate style.*

Model answer

If you know the name of the person, begin *Dear Mr Smith/ Dear Ms Jones*, etc.

In one paragraph, briefly describe yourself/your situation.

In the next paragraph, make it clear why you are applying for a scholarship and why you would be a suitable candidate. Make sure you cover all the points in the question.

Use a formal ending.

Dear Sir/Madam,

I would like to apply for one of the scholarships I saw advertised in your prospectus.

At present, I am training to be a secondary school teacher of English and I finish my course at the end of June. However, I feel I still have a lot to learn about the language and culture of the English-speaking world and would benefit considerably from a course in an English-speaking country.

The reason I am applying for a scholarship is that I cannot afford the cost of studying abroad. I have no income except for my student grant, so if I am fortunate enough to be given a scholarship, I would have to work part-time to save some personal spending money. My parents will borrow some money for my airfare if I am successful.

I would appreciate being given the opportunity to study at your college and would be very grateful if you would consider my application.

Yours faithfully,

Kesia Bonnet
Kesia Bonnet

Do not include a postal address.

Say why you are writing and what you are responding to (e.g. an advert, a prospectus).

Use a (semi-)formal, neutral style. (Remember: avoid contractions, colloquial language, direct questions and informal punctuation such as exclamation marks.)

Be polite and positive, but not too much!

Sign your name and then print your name clearly underneath.

If you have used the person's name, end *Yours sincerely*.

Further practice

You see this advertisement in an English-language newspaper.

Enquiries welcome

Our computer games company is planning to open a new research centre. We would welcome initial enquiries (but not full applications) from anyone who might be interested in working for us. Please indicate why our company might interest you, and your special skills. At this stage, we can only give basic information such as the types of positions that might become available.

*Write your **letter** in **140–190** words in an appropriate style.*

Part 2: Report

Task

Your college has been asked to accept a group of 50 students from another country for two weeks. Your principal has asked you to write a report. What would be the advantages and disadvantages of accepting this group? What would you recommend?

*Write your **report** in **140–190** words in an appropriate style.*

Model answer

Use headings.	**Report on proposed visit by 50 overseas students**
State the aim of the report and where you got the information.	**Introduction** The purpose of this report is to consider the advantages and disadvantages of accepting a large group of students from overseas for two weeks. I have discussed the issue with all the senior members of college staff.
Divide the report into relevant sections, linked to the question.	**Advantages**
Use an impersonal style when quoting.	All those I interviewed believe that for students, this would be an exciting opportunity to explore a foreign culture, both in the classroom and socially. Overall, they thought the visit would be stimulating for the college at a quiet time of the year.
Balance the positive and negative points fairly.	**Disadvantages** Some members of staff are concerned that:
Listing/Numbering points can make your report easier to read.	1 there would be insufficient seating in the library at busy times. 2 the visitors might be more interested in enjoying themselves than studying. 3 the restaurant queue would be very slow at lunchtime.
	Conclusion and recommendation
Generalise.	Clearly, the visit might involve some practical difficulties, but on the whole, everyone thought that it should be seen as an opportunity not to be missed. I would therefore suggest that the college accepts the group.

Use a clear, neutral style throughout.

Only give the recommendations at the end.

Further practice

Your English teacher has asked you to write a report on what students think of the college website. What do they like? What do they think are its weaknesses? How could it be improved?

*Write your **report** in **140–190** words in an appropriate style.*

Part 2: Review

Task

You see this announcement in an English-language magazine.

> # REVIEWS NEEDED!
> We are hoping to add a travel section to our college magazine, designed by the students. We would like you to write a review about a town or a city anywhere in the world that you have recently visited and liked. Why did you like it? What did you do there? Would you recommend it to others?
>
> The best reviews will be published in the magazine.

*Write your **review** in **140–190** words in an appropriate style.*

Model answer

It is a good idea to give your review an interesting title.

Say what you are reviewing and try to get the reader's interest.

Add vivid language to add interest.

Summarise your view, using different words from the introduction, and include a recommendation.

Give your opinion of what you are reviewing linked to the question. Remember a review is not just a list of facts – it's largely your opinion.

Give a few details of what you are reviewing linked to the question but only focus on those that you think are most important.

Seville, a wonderful city!
What a place! I recently spent a long weekend in Seville, in the south of Spain. It was the best mini-break I've ever had!

The best thing about Seville is that it's compact, so many of its main tourist attractions are close to the city centre. I headed straight to the world-famous cathedral and then on to one of the many art galleries. I discovered so many famous monuments and museums as I walked around in the glorious sunshine.

I also loved Seville because it was very relaxing and there was plenty to do for free. When I was hungry, I had a choice of hundreds of cafés or restaurants, all at good prices, serving delicious Spanish food. On my second evening there, I went to a fantastic flamenco dancing show.

So, with all its attractions, I recommend that you go to Seville! In the end, it's the people who make a place, and the locals certainly made me feel welcome!

Further practice

You see this announcement in an English-language magazine.

> # REVIEWS NEEDED!
> We are starting a new section in our newspaper about technology. Write us a review of an item you have bought recently. What is the product for? What is it like? Is it useful? Would you recommend it to others?
>
> The best reviews will be published in the magazine.

*Write your **review** in **140–190** words in an appropriate style.*

Punctuation

Punctuation mark		Uses	Examples
Apostrophe	'	• to show someone owns something • to indicate a contraction	*Tom's car* *He isn't here.*
Capital letter	B	• to begin sentences, for the pronoun I, names, countries, cities, days of the week and months (not seasons) of the year	*Graham and I play tennis on Saturdays in June.*
Colon	:	• to introduce a list • in formal writing, before a phrase that gives more information about the main clause	*There are three possibilities: first, we could ...* *The house was small: it had a kitchen and one bedroom.*
Comma	,	to divide a sentence into sections to make it easier to understand: • before and after a non-defining relative clause • to separate items in a list • to separate a tag question from the sentence • to separate an introductory word or phrase from the rest of the sentence • before or after reporting verbs (e.g. *he said, he told me*), when writing down someone's exact words	 *Another man, who looked a lot younger, was drinking coffee.* *The man was wearing black trousers, a white shirt and a blue tie.* *It's hot, isn't it?* *By the way, how are you?* *She said, 'I'm tired.'* *'I'm tired,' she said.*
Dash	–	• to separate a statement that is extra to the main idea	*I love pasta – particularly spaghetti – and other Italian food.*
Exclamation mark	!	• to express emotional emphasis in informal writing	*What a lovely day!*
Full stop/point/period	.	• to show the end of a sentence • in abbreviations	*That's very clear.* *e.g., etc.*
Question mark	?	• at the end of a direct question	*Are you tired?*
Semi-colon	;	• to separate two main clauses that have a link in meaning	*It was late; it was getting dark.*
Speech marks (Quotation marks/Inverted commas)	"...'" '...'	• when we write down the exact words someone says; they can be double ("...") or single ('...')	*"I'll help you," she said.* *'I'll help you,' she said.*

Spelling

1 Words ending in one -e
- Remove -e before -ing:
  love → lov**ing**
  (but NOT before -ee: agree → agree**ing**)
- Keep -e before -ly:
  fortunate → fortunate**ly**
  (but NOT in -le adjectives: probable → probab**ly**)
- Keep -e before -ment:
  advertise → advertis**ement**

2 Verbs ending in -ie
Change -ie to -y:
lie → l**ying**

3 Words ending in consonant + -y
Change -y to -ie:
try → tr**ies** → tr**ied**
baby → bab**ies**
happy → happ**ier** → happ**iest**

4 Words ending in vowel + -y
Keep -y:
play → play**s** → play**ed**
But note:
day → da**ily**
lay → la**id**
say → sa**id**
pay → pa**id**

5 Words ending in -c before -ed/-ing
Change -c to -ck before -ed/-ing:
panic → pani**cked**
picnic → picni**cking**

6 Words ending in one consonant
Double the final consonant before -ing, -ed, -er, -est for:
- one-syllable words with one vowel + one consonant:
  stop → sto**pping** → sto**pped**
  hot → ho**tter** → ho**ttest**
- two- or three-syllable words with the final syllable stressed:
  be'gin → be'gi**nning**

Do not double the final consonant of:
- words with two vowels before the final consonant:
  rain → rain**ing**
  look → look**ed**
  cheap → cheap**er**
- words with two final consonants:
  start → star**ted**
  rich → rich**er**
- two- or three-syllable words with the final syllable **not** stressed:
  'enter → 'enter**ing**
  (But note in British English: double final -l after one vowel: 'trave**l** → 'trave**lling**)

- words ending in -y or -w:
  stay → stay**ed**
  slow → slow**er**

7 Nouns ending in -o
Add -es in the plural:
potato → potato**es**
tomato → tomato**es**

8 Nouns ending in -our
Remove -u in the adjective:
hum**our** → hum**orous**

9 Endings often misspelt
- Adjectives:
  -ible/-able: sens**ible**, respons**ible**; comfort**able**, suit**able**
  -ful: beauti**ful**, hope**ful**
  -ent: independ**ent**, conveni**ent**, excell**ent**
  -ous: anxi**ous**, consci**ous**, delici**ous**, fam**ous**, vari**ous**
- Nouns:
  -al/-le: arriv**al**, refus**al**, princip**al**/princip**le**
  -er/-or: act**or**, operat**or**, visit**or** but driv**er**, employ**er**, writ**er**
  -ent/-ant: excitem**ent**, employm**ent** but assist**ant**, serv**ant**
  -ness: happi**ness**, weak**ness**
- Verbs:
  -ise/-ize: surpr**ise**, exerc**ise**
  British English, usually: real**ise**, modern**ise**, recogn**ise**
  American English: real**ize**, modern**ize**, recogn**ize**

10 Some useful rules
- -ise (verb)/-ice (noun):
  adv**ise**/adv**ice**, pract**ise**/pract**ice**
- -i before -e except after -c:
  n**ie**ce/rel**ie**ve; dec**ei**ve/c**ei**ling
  (Exception: foreign)

11 Words often misspelt

accommodation	heard
address	heart
affect (v)/effect (n)	immediate
because	juice
bicycle	loose (adj) /luːs/
business	lose (v) /luːz/
busy	medicine
committee	necessary
disappoint	pronunciation
embarrass	recommend
Europe	separate
familiar	similar
guilty	until

Expert speaking

Module 3B: Speaking (pages 42–43)

Exercise 9: Long turn

Why might dogs be useful for this kind of work?

Module 4B: Speaking (pages 56–57)

Exercise 5: Collaborative task

Interlocutor: Now, I'd like you to talk about something together for about two minutes.

I'd like you to imagine that a college wants to persuade students to take up more sports. Here are some sports they are thinking of encouraging and a question for you to discuss. (*Point to the spidergram on page 56.*)

First you have some time to look at the task.

(*Allow 15 seconds.*)

Now, talk to each other about the advantages of these sports.

(*Stop the candidates after 2 minutes.*)

Thank you. Now you have about a minute to decide which sport would be best to encourage.

(*Stop the candidates after 1 minute.*)

Thank you.

Module 6B: Speaking (pages 84–85)

Exercise 8: Long turn

Task 2

Look at the photos below.

Student B, compare the photos and say why people might enjoy concerts like these.

Student A, listen to Student B without interrupting. Stop him/her after one minute and say briefly whether music is important to you and why.

Why might people enjoy concerts like these?

Module 7B: Speaking (pages 98–99)

Exercise 8a: Long turn

Task 1

Interlocutor: In this part of the test, I'm going to give each of you two photographs. I'd like you to talk about your photographs on your own for about a minute, and also to answer a question about your partner's photographs.

(*Candidate A*), it's your turn first. Here are your photographs. (*Point to the photos on page 99.*) They show people wearing different types of clothes in an interview situation.

I'd like you to compare the photographs and say why the people are dressed in this way. All right?

(*Stop the candidate after 1 minute.*)

Thank you.

(*Candidate B*), what kind of clothes do you feel most comfortable wearing? (Why?)

(*Stop the candidate after 30 seconds.*)

Thank you.

Exercise 8b: Long turn

Task 2

Student 2

Interlocutor: In this part of the test, I'm going to give each of you two photographs. I'd like you to talk about your photographs on your own for about a minute, and also to answer a question about your partner's photographs.

(Candidate A), it's your turn first. Here are your photographs. (Point to the photos below.) They show people wearing different types of clothes in a social situation.

I'd like you to compare the photographs and say how these different situations affect the way people are dressed. All right?

(Stop the candidate after 1 minute.)

Thank you.

(Candidate B), what clothes do you like to wear on formal occasions? (Why?)

(Stop the candidate after 30 seconds.)

Thank you.

Students 1 and 3

How do these different situations affect the way people are dressed?

Module 8B: Speaking (pages 112–113)

Exercise 1: Vocabulary: Free-time activities

2 Kristen Stewart juggles.

4 Ronaldinho sings karaoke.

1 Taylor Swift makes jam.

6 Colin Farrell does line dancing.

5 Claudia Schiffer collects insects.

3 Ryan Gosling knits.

Module 9B: Speaking (pages 126–127)

Exercise 4: Collaborative task

Interlocutor: Now, I'd like you to talk about something together for about two minutes.
I'd like you to imagine that a visitor from another country asks you which is the best place to do some shopping. Here are some places they are thinking of going to and a question for you to discuss. (*Point to the spidergram on page 126.*)
First you have some time to look at the task.
(*Allow 15 seconds.*)
Now, talk to each other about the advantages of shopping in these places.
(*Stop the candidates after 2 minutes.*)
Thank you.
Now you have about a minute to decide which place would be best for the visitor to shop in.
(*Stop the candidates after 1 minute.*)
Thank you.

Module 10B: Speaking (pages 140–141)

Exercise 5a: Long turn

Task 1

Interlocutor: In this part of the test, I'm going to give each of you two photographs. I'd like you to talk about your photographs on your own for about a minute, and also to answer a question about your partner's photographs.
(*Candidate A*), it's your turn first. Here are your photographs. (*Point to the photos on page 141.*) They show people using different forms of transport.
I'd like you to compare the photographs and say how the people might be feeling in these situations. All right?
(*Stop the candidate after 1 minute.*)
Thank you.
(*Candidate B*), what is your favourite form of transport? (Why?)
(*Stop the candidate after 30 seconds.*)
Thank you.

Exercise 5b: Long turn

Task 2
Student 2
Interlocutor: In this part of the test, I'm going to give each of you two photographs. I'd like you to talk about your photographs on your own for about a minute, and also to answer a question about your partner's photographs.
(*Candidate B*), it's your turn first. Here are your photographs. (*Point to the photos on page 212.*) They show different types of dancing.
I'd like you to compare the photographs and say why the people might have chosen these forms of dancing. All right?
(*Stop the candidate after 1 minute.*)
Thank you.
(*Candidate A*), which of these kinds of dancing would you prefer to do? (Why?)
(*Stop the candidate after 30 seconds.*)
Thank you.

Expert speaking

Students 1 and 3

Why might the people have chosen these forms of dancing?

A

B

Module 11B: Speaking (page 156)

Exercise 2: Collaborative task

Student 1

Interlocutor: Now, I'd like you to talk about something together for about two minutes.
I'd like you to imagine that a college is thinking of offering advice to students about how to keep healthy during the winter months. Here are some ideas they have and a question for you to discuss.
(*Point to the spidergram below.*)
First you have some time to look at the task.
(*Allow 15 seconds.*)

Now, talk to each other about how these suggestions would improve the students' health during the winter months.
(*Stop the candidates after 2 minutes.*)
Thank you. Now you have about a minute to decide which suggestion would be best for the students.
(*Stop the candidates after 1 minute.*)
Thank you.

Students 2 and 3

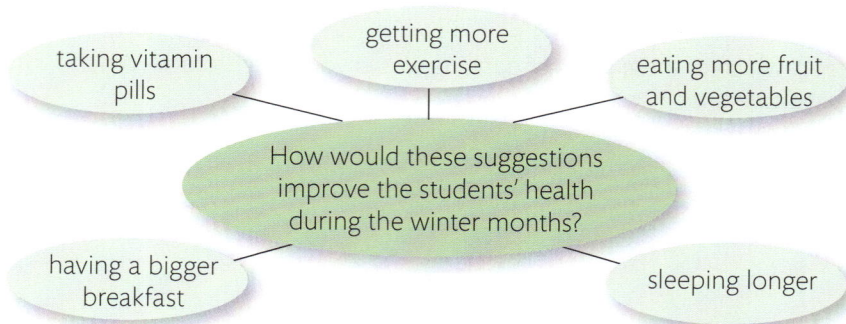

taking vitamin pills

getting more exercise

eating more fruit and vegetables

How would these suggestions improve the students' health during the winter months?

having a bigger breakfast

sleeping longer

Module 12B: Speaking (pages 168–169)

Exercise 4: Conversation

Likes and dislikes
- How do you like to spend your evenings? (What do you do?) (Why?)
- Do you prefer to spend time on your own or with other people? (Why?)
- Tell me about a film you really like.
- Do you like cooking? (What sort of things do you cook?)

Special occasions
- Do you normally celebrate special occasions with friends or family? (Why?)
- Tell us about a festival or celebration in (candidate's country).
- What did you do on your last birthday?
- Are you going to do anything special this weekend? (Where are you going to go?) (What are you going to do?)

Media
- How much TV do you watch in a week? (Would you prefer to watch more TV than that or less?) (Why?)
- Tell me about a TV programme you've seen recently.
- Do you use the internet much? (Why/Why not?)
- Do you ever listen to the radio? (What programmes do you like?) (Why?)

Exercise 5b: Long turn

Which do you think makes the most interesting interview?

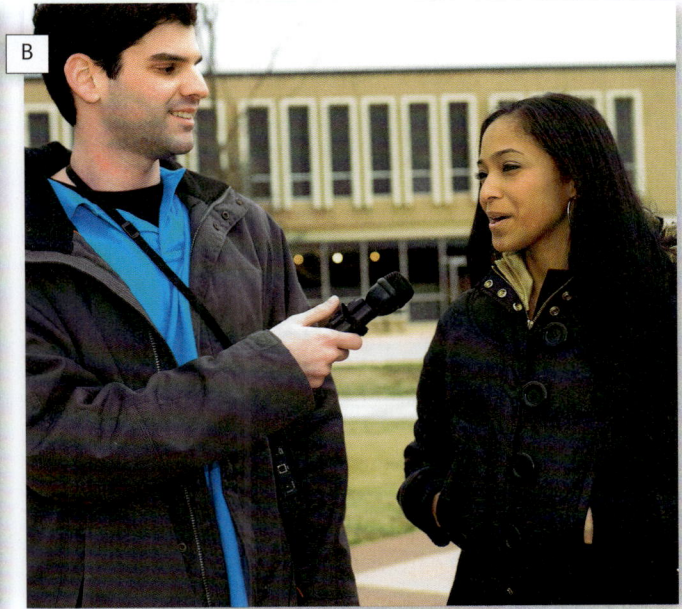

A

B

Exercise 6: Collaborative task

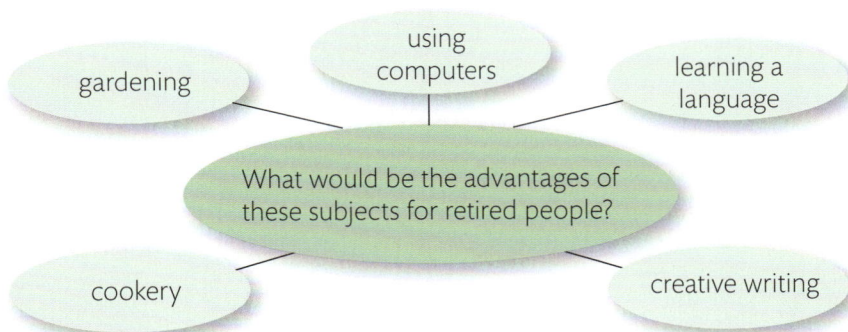

gardening

using computers

learning a language

What would be the advantages of these subjects for retired people?

cookery

creative writing

Pearson Education Limited
Edinburgh Gate
Harlow
Essex CM20 2JE
England
and Associated Companies throughout the world.

www.pearsonELT.com

© Pearson Education Limited 2014

First published 2014
ISBN: 978-1-4479-6200-7
Set in Amasis and Mundo Sans
Printed in Slovakia by Neografia

Acknowledgements

We are grateful to the following for permission to reproduce copyright material:

Cartoons

Cartoon on page 163 from *The Talented Mr Ripley*, Penguin (Patricia Highsmith), reproduced by permission of Penguin Books Ltd.

Logos

Logo on page 120 from Shelter logo, www.shelter.org.uk, reproduced with permission. Logo on page 120 from WWF logo, copyright (c) WWF, reproduced with permission. Logo on page 120 from Oxfam logo, reproduced with the permission of Oxfam GB, Oxfam House, John Smith Drive, Cowley, Oxford OX4 2JY, UK www.oxfam.org.uk. Oxfam GB does not necessarily endorse any text or activities that accompany the materials. Logo on page 120 from Age UK logo, www.ageuk.org.uk, reproduced with permission.

Text

Extract on page 9 adapted from "Our lost childhood" by Lorna Martin, The Observer 19th September 2006, copyright © Guardian News & Media Ltd, 2006; Extract on page 51 adapted from Lewis Pugh for extracts about Lewis Pugh, reproduced with kind permission. Extract on page 93 adapted from "Me and my big mouth" by Andrew Buncombe, The Independent 17th June 2006, copyright © Independent News & Media Ltd, 2006. Extract on page 135 adapted from "Welcome to America" by Dom Joly, The Times 15 October 2006, www.travel.timesonline.co.ukcopyright © News UK, 2006. Extract on page 163 from *The Talented Mr Ripley*, Published by Cornerstone (Patricia Highsmith) pp.87-88, reprinted by permission of Penguin Books Ltd.

In some instances we have been unable to trace the owners of copyright material, and we would appreciate any information that would enable us to do so.

The publisher would like to thank the following for their kind permission to reproduce their photographs:

(Key: b-bottom; c-centre; l-left; r-right; t-top)

Alamy Images: 79tl/A, Adrian Sherratt 105br, Aleksey Boldin 70tr, Allstar Picture Library 89tl, Ambient Images Inc 77tl, Blend Images 115tl, Dave Porter 108tl, David Bagnall 124tl, David Kilpatrick 136tl, Digital Vision 138tl, dpa picture alliance archive 112c, Engel & Gielen / LOOK Die Bildagentur der Fotografen GmbH 141tr, epa european pressphoto agency b.v. 119b, Hemis 68tl, Heritage Image Partnership Ltd 59cr, Ian Shaw 7br, imageBROKER 79cl/C, Jack Sullivan 208r, Jenny Matthews 28tc/c, 121tl, JEP Live Music 80bl/F, John Sturrock 21br, Juergen Henkelmann Photography 12bl, Karl Johaentges / LOOK Die Bildagentur der Fotografen GmbH 141tl, LMR Group 24cl, Marc Hill 7tr, Mike Abrahams 21tl, Photo Mere Travel 3 54tl, Photofusion Picture Library 131bl, Pictorial Press 80l/B, Roberto Herrett 137cr, steven gillis hd9 imaging 133tr, The Photolibrary Wales 30tl, uptheres 63l, Wayne Hutchinson 43tl; **Corbis:** Ariel Skelley / Blend Images 91t, Bettman 165r, Carl & Ann Purcell 54tr, Chuck Savage 14tl/A, © Corbis 31cr, Digital Art 63tr, Dung Vo Trung / Sygma 74bl, Franz Lanting 44t, Franz-marc / Frei 84tl, Jed Share and Kaoru 105bl, Jon Feingersh / Blend Images 105tl, Jose Luis Pelaez, Inc. / Blend Images 96tr, Larry Williams Associates 43tr, Nick White / Image Source 84cl, Randy Faris 14tc/C, Reuters 80tl/A, Ron Watts 170tl, Tim Draper / Design Pics 96tl, Tomas Rodriguez 100b, Tony Demin 115tr, Wally McNamee 212tl; **DK Images:** Andy Crawford 116cr, Claire Cordier 107t; **Fotolia.com:** Actionpics 57tr, Adrien Roussel 14t/B, algre 140cl (van), Andres Rodriguez 56-57tc, Andrey Kiselev 103bl, apops 77b, Artanika 147tl, auremar 49tr, CandyBox Images 91b, Darren Falkenberg 48cl, Deklofenak 133tl, Dmitry Berkut 140cl (Boat), Dmitry Pichugin 35b, Dusan Kostic 68tr, Eric Isselée 42l/F, fisherman3d 140tl (Scooter), Gina Smith 103tl, Igor Mojzes 7cl, 147br, JackF 42l/E, Jeroen van den Broek 208l, joesive47 42l/H, Jorg

Hackemann 38tl, lexmomot 119tl, lightwavemedia 147tr, Ljupco Smokovski 56tl, M.R.Swadzba 35t, MasterLu 38cl, merydolla 164tl, Mikhail Tolstoy 152tr, mlehmann78 47tl, Monkey Business 28tc/B, 49br, 131tl, naturesauraphoto 42l/C, Oliver Klimek 42l/A, Pixelshop 155tl, Rido 105tr, RRA 16tl, surangaw 46cr, TaniaLerro 126tl, timages 37t, Tyler Olsen 129, Uwe Annas 169tl, Vitas 133bl, WavebreakmediaMicro 28tl/A, 99tl, xalanx 9tc, yanlev 147bl; **Getty Images:** 2006 CBS Worldwide Inc 80l/E, AFP 51t, Andreanna Seymore 14tr/D, Andrey Smirnov / AFP 161tr, Andy Sacks 21bl, Archive Photos 80l/C, Bloomberg 122tl, Bonnie Jacobs 213cr, Chien-Min Chung 159tl, Dave M. Benett 17tl, Hero Images / Digital Vision 24tr, Huw Jones / Lonely Planet Images 26cl, Ian Dickson / Redferns 80l/D, John Dominis / The LIFE Picture Collection 91bl, Macduff Everton 16tr, Matt Cardy / Stringer 93tl, National Geographic 75bl, Photoshot / Hulton Archive 23t, Popperfoto 75tl, Ryan McVay / Photodisc 210cr, Samir Hussein / Wireimage 150tr, Tim Graham 210cl, Tobi Corney 21tr; **NASA:** 67l; **Pearson Education Ltd:** Studio 8 9tr, Gareth Boden 213cl, Rob Judges 70tl, Sozaijiten 42l/G, Ian Wedgewood 28tr/D; **PhotoDisc:** 1998 40t, 42l/B; **Press Association Images:** Corrado Giambalro / AP 61tl; **Rex Features:** Action Press 79cl/B, Associated Newspapers 137br, Ken McKay 79bl, 90tl, Phanie Agency 63br; **Science Photo Library Ltd:** 146tr, CRISTINA PEDRAZZINI 148tr; **Shutterstock.com:** Alex Staroseltsev 42l/D, argus 65tl, Arieliona 33tl, baranq 99tr, cinemafestival 173tl, DFree 112cr, Dusan Jankovic 161bl, Featureflash 89bl, 112cl, Helga Esteb 112tr, Jan Kranendonk 87l, JetKat 140bl (Plane), Joshua Haviv 135t, KR MEDIA Productions 83tr, Luckyphoto 126tr, M. Shcherbyna 119tr, Martin Good 209tr, Maxisport 112tc, Monkey Business Images 149t, pamuk 140bl (Metro), posztos 38bl, Prod-akszyn 169cl, s_buckley 11bl, Sean Pavone 161br, Sheff 166tr, Stocklite 133br, Vibrant Image Studio 140tl (Bus), Vitalii Nesterchuk 49l, wavebreakmedia 156tl, yakub88 209tl; **Carole Spike-Robertson:** 168; **SuperStock:** Fotosearch 212tr; **The Kobal Collection:** Summit Entertainment 112tl; **TopFoto:** NORRINGTON Nigel / ArenaPAL 88br, Spectrum / HIP 77tr; **www.CartoonStock.com:** Cornered / Mike Baldwin 124b

All other images © Pearson Education

Every effort has been made to trace the copyright holders and we apologise in advance for any unintentional omissions. We would be pleased to insert the appropriate acknowledgement in any subsequent edition of this publication.

Illustrated by David Semple.